Hans De Bree

World War II U.S. Made, Fully Machine-Embroidered, Cut-edge, Shoulder Sleeve Insignia

AND HOW THEY WERE MANUFACTURED

A COLLECTOR'S GUIDE

All scans and pictures of SSI are from the author's private collection except where mentioned otherwise.

Library of Congress Control Number: 2013939332

Type set in Bodoni BT / Helvetica Neue LT Pro / Minion Pro

ISBN: 978-0-7643-4355-1
Printed in China

Published by Schiffer Publishing, Ltd.
4880 Lower Valley Road
Atglen, PA 19310
Phone: (610) 593-1777; Fax: (610) 593-2002
E-mail: Info@schifferbooks.com

In Europe, Schiffer books are distributed by:
Bushwood Books
6 Marksbury Ave.
Kew Gardens
Surrey TW9 4JF England
Phone: 44 (0) 20 8392 8585; Fax: 44 (0) 20 8392 9876
E-mail: info@bushwoodbooks.co.uk
Website: www.bushwoodbooks.co.uk

DEDICATION

This book is dedicated to all the men and women who fought for liberation and freedom.

With special dedication to Pvt Joseph Martino, 259th Inf Regt – 65th Inf Div, who was in Europe from January to October 1945.

Philadelphia, PA, summer 1944.
(Courtesy of Joe Martino)

"I always remembered him walking up those steps after he got out of the taxi coming home..."

- Joe Martino

CONTENTS

Forewords 6
Acknowledgments 8
Introduction 9
Terminology 11

CHAPTER 1: Subdivisions – Periods of Construction 12
1 WWI period (1918 – early 1920s) 12
2 Early (1920s – early 1930s) 16
3 From the end of the 1920s / early 1930s until the early 1940s 17
4 From the early 1940s 31
5 From 1957 32
6 From 1968 33

CHAPTER 2: World War II 35
1 Wool SSI – Felt SSI 35
2 Fully machine-embroidered on cotton twill, cut-edge SSI 37

CHAPTER 3: WWII U.S. Made Fully Machine-Embroidered Cut-edge SSI 38
1 Manufacturing 38
2 Types of base fabric or backing 52
3 Design thread or main thread 60
4 Back thread 64
5 Embroidery styles or patterns 88
6 Examples of SSI with different embroidery styles 149
7 OD / Brown / Green border or no border 166
8 Elements or details added by the serviceman himself 186
9 Examples of units and their SSI where the period plays an important role 189

CHAPTER 4: How to Determine When a SSI is Original WWII-era Made? 199

CHAPTER 5: Reproductions and Copies 212

CHAPTER 6: Comparison with the Post-WWII German Made Fully Machine-Embroidered Cut-edge SSI for U.S. Units 237

CHAPTER 7: Comparison with the WWII British Made Fully Machine-Embroidered Cut-edge SSI for U.S. Units 258

CHAPTER 8: Variations of WWII U.S. Made, Fully Machine-Embroidered Cut-edge SSI (Examples) 269

1 In general – "The Institute of Heraldry" 269

2 Errors 276

3 Variations 283

4 WWII varieties of SSI with OD background 305

CHAPTER 9: Ways of Collecting 311

Bibliography 317

FOREWORD

A couple years back I received an e-mail from a collector named Hans De Bree. who lives in Belgium. He had many questions about the manufacture of United States Army shoulder sleeve insignia (commonly called patches) during the Second World War. I must confess that, as much as I may have wanted to answer Hans' questions, I did not know the very specific answers that he was seeking.

However, Hans De Bree is not a person to be discouraged, and question by question and answer by answer he has put together what I believe is an outstanding discourse on the topic of patches.

The earliest of references on WWII patches were concerned only with identification of the particular units or components that the insignia indicated. Some of these were produced during and just after the war itself. Perhaps the best known works in this category are the 1944 special issue of the *National Geographic* magazine and Richard W. Smith's 1981 book. However, the modern collector is faced with distinguishing postwar manufactured patches and growing numbers of fakes and reproductions. These early works were of no help in that regard.

In the early years, no patch was worth more than a few bucks, and most of them were only a couple cents. My own very first patch was out of a box of cereal. If the example you had of a particular one was a fake or reproduction, no big deal.

It is surprising that immediately after the war reproductions of patches were being produced for collectors, and that production continues with even greater sophistication to this day. Today some of the more uncommon patches are selling for real money, and it is no longer a big deal if you acquire a fake.

An informed and advanced collector needs to read what Hans De Bree has learned in his investigations. It is time to move on and ask those very specific questions about the manufacture of patches, methods of dating, and the means to spot fakes and reproductions. Others, such as Christopher P. Brown and the Kellers, have written books with an eye to answering some of these questions, but what Hans has written here is as detailed as anything I have seen yet.

Howard G. Lanham, M.D.
Westminster, Maryland, U.S.A.
December 2011

FOREWORD

Mr. De Bree has written the defining, benchmark book for U.S. Army shoulder sleeve insignia (SSI) for the twenty-first century. Incredibly and exhaustingly researched, Mr. De Bree has set the bar so very high for anyone contemplating a follow up book.

His documentation and research is equaled by the hundreds of color plates, his detailed description of manufacture location, manufacture time, type of manufacture, discussions with experienced collectors, and his own collecting experience – in short, even advanced collectors will appreciate the skill with which Mr. De Bree lays out the highs and lows of collecting SSI. Want to examine embroidered on felt? The difference between wool and felt? What a woven SSI looks like? When were certain SSI made a certain way, where worn – and at what locations? All these questions and more are answered in this authoritative study.

As many collectors rely on the web for direction, and unknowingly read information that may be of dubious value, this book is absolutely invaluable. For those who are unable to attend shows, this book should be their one reliable resource – their protection against dealers who are salesmen rather than historical experts. With the increasing values in better insignia, a well-armed collector who does not obtain this book is setting himself up for some severe financial mistakes.

This book answers the questions of both novice and experienced collectors, leading the reader step-by-step in learning what is original, what is period, and more importantly, why. Mr. De Bree has taken the collector down a road that I wish had existed when I first started collecting 50+ years ago.

I know that today's collectors are unwilling to spend their collecting funds on a good research library, but many seem to agree that the important question is, which one book should they spend their funds on? This is it. This is the book that everyone who collects wishes had been written. Because of Mr. De Bree's efforts, this is the one book every collector needs.

David A. Kaufman,
Editor of ASMIC's The Trading Post
Chatsworth, California, USA
March 2012

ACKNOWLEDGMENTS

I would like to thank those who made this work possible for their contributions of material and information:
Joe Martino, Dr. Howard G. Lanham, Jay A. Graybeal (Chief Curator at the Army Heritage Museum – U.S. Army Heritage & Education Center, Carlisle, PA), William Scott, David A. Kaufman (Editor of *The Trading Post*, the official quarterly publication of ASMIC), Craig Pickrall (Co-Founder / Co-Administrator of the U.S. Militaria Forum), Bruce Brooks, Eric Czerwinski, Lars Kleine, Christian Lefebvre, Don & Sophia van den Bogert (Pararesearchteam.com), and the professional guidance of Bob Biondi, Ian Robertson, Stacey McNutt, and Karen Choppa at Schiffer Publishing, Ltd.

…And my sons Matthias and Jochen, and Carolien for their patience during those busy two years.

INTRODUCTION

Cloth insignia identifying units or shoulder sleeve insignia (SSI) were a relatively new component of the modern United States (U.S.) military uniform and originated during World War I, when Gen. John J. Pershing authorized limited use. Unit insignia already existed prior to that time, but were of a distinctly different character. For example, there were corps badges of the Civil and Spanish American War, but they were not worn on the sleeve and denoted division only by color. After both wars, the insignia were dropped and did not continue as a tradition in the small peace time army. It was only after WWI that the designs of the various SSI had continuous use as divisional insignia.

During WWII, large numbers of SSI were made by dozens of domestic and foreign manufacturers, and were issued to many of the approximately 16 million U.S. GIs, sailors, airmen, paratroopers, and Marines from the stocks maintained by the supply service of their respective branches. Each patch, as these SSI were commonly called, represented a specific military unit of which the serviceman was a part.

This is a reference book for collectors (novice and experienced), and is focused on the WWII U.S. made, fully machine-embroidered, cut-edge SSI. It aims to provide guidelines that can be considered when determining whether a SSI is an original WWII-era manufactured one or not. Also, the differences in SSI manufacture are explained in such a way as to create a time line in a patch collection. Knowing these details will add to the personal value of a collection, and makes it much more than simply just having a group of patches. In addition, my purpose is to help a collector avoid spending money on something that is not what it seems to be (for example: a copy; a reproduction of a WWI, Interwar, or WWII SSI; or a post-WWII SSI).

This information will add to the experience one builds as a collector, because it is difficult to differentiate postwar SSI and well-made (modern) copies from WWII-era made SSI. The same manufacturing technique for these SSI was used for years after the war ended.

Many remaining stocks of WWII patches were still issued well into the early 1950s and the period of the Korean War. If one considers the following guidelines, chances are that many SSI from the 1950s still represent WWII-era made shoulder patches. (Note: the WWII SSI were manufactured well after the war, as late as 1952, to fulfil the WWII U.S. Government contracts, and were authorized as former unit insignia worn on the right shoulder even when these units were no longer an active component of the Army.)

This book is written primarily from my experience. After seeing thousands of SSI and after reading many publications, forums, and collectors' opinions, some findings and theories are established. What follows is a detailed and comprehensive picture of these particular WWII SSI. There are still many uncertainties and assumptions that I need to acknowledge because after all, at this time it is difficult or sometimes even impossible to find out what lead (for example) the manufacturers used for a certain embroidery style, or how to stop or maintain the use of the olive drab (OD) colored thread on the back of the patch.

I do not intend to show all WWII SSI in this book. There are many other titles already written that do this. However, many examples and details are illustrated to clarify my particular interpretations, in the hope of making it easy for the collector to follow my comments about patch manufacture in general.

However, even with all this information a collector may be uncertain regarding a particular SSI. In this case, the rule will always apply, "IF YOU DOUBT, DON'T BUY IT!"

The SSI manufactured in other countries are known as theater-made SSI, and are not discussed in this book. These are part of an even bigger and more varied picture, and including them would make the focus of this work more difficult.

Just a little help for the reader

In the text there are often references to pictures in the book. Also, underneath each picture a specific number is mentioned. The picture's number is an indication in what chapter and heading it can be found, or in which you are reading. The first two figures of the number are related to the chapter, and the third figure (just after the hyphen) is that chapter's heading in which the picture can be found. When the chapter is not divided into headings, this third figure is a "0," i.e., Fig. 03-412 is the 12th picture of heading (4) of chapter 3; Fig 05-008 is the 8th picture of chapter 5, which has no subdivisions at all.

Finally, some abbreviations are used in the text:

SSI	shoulder sleeve insignia
U.S.	United States
WWI	World War I
WWII	World War II
OD	olive drab
Inf	Infantry
Arm	Armored
AB	Airborne
Div	Division
HQ	Headquarters
Lt.-Gen.	Lieutenant-General
TIOH	The Institute of Heraldry

Happy reading and good patch hunting!
H. De Bree

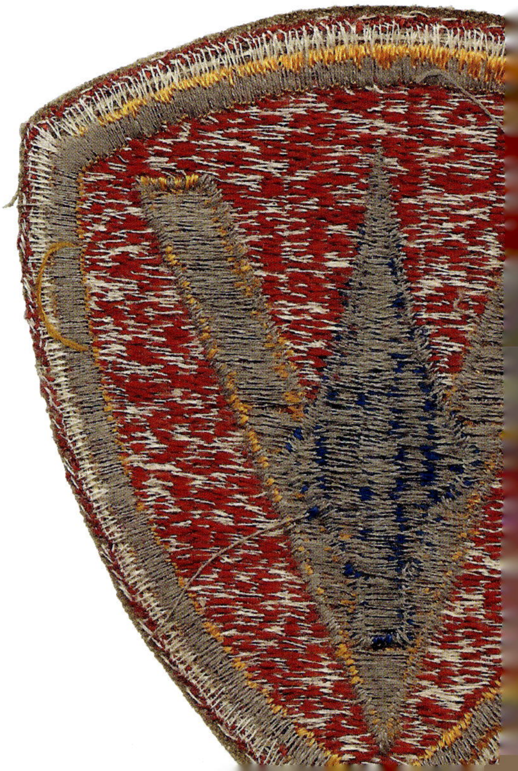

TERMINOLOGY

The design of the shoulder sleeve insignia (SSI)

CHAPTER 1
Subdivisions – Periods of Construction

Depending on the method of construction, certain periods can be distinguished.

1 | WWI PERIOD (1918-EARLY 1920s)

From 1918, most of the U.S. Army SSIs were approved by the General Headquarters, American Expeditionary Forces (GHQ, AEF). Commanding generals of armies, corps, divisions, and many other U.S. Army units sent telegrams to the GHQ, AEF with their requests for approval, enclosed with complete descriptions and drawings of the designs. Nevertheless, there was a wide variety in the final appearance of these SSIs. (Note: The U.S. entered The Great War in 1917.)

- Either a SSI cut from one certain piece of fabric (wool, felt, cotton, leather, etc.), whether or not by the serviceman himself, and sewn on the uniform. The cut letter "A" in black felt for the WWI 1st U.S. Army, not reinforced at first before being sewn on the uniform, is a good example of such SSI;
- Or, different pieces of colored fabric cut out and glued or sewn together to a SSI (felt on felt / felt on wool / wool on wool), which subsequently were sewn on the uniform;
- Or, hand-embroidered cotton, rayon, or wool thread on felt or wool base fabric. Characteristic is the looser and less dense (no nicely jointed or contiguous threads) or rougher embroidery;
- Or, to a lesser extent, machine-embroidered cotton or rayon thread on felt or wool, with also looser embroidery. Here, often a machine with a single needle was used by which the embroidered forms and threads had a looser and cruder impression. The design was drawn on the base fabric, and the maker simply followed the drawing with that one needle.

The shapes of the SSI or their different components are rougher, sometimes more odd or less well finished than later models (e.g., in the next period). Especially in the WWI period and shortly thereafter, sometimes very large SSI will show up on the left shoulder of the uniform.

NOTE	Difference between felt and wool
	- Felt is pressed wool, without structure - Wool tissue is woven and can appear with or without structure

Fig. 01-101: Front of a small WWI period leather on leather 36th Inf Div SSI.

Fig. 01-102: Front of a very large WWI period machine-embroidered 36th Inf Div SSI on olive drab (OD) wool.

Below is an example of the machine-embroidered 79th Infantry Division (Inf Div) SSI on OD wool, made around 1918-1920. It is larger than its known WWII counterpart.

Fig. 01-103: Front and back of a WWI period 79th Inf Div SSI.

Fig. 01-104: Front of a very large felt 1st U.S. Army Artillery SSI.

The following is an example of a felt WWI period (late 1918-1920) 1st U.S. Army Artillery SSI. It is a very large "A" simply cut out of a piece of black felt. The fabric of the OD wool uniform was the background of this patch.

At the time, 1st Army Commander Lt.-Gen. Hunter Liggett's "Memorandum 45" (December 14, 1918) designated the Army's Artillery by red and white divided horizontal blocks between the lower legs of the "A."

In this period one of the most unique types of SSI were made: the Liberty Loan Patch. They are woven (not embroidered) using the same technique as a modern shirt label. The fact that the Liberty Loan SSI are woven can be seen on the back. With these SSI, the back colors are reversed from the front (such as the WWII and post-WWII German and Italian theater-made woven SSI). This typical feature can clearly be seen in the following illustrations.

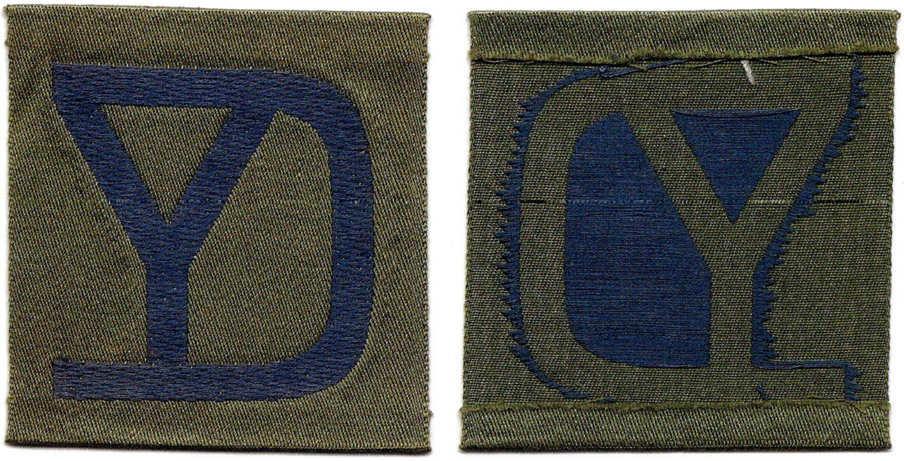

Fig. 01-105: Front and back of a 26th Inf Div Liberty Loan patch manufactured with two different colors of thread (OD and blue). The woven patch shows reversed colors at the back.

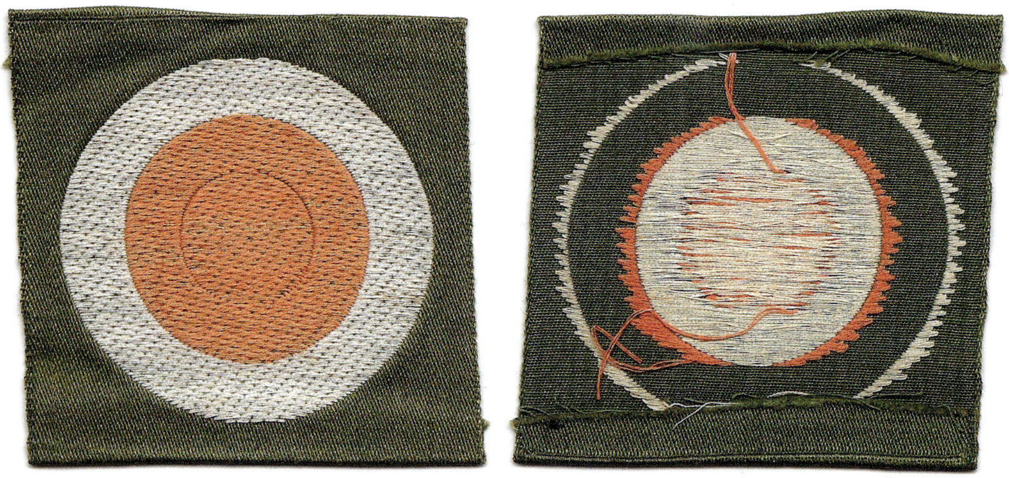

Fig. 01-106: Front and back of a 37th Inf Div Liberty Loan patch made with three different colors of thread (OD, white, and pink). Also, here the woven patch shows the typical reversed colors at the back.

Liberty Loan Patches were manufactured by the Treasury Department for Liberty Loan Campaigns, in conjunction with the War Loan Program, to sell war bonds and to raise the necessary funds in the USA for the war. During WWI, they were sold at stores, banks, and anywhere else that the government thought they could be sold to get the necessary money for the war. For the U.S. military they were posted at Points of Embarkation, as well as PX stores (Post Exchange stores) overseas.

So the Army did sell these kind of patches to returning veterans. That way some of these patches ended up in their respective units, especially those who returned home from the war. Many of them were sewn onto uniforms, as the Liberty Loan Patches were of much better quality than the patches that were issued to the soldiers, since the Liberty Loan Patches were woven and had better detail.

Fig. 01-107: Front and back of a Tank Corps Liberty Loan patch. Even with four colors (OD, yellow, pink, and blue), the woven patch shows reversed colors at the back.

2 | EARLY 1920s – EARLY 1930s (TRANSITIONAL PERIOD)

During this period we see the further refining, standardization, and industrialization (on a small scale basis) of the manufacturing method of the WWI-period SSI. The larger SSI seen during the WWI period were no longer manufactured. During this period:

- Either different colored pieces of fabric cut out and glued or sewn together to a SSI (felt on felt / felt on wool / wool on wool);
- Or hand- or machine-embroidered on felt or wool, but still with a much looser embroidery than the later specimen. Also, a machine with a single needle to embroider was used by the maker, following a design which was drawn at first on a base fabric.

Fig. 01-201: Felt on felt – front and back.

Fig. 01-202: Felt on OD wool – front and back.

3 | FROM THE END OF THE 1920s / EARLY 1930s UNTIL THE EARLY 1940s

- Embroidered cotton or rayon threads on felt or wool base cloth, using an embroidery machine, and then cut to the size and shape of the SSI.

At the start of this period SSI were embroidered with a machine having a single needle as described earlier. In a later period, more particularly from the 1930s, more and more SSI were needed and patch manufacturing on a large scale basis was necessary. For that reason the commercial Schiffli embroidery machine was introduced to embroider SSI and was used from then on (see further on in this book).

From this period, and because of the use of the embroidery machine, we can nicely see close and contiguous embroidery.

Fig. 01-301: Front and back of an early 1930s 26th Inf Div SSI partially machine-embroidered on OD wool.

Fig. 01-302: Front and back of a 1930s 40th Inf Div SSI partially machine-embroidered on dark blue felt.

Also, a combination of the preceding methods (headings (2) and (3) of this chapter) was applied. With the 2nd Inf Div SSI on felt below, the Indian head and feathers are very nicely embroidered, probably with an embroidery machine. This is an early 1930s-period SSI.

Fig. 01-303: Front of an early 1930s 2nd Inf Div SSI felt on felt SSI, and partially machine-embroidered.

Fig. 01-304: Back of the 2nd Inf Div SSI illustrated in Fig. 01-303.

Other examples of Interwar period SSI **machine-embroidered on wool base fabric** (from the 1930s to 1941) follow below. These were still used during the early years of WWII.

Fig. 01-305: Front and back of a 6th Inf Div SSI on OD wool.

Fig. 01-306: Front and back of a 35th Inf Div SSI on Officer's dark wool elastique.

Fig. 01-307: Front and back of a 35th Inf Div SSI on OD wool.

Fig. 01-308: Front and back of a 31st Inf Div SSI on OD wool, reinforced with gauze (as stabilizer).

Fig. 01-309: Front and back of a 36th Inf Div SSI on OD wool with no reinforced back.

Fig. 01-310: Front and back of a 44th Inf Div SSI on OD wool with no stabilizer at the back (not reinforced).

In this period (1930s), the partially machine-embroidered khaki cotton twill patch, or short khaki cotton twill patch, was introduced and used in the U.S. They were manufactured on cotton twill as a base fabric instead of wool or felt, with the khaki color of the fabric as the background color. These patches were worn even during WWII.

Just as with the examples of the 26th and 36th Inf Div SSI on OD wool (illustrated above) and several others of such kind, the design of these SSI was only machine-embroidered on KHAKI (or TAN) cotton twill cut into a round, square, rectangular, or diamond shape, and then finished with a fine stitched border of khaki-colored rayon thread. The latter was to avoid the unravelling of the cotton twill-base material used for the SSI and to have a nicer finish once the patch was sewn on the uniform.

These SSI were used on the summer uniform (e.g., for hotter southern regions in the U.S. and hot regions abroad), which had the same khaki color as the cotton twill those SSI were embroidered on. A khaki-colored sewing thread was needed to sew the patch on that particular uniform.

Fig. 01-311: Front and back of a small bordered pre-WWII 36th Inf Div SSI, partially machine-embroidered on khaki cotton twill-base fabric.

Fig. 01-312: Front and back of a small bordered pre-WWII 26th Inf Div SSI, partially machine-embroidered on khaki cotton twill-base fabric.

In addition to these pre-WWII khaki cotton twill SSI and also those made in the pre-WWII period (prior to 1941 – see further on), one needs to know that there are also fully machine-embroidered SSI on KHAKI-colored wool. Some patches were manufactured on that specific color of wool base fabric, just as the ones on OD wool illustrated above. The border is of khaki color and had the same purpose as why the cotton twill patches were manufactured: to serve on the khaki-colored summer uniform. Probably these were never made in large quantities because they are rare, but now and then one can be seen. A good example is the early 1940s 12th Armored Division SSI below.

Fig. 01-313: Front and back of a 12th Arm Div SSI, fully machine-embroidered on khaki-colored wool base fabric.

REMARK: During the WWII period, partially machine-embroidered khaki cotton twill patches were also manufactured in the U.S. However, the borders on pre-WWII era U.S. made cotton twill patches appear to be much thinner than their WWII (1941-1945) counterparts. These WWII khaki cotton twill patches have the usual wide border, such as the common WWII U.S.-made fully machine-embroidered cut-edge SSI. The latter needed a wider border to meet the higher quality standards of that time, as they were manufactured according to the cut-edge principle (see further on): the border was machine-embroidered, at first during the embroidery process, and then the SSI was cut around that border. The pre-WWII ones were cut at first after embroidering the design on the cotton twill, and then finished with a fine stitched border around the edge. Compare this feature with the early-WWII khaki cotton twill 1st U.S. Army SSI below.

Fig. 01-314: Front and back of an early-WWII U.S. made, partially machine-embroidered on khaki cotton twill-base fabric, cut-edge 1st U.S. Army SSI.

Another way of construction in this period was folding the edges of the base fabric: the **FOLDED BORDER**. This was applied also to avoid the unravelling of the base material after being cut into separate SSI.

In the following example of the 26th Inf Div, the base fabric is olive drab colored (OD) wool. There is no border stitched as illustrated above, but the SSI is simply folded into the required size and shape. With this example, the SSI was stitched at the edge to maintain the fold, done with a conventional sewing machine because of the very regular stitch which can be seen. It could have been done either by the manufacturer as a nice completion (as a quality label), or by the GI himself, or on the GI's request by a tailor or relative before being sewn. In either way, this simplified fixing the SSI on the GI's uniform. This example, while it is felt on wool instead of embroidery, is nevertheless an SSI from the period of the early 1930s.

This way of finishing (the folded border) was also applied to the previously illustrated SSI on khaki cotton twill. An example of a 4th Inf Div SSI with such kind of border can be seen on the following page. The SSI on OD wool would have been likely foreseen on OD-colored uniforms, while the SSI on khaki cotton twill was worn on the khaki-colored summer uniform.

Fig. 01-315: Front and back of a pre-WWII 26th Inf Div SSI – Felt on wool SSI with folded border.

Below is an example of the khaki cotton twill 4th Inf Div SSI with a border to be folded. The border has not been folded yet, but needs to be when sewn on the uniform by the GI.

Fig. 01-316: Pre-WWII 4th Inf Div SSI – Partially machine-embroidered on khaki cotton twill-base material, cut for a border to fold.

Fig. 01-317: Back of the patch illustrated in Fig. 01-316, reinforced with gauze (as stabilizer).

Here is a comparison to the previous SSI: an early-WWII partially machine-embroidered khaki cotton twill 4th Inf Div SSI with a machine-embroidered khaki border. This border is noticeably wider than the pre-WWII made khaki cotton twill patches have. During the WWII period, the manufacturers used to make such typical borders to the fully machine-embroidered cut-edge SSI (from early 1941 – see theory below), and also applied this kind of border to their WWII khaki cotton twill counterparts during the embroidery process, before being cut around that border.

Fig. 01-318: Front and back of an early-WWII cut-edge 4th Inf Div SSI – Partially machine-embroidered on khaki cotton twill, with wider machine-embroidered khaki border.

POSSIBLE THEORY: Why certain Divisions had wool/khaki twill SSI and others had not, and the beginning of the fully machine-embroidered cut-edge SSI.

Pre-WWII to early-WWII fully or partially machine-embroidered variations of SSI on respective wool (OD-colored wool and Officer's dark wool elastique) and khaki cotton twill-base fabric, as the ones of the 31st, 35th, 36th, and 37th Infantry Divisions (Inf Div) are not that uncommon. You do see that kind of manufacture on patches that were used in the early 1940s, and also in veterans' lots. Elements of these Inf Div existed prior to the war as National Guard units in the U.S., and were inducted into Federal Service in the course of 1940 and 1941 (mobilization). You will notice that this date is prior to December 7, 1941, and the entry of the U.S. into WWII.

After the Germans overran Europe in 1940 the U.S. leadership became alarmed, but public opinion was still against entering another European war, and even more against any kind of involvement in a land war in Asia. However, there was enough support for defense of the western hemisphere that the Army was able to get money from Congress to expand.

On August 27, 1940, Congress approved induction of the National Guard into Federal Service from their home states for what was called a limited emergency. The logistics of inducing so many soldiers at the same time were complicated (e.g., it was not until November 25, 1940, that the 31st Div was called up). During 1940, the following National Guard Divisions, whose serial began with the number 26 and continuing to number 45, were called up: 27th, 30th, 31st, 32nd, 35th, 36th, 37th, 41st, 44th, and 45th. Other Divisions were called up for mobilization in 1941.

Anyhow, one might have a theory that these machine-embroidered on wool and khaki twill variations also happen to be for many of the National Guard Divisions federalized in 1940. It is for sure that a large supply of new uniforms and insignia were also needed at the time, and it may be that this style was typical of what was being produced at the time, before the fully machine-embroidered cut-edge SSI became the dominant type manufactured in the U.S.

This is just a theory, but of those 10 divisions one can picture these on wool/khaki twill variations and cannot think of any common wool/khaki twill variations for divisions that were called up after 1940, except for the 26th Div (inducted on January 16, 1941), the 28th Div (inducted on February 17, 1941), and the 29th Div (inducted on February 3, 1941). In the case of the 26th, 28th, and 29th Inf Div, January and February 1941 is close enough for this theory to still work.

Of the 33rd and 34th Inf Div, inducted into Federal Service on March 5, 1941, and February 10, 1941, respectively, there are practically no SSI partially embroidered on wool/khaki twill ever seen. And if there are, they are very hard to find, because probably they were never made in large numbers.

The Regular Army Divisions were from #1 to #25. Only a few of these Div (1st Inf Div to 9th Inf Div, activated between 1918 and 1940) had partially machine-embroidered SSI on wool/khaki twill. The Americal Div, 24th, and 25th Inf Div were activated overseas in a later period, which could explain the (probably) nonexistence of these SSI on wool/khaki twill. (Activation dates were: Americal Div: May 27, 1942; and both the 24th and 25th Inf Div on October 1, 1941.)

Of the National Army Divisions formed in WWI from drafted personnel and starting with the number 76, and which were the basis of the Organized Reserve Divisions of WWII, wool/khaki twill SSI are never seen. These Inf Div, together with the 10th Mountain, 42nd, 63rd, 65th, 66th, 69th, 70th, 71st, and 75th Inf Div were activated from 1942.

To conclude, it appears that wool/khaki twill SSI only were manufactured in the U.S. until the beginning of 1941. Good examples are the early-WWII Armored Div SSI fully machine-embroidered on OD wool. It is a good chance that from then on the fully machine-embroidered, cut-edge SSI on cotton twill-base fabric were introduced.

An additional question could be asked: why are there U.S. made fully machine-embroidered OD wool SSI of late activated U.S. Armored Divisions (Arm Div)? These of the 13th Arm Div (activated October 15, 1942) and 22nd Arm Div (was not even organized during WWII) are good examples and do exist.

In the early years of WWII (1940, when the first of sixteen WWII Arm Div were activated), the U.S. Army might have planned to form more Armored Divisions than they activated during WWII, and therefore might have ordered to manufacture all these SSI in advance. For example, the felt 7th, 8th, and 9th Ranger Battalion Scrolls, and the fully machine-embroidered on cotton twill cut-edge 18th Arm Div patch (also see Fig. 03-916 further on in this book) were also manufactured in anticipation of activation, but were never formed. This would explain the existence of some of those fully machine-embroidered OD wool SSI. Probably only a small number were ordered and manufactured, which also could explain their rare appearance these days.

AN IMPORTANT REMARK ABOUT THE CONSTRUCTION: The unstructured wool or felt base material was less strong than the later applied cotton twill to hold the loops of the embroidery. Because of that the embroidery style was often more open and irregular (like it was very used). That is the reason why in many cases a reinforcement (also called "stabilizer") of black or white mesh or gauze was added at the back of the pre-WWII dated wool/felt SSI. When cotton twill-base fabric was used for the pre-WWII era made SSI for the cotton twill patches, we often see that this kind of reinforcement was continued, although it was unnecessary (see Fig. 01-318 previous). Most likely, it all had to do with the quality label of the manufacturer.

Fig. 01-319: A 44th Inf Div SSI, fully machine-embroidered on OD wool base fabric without reinforced back. Although this is an unused SSI, the little irregularity of the embroidery is because of the less strong OD wool base fabric. This patch shows both nice contiguous and open embroidery.

Fig. 01-320: A 3rd U.S. Army SSI on OD wool with black mesh reinforced back. This is a typical pre-WWII open embroidery pattern (see chapter 3, heading 5) which remained very regular in spite of the less strong wool base fabric. The reinforcement (also called stabilizer) kept the embroidery loops in place.

Other examples are these two pre-WWII SSI below, both with the typical Gemsco embroidery style (see further on in this book). The one manufactured on OD wool (8th Inf Div SSI) was *not* reinforced at the back, and shows a more open manufacture style than the other (36th Inf Div SSI), which is partially machine-embroidered on cotton twill (even with white gauze stabilizer at the back). The details of both fronts are also added below to compare the density or contiguousness of the embroidery style.

Fig. 01-321: Front and back of a pre-WWII 8th Inf Div SSI, fully machine-embroidered on OD wool base material without reinforcement (stabilizer) at the back.

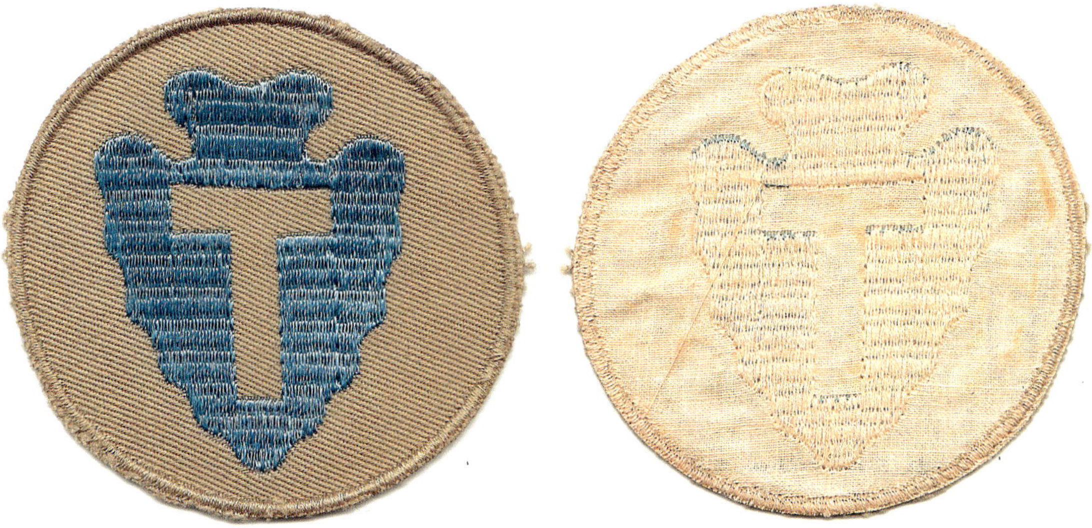

Fig. 01-322: Front and back of a pre-WWII 36th Inf Div SSI, partially machine-embroidered on cotton twill-base fabric with stabilizer at the back. Even without the reinforcement (stabilizer), the cotton twill-base material is strong enough to hold the embroidery loops.

Fig. 01-323: Detail of the front of the OD wool 8th Inf Div SSI illustrated in Fig. 01-321. Although a similar style can be seen, it has a slightly more open and a little less regular embroidery style than the one on cotton twill-base material illustrated in Fig. 01-324 below.

Fig. 01-324: Detail of the front of the 36th Inf Div SSI illustrated in Fig. 01-322, with a very regular embroidery pattern.

4 | FROM THE EARLY 1940s

- Around 1941, the fully machine-embroidered cut-edge SSI, with or without OD border (Olive Drab border), were introduced and are the subject of this book. These were embroidered on a piece of cotton base fabric, also called cotton twill or backing.

All U.S. made fully or partially embroidered SSI were made using an embroidery machine, even those on felt or wool (see further on).

Fig. 01-401: Front and back of a WWII U.S. made, fully machine-embroidered on cotton twill cut-edge 102nd Inf Div SSI.

NOTE

Towards the end of WWII, SSI might be worn on both shoulders on the uniform: as an active duty SSI (the usual left side), and as a former combat (right side) shoulder patch when authorized.

Some SSI were sometimes embroidered to be used on the right shoulder (e.g., the 101st Airborne Div SSI with the Eagle facing the opposite direction – to the right instead of the usual left). Here, it is difficult to find out if these should be WWII or post-WWII era made.

5 | FROM 1957

The same features as described previously in heading (4) of this chapter, but with a green border, following the change in color of the U.S. Army uniform from olive drab (OD) to green.

Fig. 01-501: Front and back of a U.S.-made, fully machine-embroidered on cotton twill cut-edge 38th Inf Div SSI with green border.

Fig. 01-502: Front and back of a U.S.-made, fully machine-embroidered on cotton twill cut-edge 4th Armored Div SSI with green border which is slightly paler than the border in Fig. 01-501 here above

6 | FROM 1968

The same features as described above in heading (5) of this chapter, but with a MERROWED EDGE. The cut-edge manufacturing disappears because of the fraying of the edges. The method invented in the 1930s of new edge embroidery is now applied, and is to this date in use. Although a few patches with merrowed edges from the 1940s and 1950s have been observed, consistent merrowing of military patches did not emerge until this date.

An important feature of this method is the pig tail. This is the woven loose strands of the border that will avoid further fraying of that border. The pigtail extends beyond the patch and is often taped, glued, or sealed to the back of a patch.

Also, at this time nylon and polyester (cheaper, synthetic threads) entered production.

Fig. 01-601: Front and back of a 6th U.S. Army SSI with merrowed edge.

The merrowed edge (also called overedge stitch, overlock stitch, or rolled edge) is a protective border of thread all around the patch's edge, often referred to as a rolled edge because of its appearance, the original purpose of which was to prevent ravelling. To add this kind of stitch, a special machine which is named after the inventor, Joseph M. Merrow (in 1881, by the Merrow Machine Company, Connecticut, U.S.A.), is used. Nowadays the use of this border is widespread.

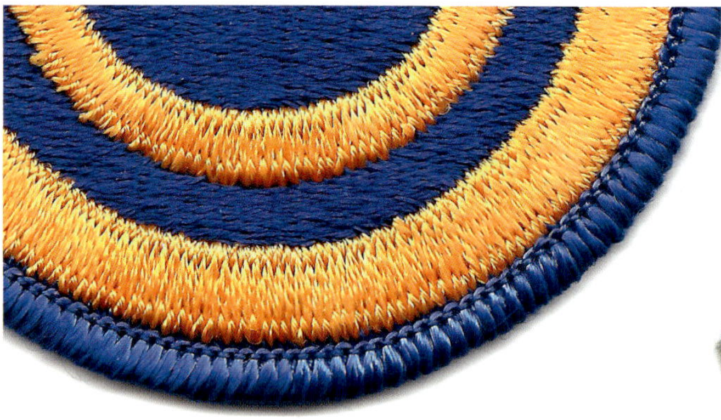

Fig. 01-602

Fig. 01-603

Fig. 01-604: Pigtail of a 79th Inf Div SSI with merrowed edge.

Fig. 01-605: Front and back of a U.S. made, fully machine-embroidered 3rd U.S. Marine Div with merrowed edge and pigtail.

CHAPTER 2
World War II

1 | WOOL SSI – FELT SSI

At the beginning of WWII, the SSI made in the 1930s (embroidered or not) were still issued to troops and worn. This means that wool and felt SSI were still part of the army uniform. A displayed original uniform jacket (see picture below) still has a 1930s felt on OD wool 5th Inf Div SSI. This is good evidence that these kind of SSI also were issued and worn during WWII (e.g., on the service dress).

Fig. 02-101: A 5th Inf Div uniform.

Fig. 02-102: Detail of Fig. 02-101: A 1930s felt on OD wool 5th Inf Div SSI.

Fig. 02-103: The same SSI as illustrated in Fig. 02-102.

During the early 1940s (1940-early 1941), some machine-embroidered on OD wool SSI were still manufactured. The wool U.S. Armored Division SSI are good examples, such as the example below of the 10th Armored Div, which was activated on July 15, 1942. This patch was manufactured on OD wool prior to and in anticipation of the Division's activation. The complete design of these patches was integrally machine-embroidered on OD wool, and then cut to shape and size (around the embroidered design). This also included the additional wool border for sewing the patch on the uniform.

Fig. 02-104: Front and back of a 10th Arm Div SSI, fully machine-embroidered on OD-colored wool-based fabric with black back thread.

Fig. 02-105: Front and back of a pre-WWII 8th Inf Div SSI, fully machine-embroidered on OD wool-based material with white back thread with no reinforcement (stabilizer) on the back.

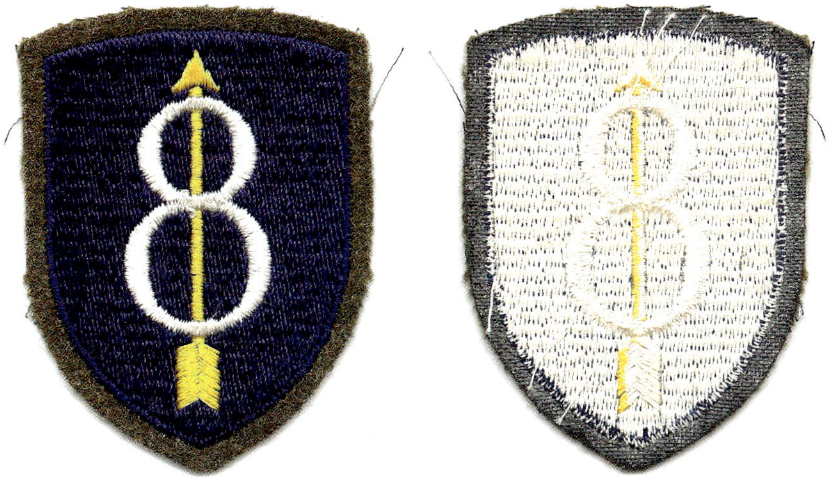

Fig. 02-106: Front and back of a pre-WWII 8th Inf Div SSI, fully machine-embroidered on OD wool base fabric with white back thread and reinforced with black mesh (as stabilizer) on the back.

2 | FULLY MACHINE-EMBROIDERED ON COTTON TWILL, CUT-EDGE SSI

In the early 1940s, a new technique for making SSI was tested and employed. Because wool and felt were not very durable, machine-embroidered SSI on wool wore out very quickly from the wear and washing. (Note: it was also practice in many dry cleaning establishments to remove the patches when dry cleaning uniforms and then sew them back on to avoid damaging them. That is why often snap fasteners on both SSI and service dress uniform were used – to remove and to re-attach the SSI more easily.)

This new commercial technique was now applied on cotton base fabric and called Cut-edge SSI, because of the specific procedure. This was used until the late 1960s, until the MERROWED EDGE SSI was introduced.

CHAPTER 3
WWII U.S. Made Fully Machine-Embroidered Cut-Edge SSI

1 | MANUFACTURING

At the end of 1940-early 1941 in the United States, a new machine-embroidery technique or process was introduced for higher quality SSI, to replace the machine-embroidered SSI on olive drab-colored (OD) wool. A possible theory of this historical fact can be read earlier in this book in chapter 1, heading (3). Using a detailed description, this new technique is discussed on the following pages. (Note: the WWII SSI were manufactured well after the war, as late as 1952, to fulfill WWII U.S. government contracts. However, the application of this new machine-embroidery technique with the "cut-edge" principle was continued until the late 1960s.)

In a logical way of thinking, during and just prior to WWII there would have been three categories of patches (and other insignia) available to soldiers.

The first of these categories were those purchased at government expense by the Quartermaster Corps (QM) and issued to enlisted men at no cost to be sewn on their uniforms. These should be the most common of the SSI types that have survived.

The second category are those SSI that were privately purchased by the soldier in question, and that he would have had to pay his own money for. Some of these could have been identical to those of the first category (from the same manufacturer source as those issued by the QM), but some were not.

The third category are those insignia that were contracted for and purchased by an entire unit, out of unit or individual funds, done outside of government channels and in small lots (local and foreign theater made). Many of the airborne insignia were done in this third way. They were approved by local authority on the unit's own initiative and manufactured, and were not provided by the QM.

When one encounters an unusual SSI manufactured in a style never before seen, it is possible that it is a privately purchased one. It is clear that some SSI were privately purchased and put on the uniform by the tailor who tailored the uniform. That would be a type of the second category. Officers bought their own uniforms, while enlisted men were issued uniforms. You are more likely to see unusual patches of the second category on officers' uniforms.

This book will only describe the manufacturing of SSI of the first category, provided of course that they are fully machine-embroidered on a specific medium.

Fig. 03-101: Front and back of a WWII U.S. made, cut edge 80th Inf Div SSI.

These SSI were not made by hand, but were MACHINE-EMBROIDERED by contracted civilian, privately owned companies on a commercial basis.

On a large piece of cotton twill-base fabric, or short COTTON TWILL (technical collector term: BACKING), rayon threads were embroidered using a large mechanized embroidery machine (the Schiffli embroidery machine, invented by Isaak Groebli, Sankt-Gallen, Switzerland, in 1863). The embroidery process was imported into the U.S.A., but was not used until the 1930s to embroider SSI on a large scale basis for the U.S. Army. From the 1940s it is the common way of manufacturing SSI.

On that particular embroidery machine, several hundreds of needles are active to make several dozens of patches at once to meet the demand for this private, largely commercial manufacturing process. The used base fabric was provided on large rolls which could be used that way on the Schiffli embroidery machine. In a few words, it is a way of manufacturing insignia by applying a two-thread system machine embroidering (with front yarn and back yarn) on a base fabric, and utilizing (on a loom) the combination of a continuously threaded needle and shuttle containing a bobbin of thread. It was operated by a single person (operator).

This kind of embroidery is called Schiffli embroidery, also Swiss embroidery, because of its Swiss origin at the end of the nineteenth century.

Fig. 03-102: An example of a Schiffli embroidery machine.

The process begins with a drawing of the SSI, which was created by a designer of that company according to the SSI's specifications and standards (see further on in this book). This drawing was enlarged to five or six times the size of the finished patch, with every stitch actually drawn in by hand. The operator on the Schiffli embroidery machine manually traced every indicated stitch line with a metal stylus, creating a punched paper template. This punched paper tape is mechanically read by a machine that directs the hundreds of needles, placed horizontally one above the other on the loom, simultaneously. That way, multiple copies of identical designs could be created.

Fig. 03-103: The operator on a Schiffli embroidery machine.

With the base fabric held in a frame covering the full width of the machine, the needles moved back and forth through the material. The yarn used to embroider the base fabric was supplied from large individual spools (or bobbins), which had to be replaced when the thread was used up (hence, the many manufacturer errors when this was overlooked, or when the wrong bobbin was installed). A different color of thread was used on each pass during the embroidering. This layered one color on top of another, creating a bas relief effect in the design. This feature is one of the differences with woven fabric, which is even (see further on in this heading). With embroidery two or three layers are common, but attempting to penetrate too many layers (thickness) tends to break the embroidery machine's needles.

As mentioned above, this kind of embroidery had its origin in Switzerland. The SSI made that way are often referred to as Schiffli patches because they are made on Schiffli looms. The shuttle, containing the bobbin and utilized on these looms, resembles the shape of a sailboat's hull, and "Schiffli" means "little boat" in the Swiss dialect of the German language.

Here it is necessary to note that, given the large amount of variety in embroidery patterns, presumably other types of embroidery machines might have been used besides the commonly used Schiffli embroidery machine. This fact remains a presumption, although many different types of embroidery machines do exist.

The vast majority of the WWII U.S. made SSI were being produced by private manufacturers on government contract, and by government specifications and standards ("The Institute of Heraldry" Drawings – see chapter 8, heading 1). These specifications specified the final appearance of the patch, but did allow some discretion by the manufacturer as to just how it would be made. It is because so many different manufacturers were involved and the need was so great that we see all these small variations in the final product. Examples of these different patterns are illustrated further on in this book.

During WWII, all embroidery threads used for making SSI were RAYON fibers.
References to this fact are:

- Kaufman, David A. "Patch Styles and Manufacture." *The Trading Post*: the official quarterly publication of the American Society of Military Insignia Collectors (ASMIC), Edition Apr-Jun 2002;
- Conejos, Sean. "Synthetically Speaking, WWII Won't Have Synthetic Threads" *The Trading Post*, Edition Oct-Dec 2011.

Rayon is a manufactured regenerated cellulose fiber. Because it is produced from naturally occurring polymers, it is neither a truly synthetic fiber nor a natural fiber; it is a semi-synthetic or artificial fiber. Rayon is known by the names viscose rayon and art silk in the textile industry. It usually has a high luster quality, giving it a bright sheen. It is cheap and feels smooth on the skin, though it is weak when wet. It was produced in large quantities through the 1930s for commercial needs. At that time the fully machine-embroidered SSI on wool were introduced and manufactured on a larger scale commercial basis. To meet the higher standards (respective) of the pre-WWII and WWII patch, these large scale productions of rayon came just in time.

IMPORTANT REMARK: Embroidery style versus weave style

In literature, on the Internet, or among collectors, two specific WWII embroidery styles which can be seen on SSI – the Gemsco embroidery style and the ribbed embroidery style (see further on in this book) – are mostly called the Gemsco and ribbed *weave* style, respectively. Although these particular SSI are embroidered, and to avoid misunderstandings regarding the fact that none of the styles discussed in this book are woven but embroidered, the term embroidery here is better placed.

For an embroidered style, one needs two threads and a medium (specific base fabric) to embroider on. On the other hand, a woven style has two threads without medium. Another feature is the fact that woven texture is even unlike the bas relief-like type of style, because of the different layers of the embroidered design. Also, at the back of a woven style, the colors are reversed from the front (e.g., WWI Liberty Loan patches – see earlier; and some WWII and post-WWII German and Italian theater made woven SSI – see the two examples below illustrated as Fig. 03-104 and Fig. 03-105). The embroidered SSI does not have this feature.

Fig. 03-104: Front and back of a WWII Italian made, woven 34th Inf Div SSI.

Fig. 03-105: Front and back of a WWII Italian made, woven 15th Army Group SSI with folded border.

In general and as written above, in the technique with the Schiffli embroidery machine, the thread loop has the shape of a double-ended small boat. See pictures below.

Fig. 03-106: Detail of a WWII machine-embroidered 9th USAAF SSI.

Fig. 03-107: Detail of a WWII machine-embroidered 33rd Inf Div SSI.

If one sews by hand, one can pull the same thread from both sides of the cloth, but a sewing and embroidery machine can work only by having two different threads on either side (both on a BOBBIN).

A main thread (on the front of the SSI, also DESIGN thread) is fixed or caught by a second thread at the back of the SSI to avoid the main thread coming loose (see pictures on the following pages). The thread on the back, in technical terms BACK THREAD, has a typical appearance in the U.S.-made SSI. This back thread will also be part of determining the originality of the SSI. More about this item will be discussed below.

When completely embroidered with threads and so completely covering the cotton twill-base fabric (no more visible backing), these SSI are called in the jargon FULLY (MACHINE-) EMBROIDERED SSI. (Note: the same terminology can be used with the SSI which were fully machine-embroidered on OD wool.)

On the following page, illustrated as Fig. 03-108, is an example of a flawed patch of the 90th Inf Div. A large part of the SSI has not been embroidered. Most likely the red rayon thread to create the "T" and the "O" of the design was used up and the operator probably forgot to replace that specific bobbin with a new one. With this example one can clearly see the way of embroidering. First the design's background was manufactured, then the design details were marked and embroidered (the "Tough Ombres" symbol). As one can see, the background did not cover the whole SSI completely. In the center of the SSI, a part of the khaki cotton twill-base material is still visible. The place where the details had to come were uncovered to save design threads and embroidering time. Only an overlap was foreseen. The red design is double embroidered to become a bas relief effect in the patch design for which Schiffli embroidery is known.

Fig. 03-108: A flawed 90th Inf Div SSI which demonstrates how a patch was manufactured.

Fig. 03-109: Detail of the back of an 8th Inf Div SSI. The loops of the two different threads can clearly been seen. The main thread is fixed or caught by a second thread (back thread) at the back of the SSI.

Fig. 03-110: Detail of the back of a 135th AB "Phantom" Div SSI.

A border was machine-embroidered around the design which was always focused inward. This means that the thread of the border is always perpendicular to the cut-edge. This would in effect lock in the embroidery and prevent ravelling of the SSI.

Once the patches were embroidered on the cotton twill-base material (see Fig. 03-111 and 03-112) they were individually hand-cut (see Fig. 03-113).

Fig. 03-111: Several SSI of the 31st Inf Div on the same piece of khaki cotton twill-base fabric after manufacture.

Fig. 03-112: Back of Fig. 03-111.

Fig. 03-113: Front and back of an individually cut 92nd Inf Div SSI, fully machine-embroidered on khaki cotton twill-base fabric.

Once the SSI was individually cut, the cotton twill was further cut to the edges of the embroidery (the border). For this reason, these SSI are called CUT-EDGE SSI. At the side of the border one often sees the remnants of the cotton base fabric or backing (see Fig. 03-114 below).

Fig. 03-114: A WWII U.S. made, cut-edge 66th Inf Div patch (2nd design) with remnants of the khaki cotton twill backing at the edge of the SSI.

In this trimming, it often happened that the edge threads of the border accidentally were damaged or cut through because one wanted to cut the remnants of the backing too close to the edge. Although the SSI was damaged, the repair did not take long. For that reason, and because more and more SSI were needed in the course of WWII, these were not lost or discarded during this period. In many cases, the cut part of the border was repaired by simply stitching or embroidering with the same color of rayon thread. Due to the repairs, the SSI in that place is thicker and sometimes less flexible because of this.

Fig. 03-115: Front and back of a repaired 27th Inf Div SSI.

Fig. 03-116: A slight shift in the embroidery of a 69th Inf Div SSI.

NOTES

1 This way of repair was also often used for each part of the SSI where any threads were loose (front and/or back), as well as small portions of the SSI where no thread was embroidered and where a little part of the cotton base fabric still was visible.

2 There are also plenty of examples of SSI with a slight shift in the embroidery (due to human error, or an error in the embroidery machine), and which have never been recovered. One can see a small portion (line) of the cotton base fabric on one side next to the border, on both the front and the back of the SSI. These can be labelled as errors.

REMARK: Unfinished SSI where entire sections and pieces of embroidery are missing can also be found, but have nothing to do with the feature (slight shift) mentioned in point 2 here above. Below is an example of a WWII USAAF SSI (Fig. 03-117) where a large piece of the left wing is missing. One can even see the khaki cotton twill-base fabric. Here the thread on the bobbin to embroider that certain part of the SSI was probably used up and the bobbin had to be replaced (and may have been done too late). These were often never repaired, such as the one on the next page.

Fig. 03-117: Front and back of an unrepaired USAAF SSI.

Fig. 03-117a: An unrepaired 14th Armored Div SSI (see the red section and OD border). Nevertheless, the last added details during manufacture (divisional number, lightning bolt, caterpillar, etc.) are finished. This could mean that, during the embroidery process of this particular patch, one did not replace the empty coils of red and OD-colored thread.

After the shoulder patches were finished, they were bundled (with string – example: see Fig. 03-118 below) and packed in a box. Once labelled, they were shipped to the unit or the stock.

Fig. 03-118: Example of a factory tied bundle of U.S. IX Corps patches.

Fig. 03-119: A labelled box of 200 U.S. IX Corps SSI.

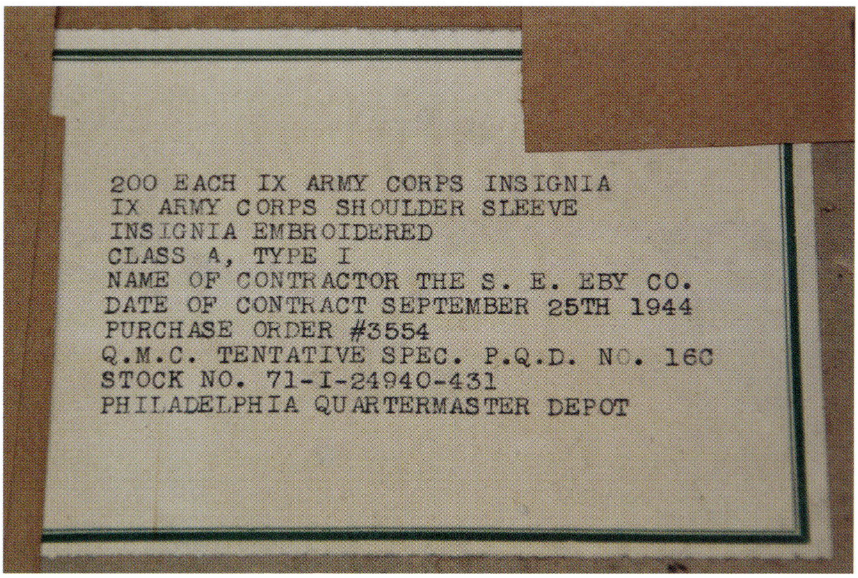

2 | TYPES OF BASE FABRIC OR BACKING

An embroidery style consists of two threads and a medium on which one embroiders. This medium, the base fabric, is also called backing in the collector world and could be any kind of fabric (wool, felt, cotton twill). (Note: a woven style needs two threads and no medium.)

During WWII, cotton twill was used as the backing material for the cut-edge SSI. It was utilized in all possible colors.

At the beginning of WWII, mainly Olive Drab-colored (OD) cotton twill was used. Later KHAKI cotton twill (also TAN cotton twill) was more utilized as backing because the OD cotton threads were needed for other applications, such as uniforms and tents.

At the end of WWII (late 1944 to early 1945), base material that was black, blue, or even yellow was used, because the backing was completely covered with embroidery and it could not be seen anyway.

The backing NEVER lights under UV light in all cases, not even on the edge!

Fig. 03-201: KHAKI or TAN cotton twill base fabric or backing.

Fig. 03-202: OD cotton twill backing – front and back of a WWII 82nd Airborne Div SSI.

Fig. 03-203: KHAKI cotton twill backing – front and back of a WWII 82nd Airborne Div SSI.

REMARKS:

- Fig. 03-202 to Fig. 03-204: The cotton twill backing had yet to be cut away by the military before the SSI was sewn on the uniform.
- In certain cases, explanations of historical facts of battles in which the unit was part are sometimes given to the remaining separate fixed threads on the backing that is often left on the SSI (see pictures Fig. 03-202 to Fig. 03-204 – the separate, embroidered threads between tab and shield of the SSI). These colored embroidery threads are needed to continue the machine embroidery from one patch to the next on the same piece of cotton twill backing, without being cut through during the embroidery process. After all, the SSI were manufactured with continuous threads coming from bobbins. Often those remnants were cut off after the SSI's completion. These separate, embroidered threads can also be seen in Fig 03-201.

Fig. 03-204: Blue cotton twill backing – WWII 101st AB Div SSI.

NOTE

About the separate threads between tab and shield (see remarks on the previous page and the figure above) with the 101st AB Div SSI in Fig. 03-204: I once was told that the three colored threads (red, white, and yellow) specified the three bridges in the vicinity of Carentan (Normandy, France) conquered by the Division during the June 1944 battle. Likely, this is because of the bridge-like appearance of the three threads. That is too good to be true! Maybe veterans saw their experiences and the unit's events in the drawing made by those threads, or maybe heroic stories are sometimes invented by sellers or distributors to upgrade the value of the SSI. Nevertheless, this fact makes this SSI very special and rarely seen.

Fig. 03-205: Black cotton twill backing – See the frayed threads at the top of the SSI (edge).

Fig. 03-206: Yellow cotton twill backing – See the frayed threads on the edge of the SSI.

Fig. 03-207: Detail of Fig. 03-206.

In a later period in the U.S. (probably late 1944 to early 1945), manufacturers went even further in their efforts to be more efficient. The color of the cotton twill backing was used *as a visible part* if permitted by the color of the SSI to save embroidery threads, and to gain time in the production process. More SSI were needed, and could be manufactured in a shorter time using this method. When a background base fabric was used, only the different colored parts of the design of the SSI were then embroidered using the process described above.

This method of partial embroidery was used as early as the 1930s and continued into the early 1940s (1941-1942), and was utilized for SSI for the summer uniform, where the khaki cotton twill backing had the same color as that kind of uniform (see above chapter 1, heading 3). These were also issued to troops and worn during WWII.

Fig. 03-208: Partially machine-embroidered on blue cotton twill backing (center) – Late-WWII U.S. made, cut-edge 3rd USAAF SSI, reinforced with gauze (stabilizer) at the back.

Fig. 03-209: Partially machine-embroidered on black cotton twill backing – WWII 2nd Inf Div SSI, not reinforced at the back.

Fig. 03-210: Blue cotton twill backing – WWII U.S. XX Corps SSI reinforced with gauze (as stabilizer).

Fig. 03-211: White cotton twill backing – WWII U.S. XXIII Corps SSI reinforced with gauze (as stabilizer).

Fig. 03-212: Green cotton twill backing – WWII 90th Inf Div SSI reinforced with gauze (as stabilizer).

Fig. 03-213: Golden orange-colored cotton twill-base fabric – A WWII eight-wheel variant of the Tank Destroyer Forces SSI, reinforced with gauze (= stabilizer).

Fig. 03-214: For comparison a WWII U.S. made, fully machine-embroidered cut-edge SSI of the same unit as in Fig. 03-213.

Fig. 03-215: Front and back of an early-WWII, partially machine-embroidered khaki (or tan) cotton twill cut-edge 1st U.S. Army SSI with wide border for wear on the summer uniform (see chapter 1, heading 3).

Do not confuse Fig. 03-215 with the following. Below is a pre-WWII example of a 26th Inf Div patch with the same application of the cotton twill (khaki-colored). But because of the fine stitched border, it is certainly not a WWII cut-edge SSI such as the previous one.

Fig. 03-216: Front and back of a pre-WWII, partially machine-embroidered khaki (or tan) cotton twill 26th Inf Div SSI for wear on the summer uniform.

3 | DESIGN THREAD OR MAIN THREAD

The main thread determines the colors and embroidered design of the insignia. During the embroidery process it is put on a large bobbin which is placed on the embroidery machine.

The embroidery of the WWII U.S. made fully machine-embroidered, cut-edge SSI has:

- No loose embroidery style, but nicely close (contiguous) threads;
- Bright colors;
- Main thread NEVER lights under UV light in all cases.

REMARK: There are exceptions with looser embroidery (less contiguous threads). This will be discussed in chapter 3, heading 5: "Embroidery styles or patterns."

Yet the SSI show different patterns or embroidery styles of WWII machine-embroidery, reflecting the various companies who made them. Some examples (details) follow.

Fig. 03-301: Detail of a WWII cut-edge 33rd Inf Div SSI.

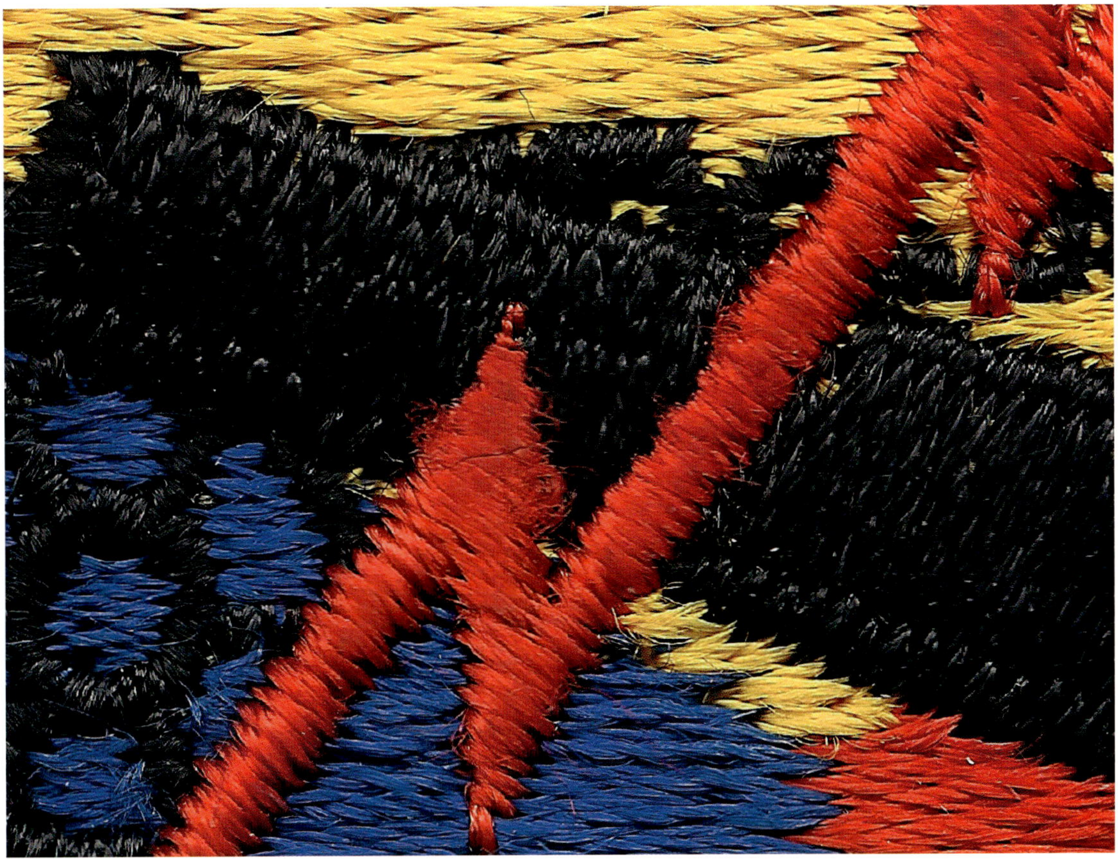

Fig. 03-302: Detail of a WWII cut-edge Armored Div SSI.

Fig. 03-303: Detail of a WWII cut-edge Allied Forces SSI.

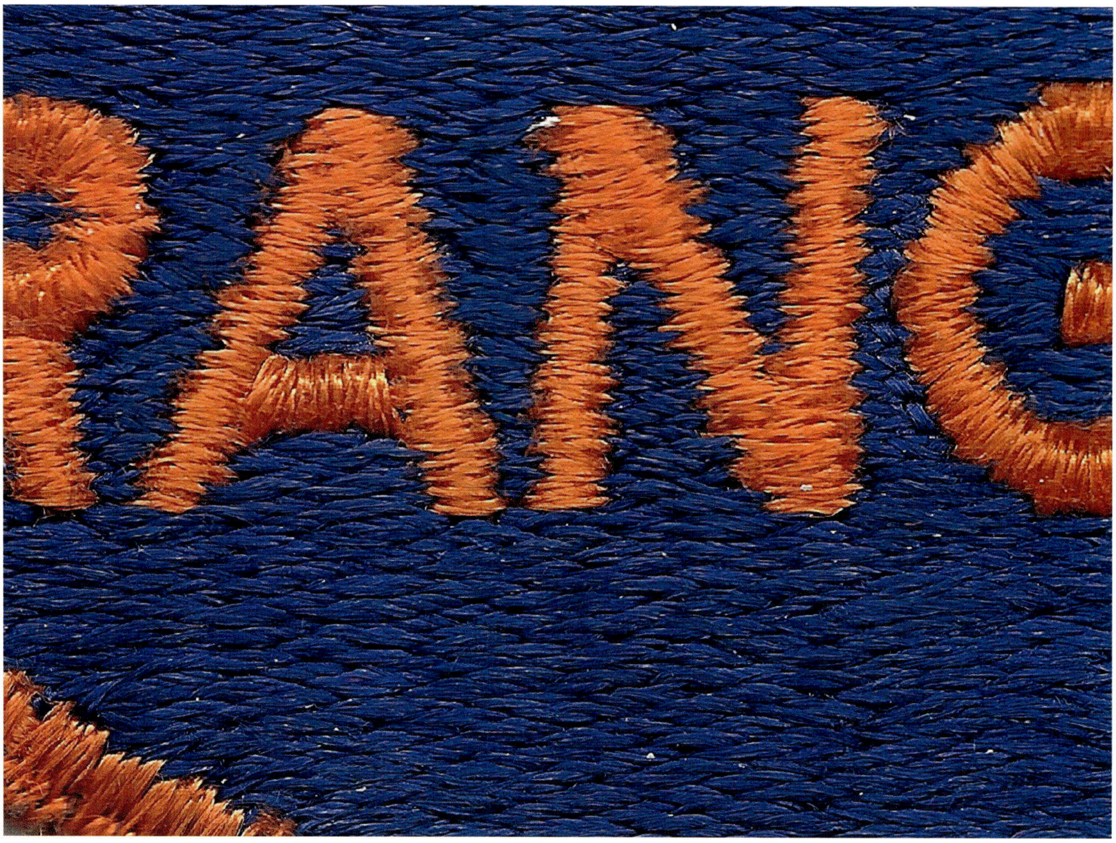

Fig. 03-304: Detail of a WWII cut-edge Rangers lozenge patch.

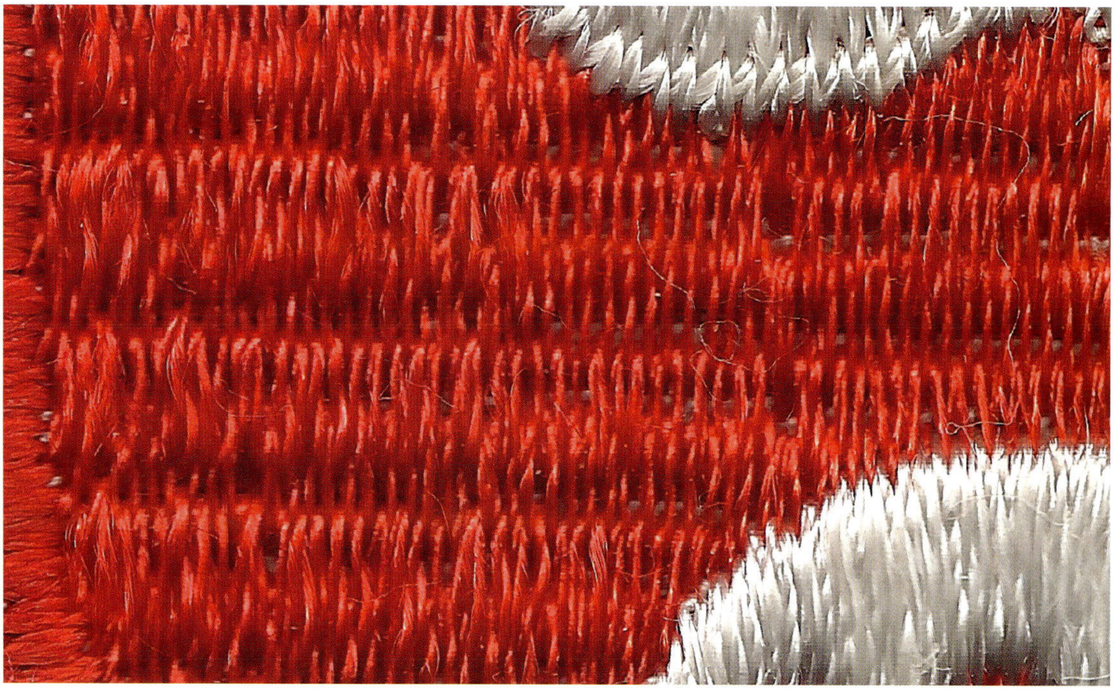

Fig. 03-305: Detail of a WWII cut-edge Airborne Command SSI – Gemsco embroidery style. (Note: Gemsco: General Merchandising Co., Milford, CT, U.S.A.)

Fig. 03-306: Detail of a WWII cut-edge 3rd Inf Div SSI – ribbed embroidery style.

Fig. 03-307: Detail of a WWII cut-edge 92nd Inf Div SSI – ribbed embroidery style.

4 | BACK THREAD

As explained before, in the machine-embroidery procedure two threads are used. When one sews by hand one can pull the same thread from both sides of the cloth. But a sewing and an embroidery machine can work only by having two different threads (and two needles) on either side (both on a BOBBIN).

The back of the U.S. made WWII SSI has threads of the same quality as the main thread. This thread at the rear side of the patch serves to keep the main thread (which determines the colors and embroidered design of the SSI) fixed on the backing, and is called in technical terms BACK THREAD. The loosening of the main thread is thus avoided. So, together with the much stronger cotton twill-base fabric, that way the durability of the SSI is increased.

Back thread is also referred to as BOBBIN THREAD or CATCH THREAD, because it is the catch thread, usually placed on a bobbin on the underside of a conventional home sewing machine or a commercial embroidery machine, that catches the main thread at the back of the base fabric. It is not clear if there is a technical difference between the two terms that would make one of them preferred. It is mentioned here because many collectors use the term bobbin thread and may not recognize the term back thread, although the term bobbin thread could be misinterpreted, because the main thread at the front of the insignia was also on a bobbin to use with the same kind of machine.

Fig. 03-401: The back of this WWII 45th Inf Div SSI is completely covered with white back thread. Sometimes this is called SNOW because of the large quantity of white color appearing on the back due to these threads.

In my opinion and experience I have built during the time of collecting, this back thread for original WWII SSI has virtually the same thickness and quality as the main thread. In no case could I identify a thinner back thread on a WWII patch. In many later made SSI (post-WWII), sometimes a difference in thickness can be seen. The back thread is sometimes thinner and has a fishing thread or nylon kind of view, although it is rayon (example: see Fig. 03-402 on the following page).

Fig. 03-402: Front and back of a post-WWII 3rd U.S. Army SSI.

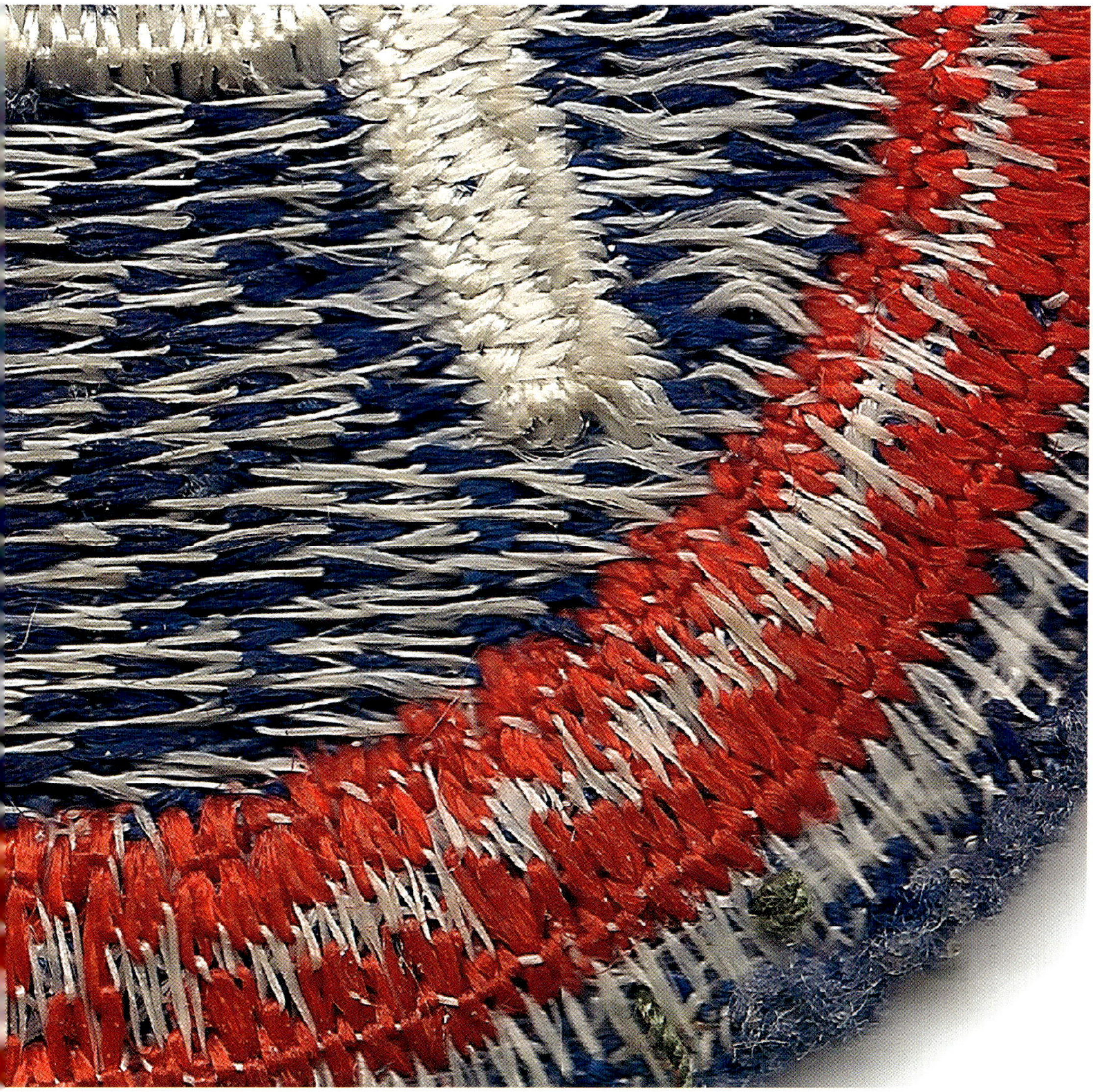

Fig. 03-403: Detail of the back of the 3rd U.S. Army patch illustrated in Fig. 03-402. Note the thinner back thread compared to the main thread.

But in most cases, post-WWII SSI are equal to their WWII counterparts (see some examples below). This is simply because the same construction technique of WWII was continued until the 1960s.

Fig. 03-404: Front and back of a 1950s Far East Command HQ SSI.

Fig. 03-405: Front and back of a 1950s 1st U.S. Army SSI.

Fig. 03-406: Front and back of a post-WWII General Headquarters U.S. Army Pacific SSI.

Fig. 03-407: Front and back of a post-WWII SSI of the Airborne Infantry component of the 8th Inf Div.

Fig. 03-408: Front and back of another post-WWII SSI of the Airborne Infantry component of the 8th Inf Div.

NOTE | Regarding Fig. 03-407 & Fig. 03-408

The 8th Inf Div was an active duty Army unit stationed in Mainz, Germany, and although mechanized, it had an Airborne Infantry component assigned to the Division from 1958 to 1973. The patches illustrated above have a cut-edge, so it would probably have been made in the 1958 to 1967 time frame.

My theory and assumption is that during WWII, the companies which made rayon threads always made the threads of the same thickness in order to have good quality SSI. During WWII, rayon was produced on the production line presumably without distinction of thickness. During this production, the viscose solution was forced through a device resembling a shower head with many small holes called a spinneret. Each hole produced a fine filament of rayon. Because of the necessary mass production there was simply no time to adjust those production lines to create rayon threads of different thickness. After being colored the rayon fibers were practically all of the same kind. Also, it is doubtful that the companies that made SSI would take the time to stock threads of different thicknesses. This remains only a theory, but one that is supported by the large number of WWII-era made SSI I have seen.

Depending on the period and the company, these back threads have a certain color that in most cases is different from the main colors of the SSI.

But most important, *the back thread NEVER lights under UV light in all cases.*

The variety of back thread used during WWII can be seen on the following pages. Also see the pictures with the examples of the back thread in the previous and following chapters. By this back thread alone, the amount of variations of patches is enormous.

The WWII back thread in detail:

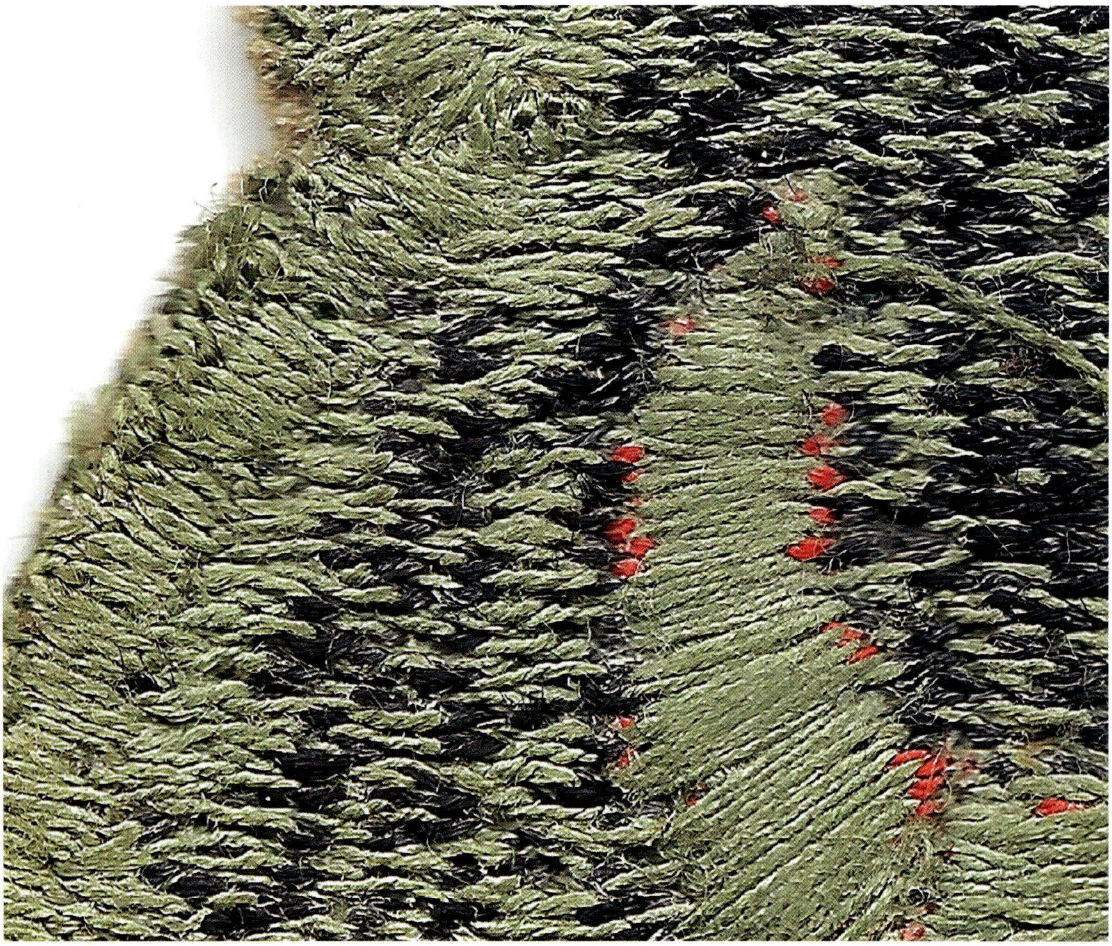

Fig. 03-409: Detail of the back of a WWII cut-edge 34th Inf Div patch with OD back thread.

Fig. 03-410: Detail of the back of a WWII cut-edge 77th Inf Div patch – OD back.

Fig. 03-411: White back thread.

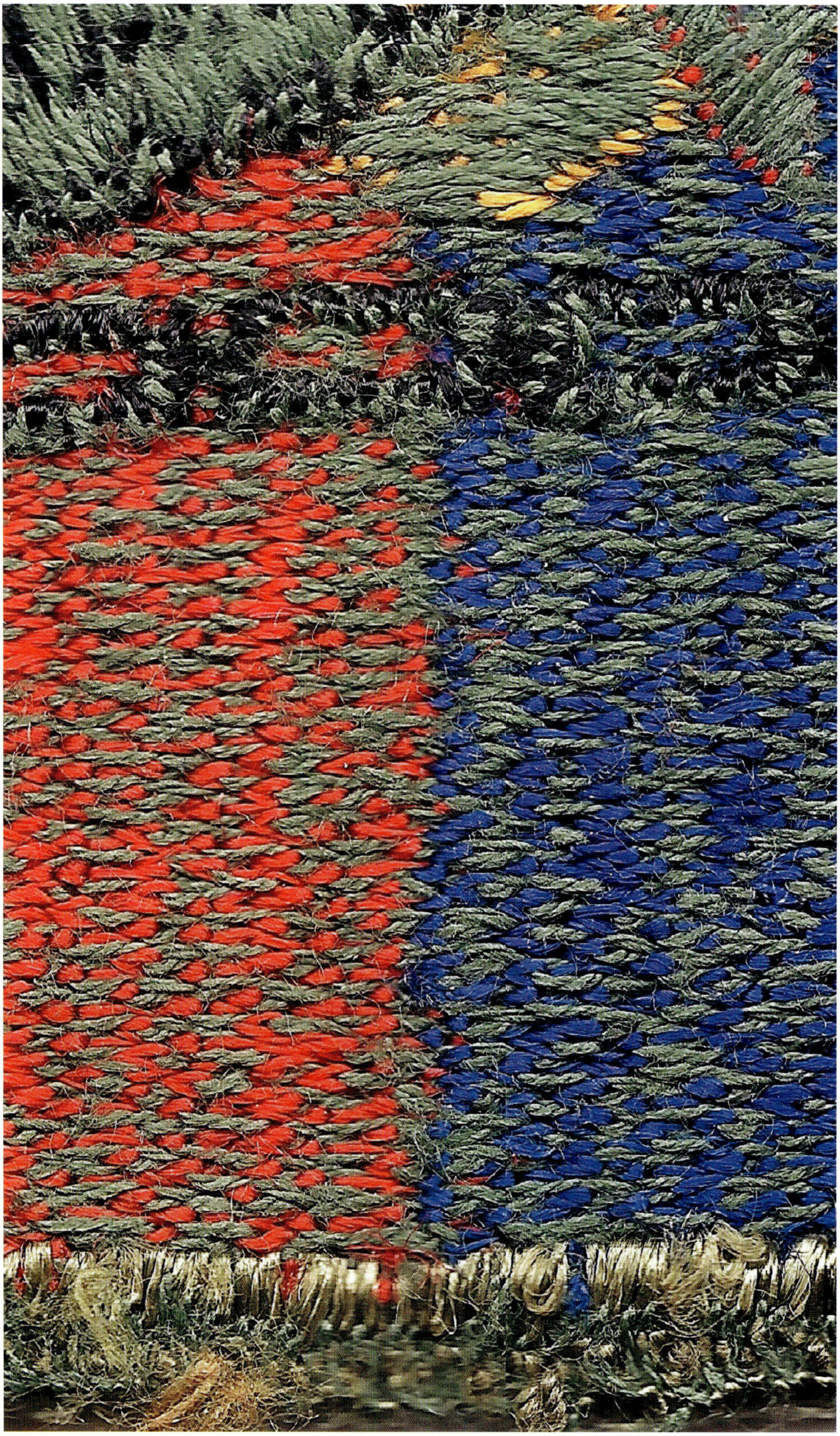

Fig. 03-412: Detail of the back of a WWII cut-edge Armored Div SSI with OD back thread.

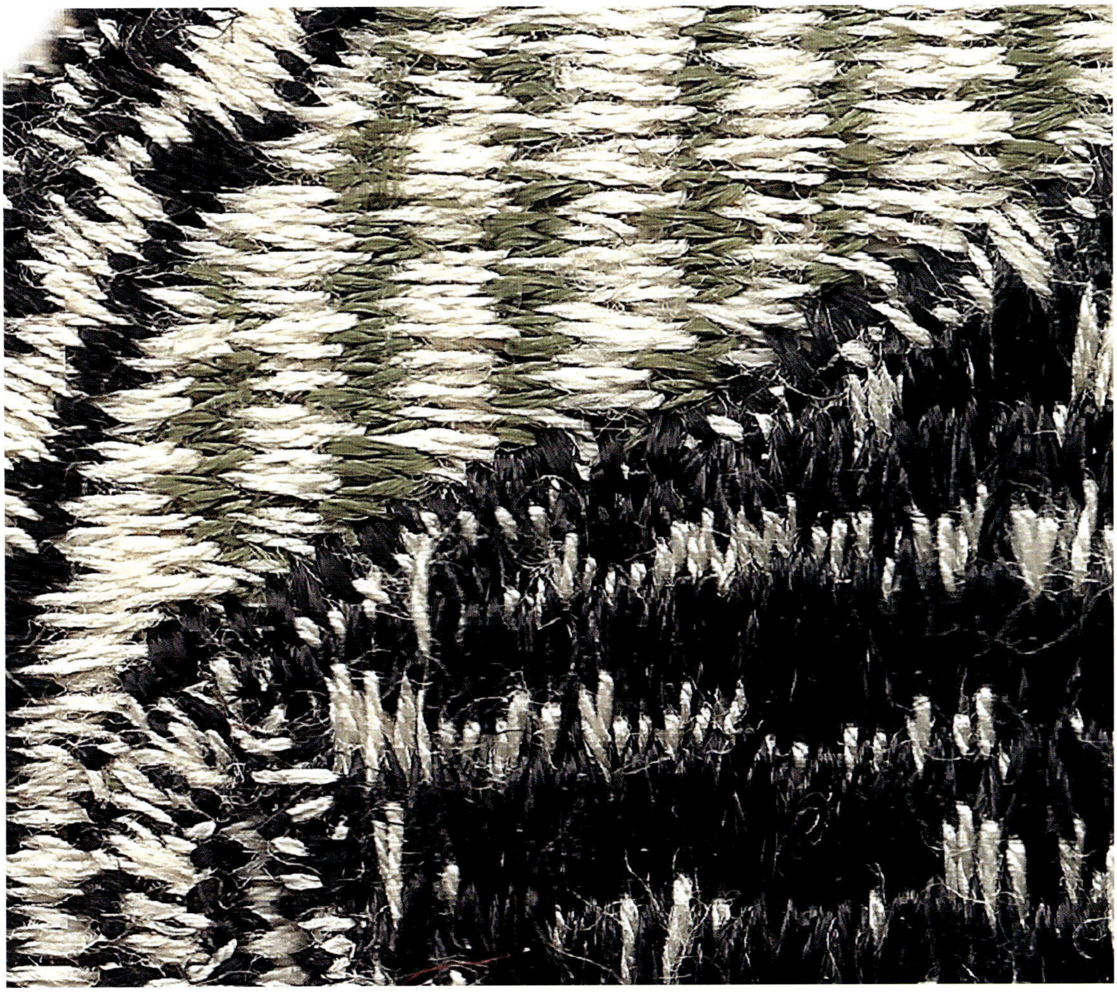

Fig. 03-413: White back – ribbed embroidery style.

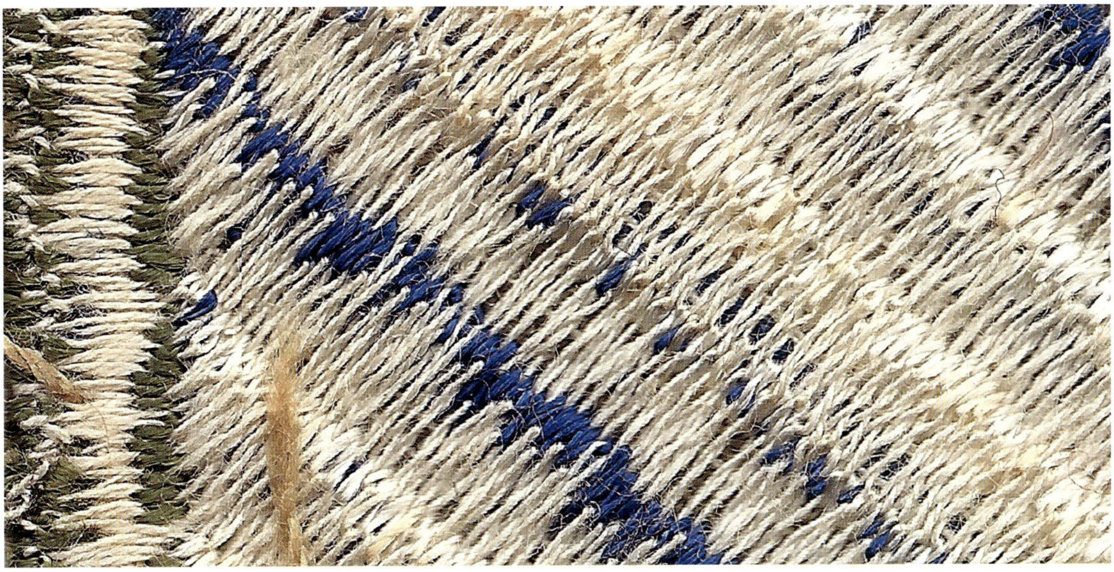

Fig. 03-414: Detail of the back of a WWII cut-edge 3rd Inf Div white back SSI – ribbed embroidery style.

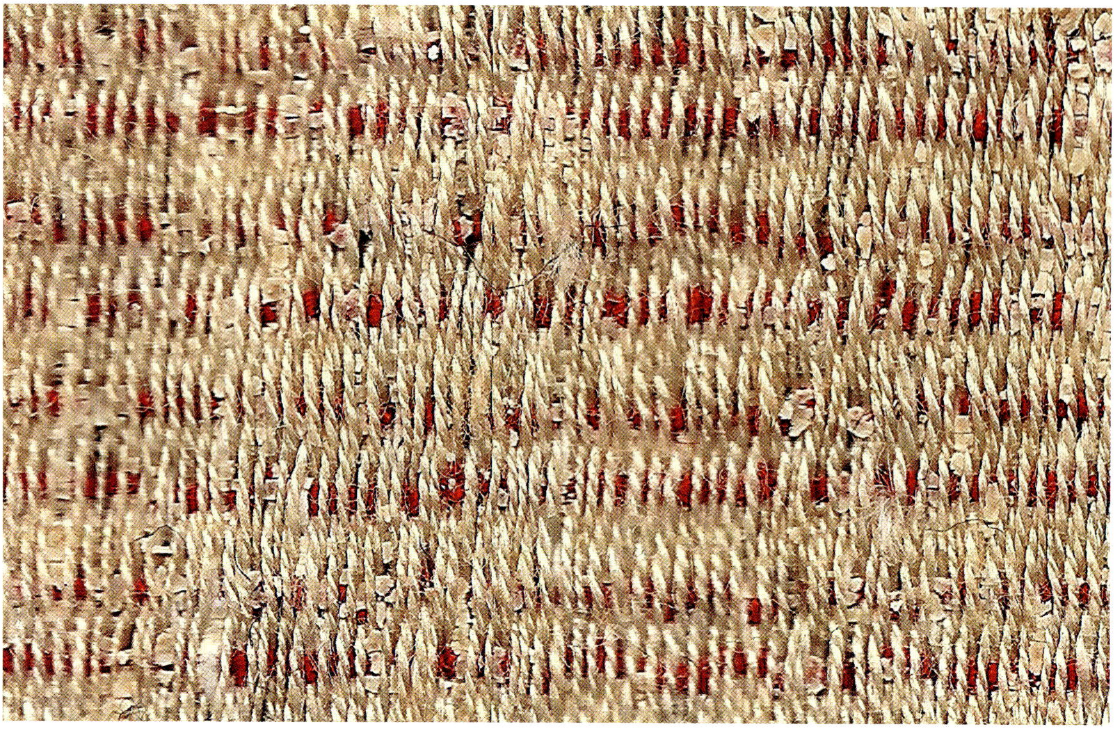

Fig. 03-415: Detail of the back of a WWII cut-edge 28th Inf Div white back SSI with Gemsco embroidery style. Note the remnants of glue or a varnish-like product.

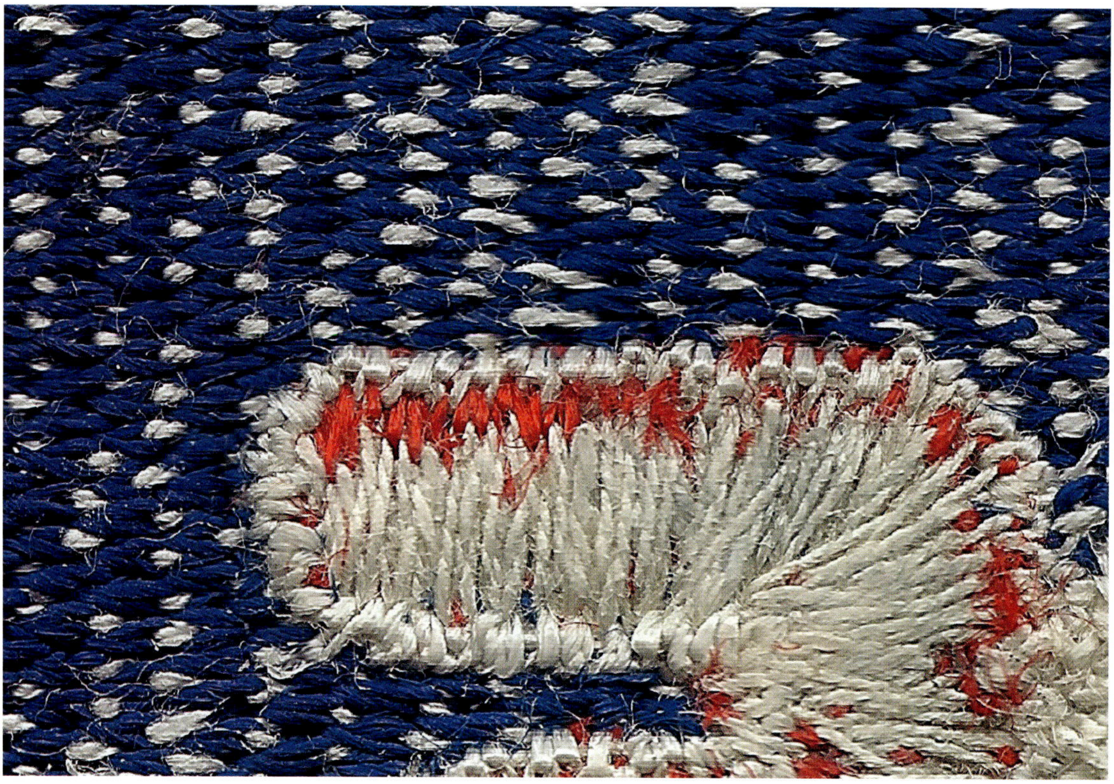

Fig. 03-416: Detail of the back of a WWII cut-edge 75th Inf Div white back SSI. Note the very small loops of the white back thread.

Fig. 03-417: Detail of the back of a WWII cut-edge 1st Inf Div white back SSI.

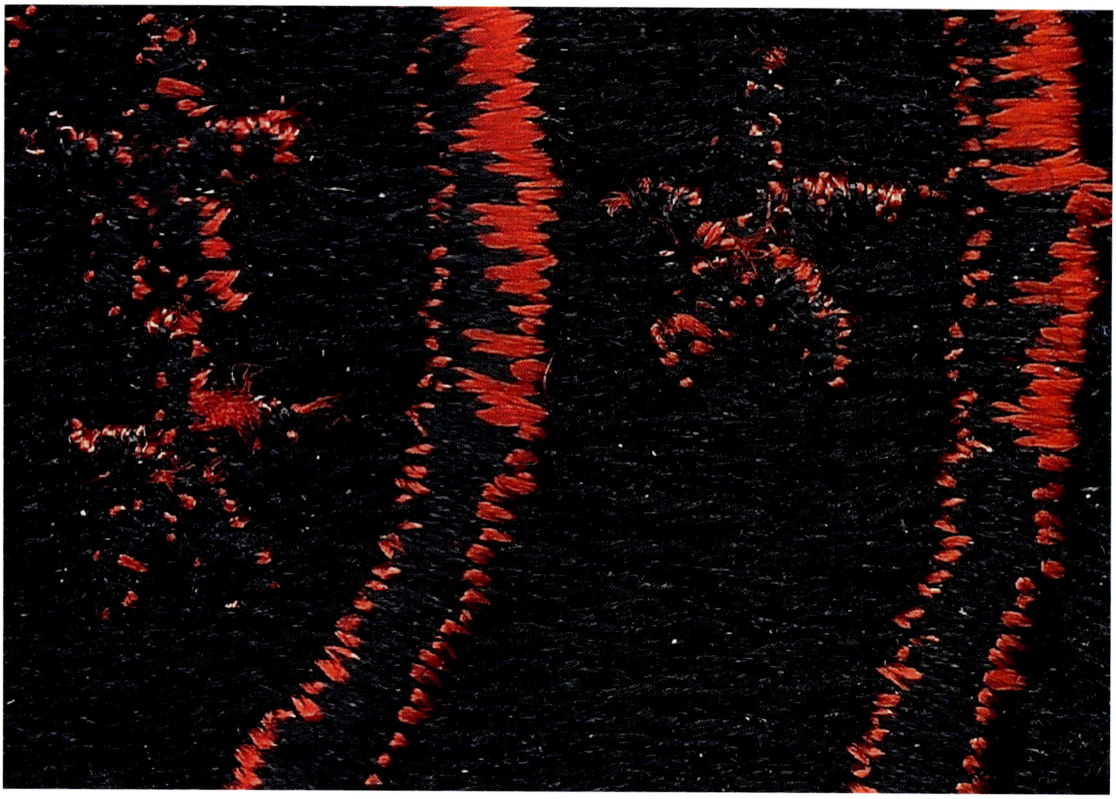

Fig. 03-418: Detail of the back of a WWII cut-edge 27th Inf Div black back SSI.

Fig. 03-419: Detail of the back of a WWII cut-edge 2nd Inf Div white back SSI. The back thread has a very regular pattern.

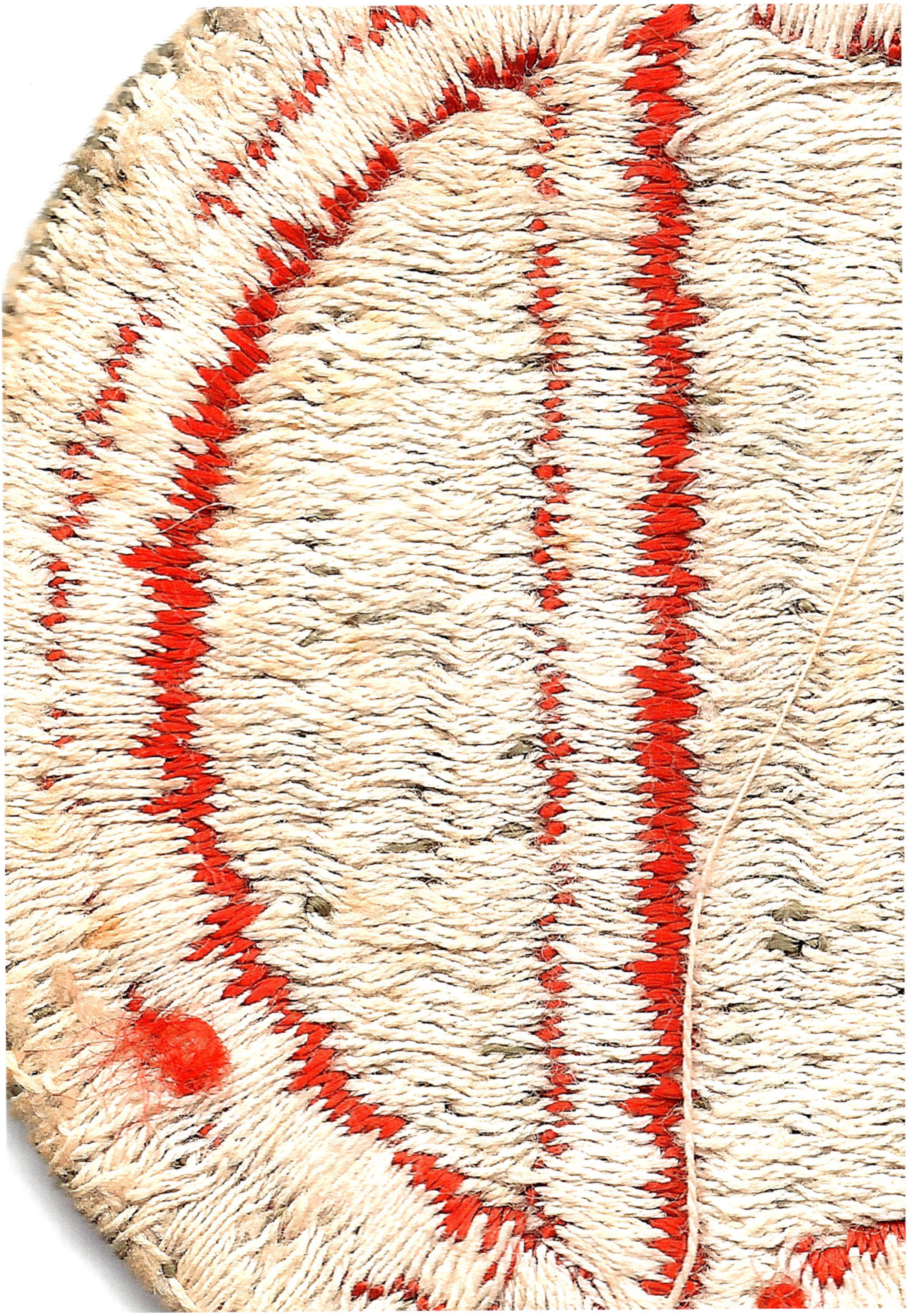

Fig. 03-420: Detail of the back of a WWII cut-edge 85th Inf Div white back SSI. The back is completely covered with white back thread.

The color of the WWII back thread ranges from olive drab (OD), black, white, grey, green, brown, and purple to light and dark blue. (Note: The term "SNOW" that often appears in literature is a reference to the degree of the appearance of whiteness caused by the used white back thread at the back of the SSI.)

What was available was used. From experience, it should be noted that these colors were used the least as the main color, and thus were sufficient in stock; except for the OD-colored fiber, which during WWII (somewhere around the end of 1942 to early 1943) was presumably changed as a back thread because that color of thread was needed for uniforms, tents, and other miscellaneous materials for military equipment. The SSI of later activated Divisions are seldom seen with OD back thread, which strengthens this assumption.

The manufacturers probably had directives to be thrifty with this kind of thread in their stocks, and to use it only when necessary (according to the U.S. government's specifications). From then on during WWII, it could have been difficult for these companies to obtain the OD thread because of these other applications.

Since the construction of the fully machine-embroidered SSI on wool or felt base fabric during the 1930s, there were already back threads of different colors:

Machine-embroidered on wool base fabric:
Fig. 03-421 to Fig. 03-426.

Fig. 03-422: White back.

Fig. 03-423: Light blue back.

Fig. 03-421: White back.

Fig. 03-424: Black back.

Fig. 03-425: Front and back of a 1st Arm Div SSI, fully machine-embroidered on OD wool base fabric, with partial black and dark blue back thread.

Fig. 03-426: Front and back of a 1st Arm Div SSI, fully machine-embroidered on OD wool backing, with white back thread.

Machine-embroidered on felt backing:
Fig. 03-427 to Fig. 03-429.

Fig. 03-427: Front and back of a 41st Inf Div SSI, fully machine-embroidered on black felt base material, with OD back thread.

Fig. 03-428: Front and back of a 41st Inf Div SSI fully machine-embroidered on black felt base fabric, with white back thread.

Fig. 03-429: Front and back of a 41st Inf Div SSI, fully machine-embroidered on black felt base fabric, with black back thread.

Most likely from early 1941 there was a conversion to cotton twill as the basic material, mainly because of its higher quality than the wool.

The same colors of back threads were also used here during WWII. But in the literature one distinguishes several periods, although this should be interpreted quite relatively. It was largely dependent on the companies which made them and the back thread they had in stock. For example, there is sufficient evidence of SSI from the same manufacturer having various colors of back thread mixed on a single patch. When the thread was used up another coil was installed to continue to process.

Fig. 03-430: Back of a WWII OD-bordered, cut-edge 31st Inf Div SSI with OD and white back thread. It is odd to see the red design thread being caught with OD-colored thread, while the thread of the OD border is caught with white thread (see the outer white circle).

Fig. 03-431: Back of a WWII OD bordered, cut-edge 95th Inf Div SSI with rare OD and white back thread.

It is clear that certain SSI do not have certain colors of back thread. For example, OD back SSI can not be seen with some units formed later in the war (from 1943). For that reason, one assumes that OD backed SSI were only manufactured during the period 1941-early 1943. Although there is no doubt that during this early-WWII period the OD-colored back thread would have been used more than any other kind of color because it was the U.S. Army's WWII uniform color, this OD-colored thread was even used as back thread until after WWII, dependent on the manufacturer's stock.

A good example of a patch that does not exist with OD-colored back thread is the WWII cut-edge 70th Inf Div SSI below.

Fig. 03-432: Front and back of a WWII cut-edge 70th Inf Div SSI. The patch is not seen in another back thread color than white yet.

PERIODS:

- Early-WWII (1941-early 1943): Particularly OD back, green back, brown back, and white back (Note: In this period the partially machine-embroidered on KHAKI cotton twill-base fabric cut-edge SSI with wide border were manufactured);
- 1943-1944: Particularly white back, but also other colors if in stock;
- End 1944-1945: Particularly white back or black back, but sometimes also OD back. (Note: In this period, the partially machine-embroidered on those other than khaki-colored cotton twill backing cut-edge SSI appear.)

Examples:

Fig. 03-435: Back of a 32nd Inf Div SSI – Pink back.

Fig. 03-433: Back of a USAAF GHQ SSI – OD back.

Fig. 03-434: Back of a USAAF GHQ patch – White back.

Fig. 03-436: Back of a 1st Allied AB Army SSI – Purple back.

Fig. 03-437: Back of a 33rd Inf Div SSI – Brown back.

Fig. 03-438: Back of a 101st AB Div SSI – Black back.

Fig. 03-439: Back of the rare 2nd Inf Div SSI with OD back thread.

Fig. 03-440: Back of the frequent occurring 27th Inf Div SSI with OD back thread.

Some SSI are frequently seen with OD back, while others are rarely seen (early-WWII). The other colors, except the white back, are rare or occasionally encountered. The fact that brown back SSI were made suggests that OD rayon was not always available. It was the color closest to OD.

In my opinion and experience, the white back patch is, during and after WWII, the most common of all SSI. A reason for this claim could be that non-colored rayon thread was cheaper than colored. If one looks very closely at the back of a WWII-period manufactured patch with a large portion of white design, one can see that the white catch or back thread has a different kind of white than the white design thread when the latter appears at the back. So the white back thread is in fact not white at all. It has more a less bright and non-colored "natural" or "dirty-whitish" impression. This rayon fiber appears to have come directly from the production line without being colored. This important feature can be seen in Fig. 03-441 and Fig. 03-442 on the following page and will be discussed further on in chapter 4.

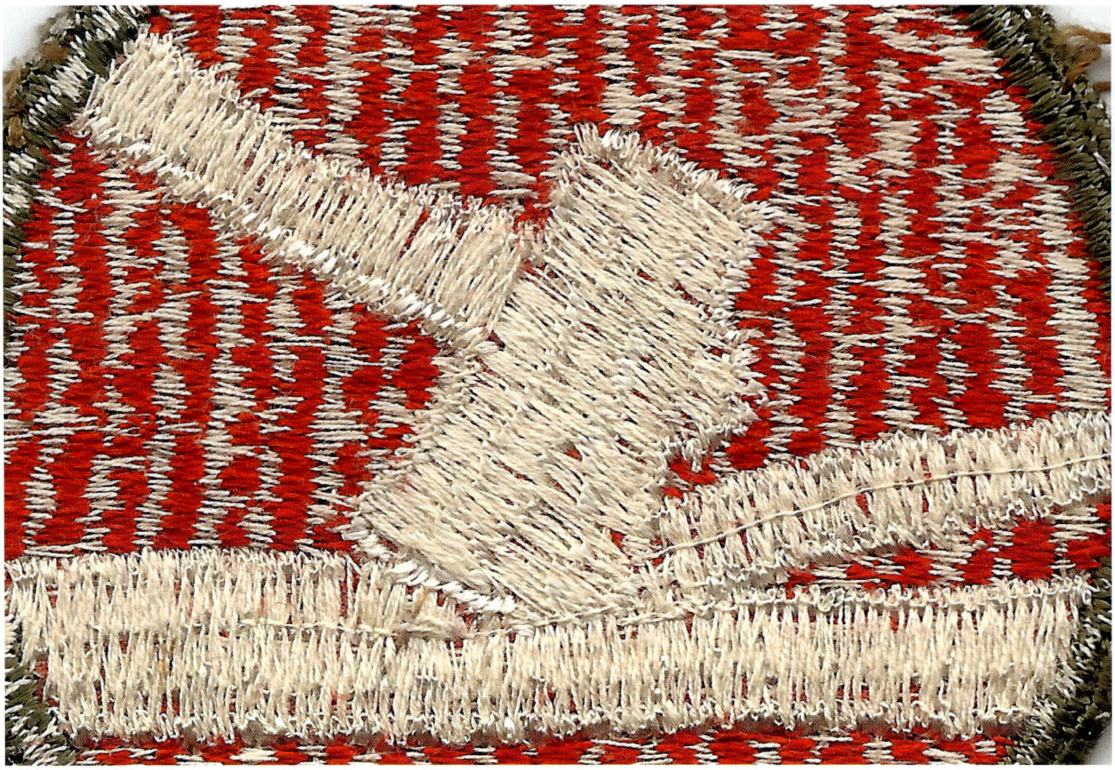

Fig. 03-441: Detail of the back of a WWII U.S. made, cut-edge 84th Inf Div SSI. Note the less brighter white of the back thread compared to the white design thread at the edges of the axe.

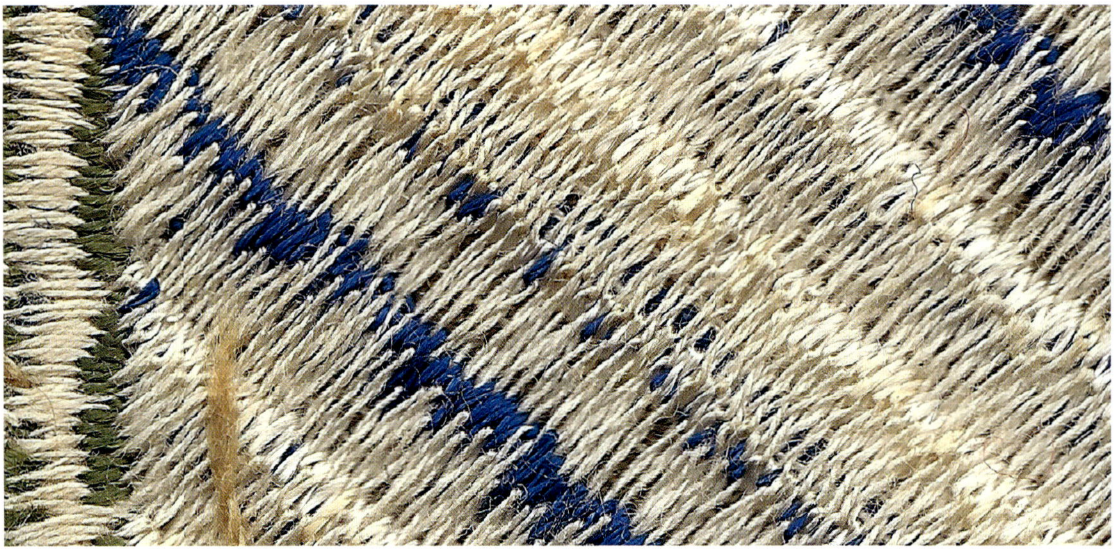

Fig. 03-442: Detail of the back of a WWII cut-edge 3rd Inf Div SSI. Also with this example, note the less brighter white of the back thread compared to the white design thread which appears in narrow parallel diagonal pattern rows next to the blue ones.

During WWII there were SSI with a full back of back thread, and also SSI with relatively little of it. This also differs from company to company and their embroidery processes: some used much of it, the others relatively few. Here several factors probably played a major role; factors very difficult to determine after more than 65 years, but here are some possibilities:

1 Due to the large amounts of SSI which had to be made, there was probably an effort to save threads during WWII;

2 There are specific embroidery patterns used by certain companies during WWII which exist as a sort of signature or quality label of the company itself (the conservative policies of company management). For example, the use of ribbed embroidery, a zigzag style or Gemsco Company embroidery (the latter is embroidery, using lots of back thread which covers the whole back of the patch in a specific way). It is obvious with these kinds of manufacture styles or patterns that the appearance of the back thread is related to the method of embroidering the main thread.

Top left is a pre-WWII 36th Inf Div SSI which has the typical Gemsco embroidery style. The pre-WWII 36th Inf Div (bottom left) has a common embroidery style. To increase the durability of the SSI, the one made by Gemsco standards even has a reinforced back with light-colored cotton fabric. The firm probably knew the SSI had to endure the hardest conditions and made the SSI of higher quality. This quality appears to be continued in the WWII era made patches by that same firm using the typical manufacture style with the back thread covering the entire back. Although both SSI are not WWII fully machine-embroidered cut-edge SSI, they are still good examples of this quality label;

3 The way of embroidering itself (technique);

4 The type of embroidery machine (technology);

5 …

However, the SSI must have back thread to be a WWII patch!

Fig. 03-443: Comparison of quality: two pre-WWII U.S. made, 36th Inf Div SSI (back and front).

Fig. 03-444: The back of a WWII U.S. made, cut-edge 65th Inf Div SSI. Only the border is practically covered with white back thread.

NOTE

In Fig. 03-444 above, the back thread of the axe is very difficult to see because of the same color of the main thread. A closer look while holding the SSI in your hands would show that there is a difference between the white-colored main thread and the white-colored back thread. The latter is less bright and more uncolored ("dirty-whitish"). This feature will be discussed further on in this book with the UV light test (see chapter 4).

Fig. 03-445: The back of a WWII U.S. made, cut-edge 33rd Inf Div SSI with Gemsco embroidery. The back is completely covered with white back thread.

Fig. 03-446: The back of a WWII U.S. made, cut-edge Americal Div SSI.

Fig. 03-447: A WWII Americal Div SSI with white back thread, completely covering the back.

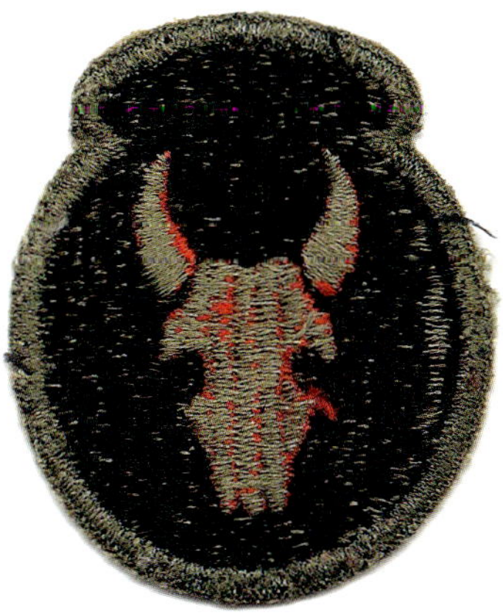

Fig. 03-448: The back of a WWII 34th Inf Div SSI.

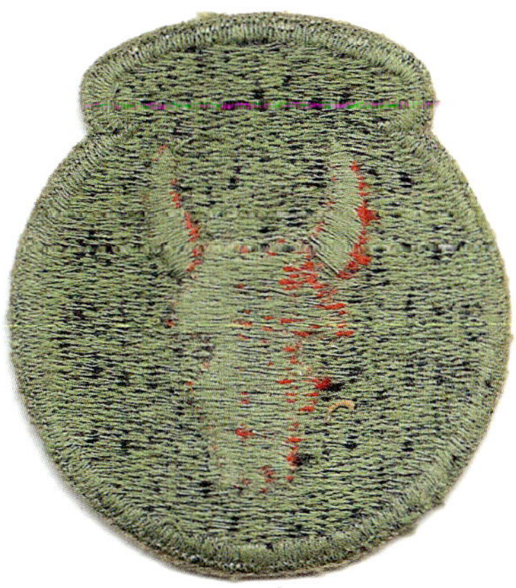

Fig. 03-449: A WWII 34th Inf Div SSI with OD back thread, completely covering the back.

Fig. 03-450: The back of an unusual WWII U.S. made, cut-edge flat top 8th Inf Div SSI.

Fig. 03-451: A common WWII cut-edge 8th Inf Div SSI with lots of white back thread.

Finally, back thread appears on the back of a patch in a particular way because of the embroidery technique that a manufacturer used. Using the appearance of this back thread on SSI of various different U.S. units, it is possible to establish that they were the product of the same manufacturer.

This involves the application of either a pre-WWII embroidery technique which was continued during wartime, or a similar technique only used during WWII. If a pre-WWII contracted company could continue during the WWII era, chances are that the technique used remained the same. This is also true with WWII contracted manufacturers who never worked for the U.S. government prior to the war. Because all these companies made dozens of SSI for several units in the homeland, the embroidery technique barely changed with a particular manufacturer.

The following examples of two different WWII units show the same appearance of back thread, although the color is different. See Fig. 03-452 to Fig. 03-455. What appears to be parallel "V"-rows of back thread can be seen in both details. Here, one could conclude that both cut-edge SSI were made by one and the same manufacturer during the war.

In the following heading of this chapter, examples of pre-WWII embroideries which were continued during WWII are illustrated and discussed.

Fig. 03-452

Fig. 03-453

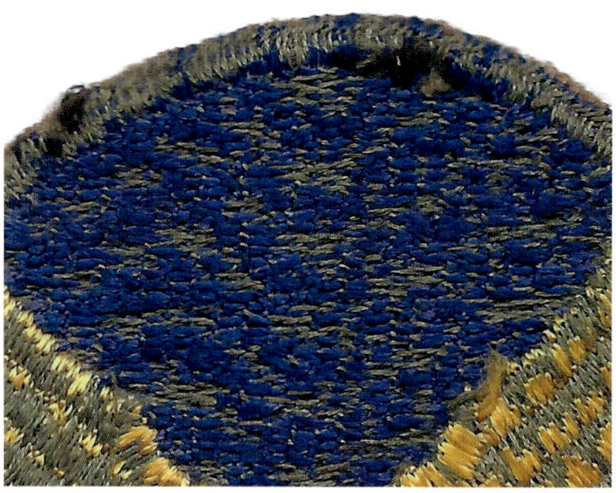

Fig. 03-454: Detail of Fig. 03-452.

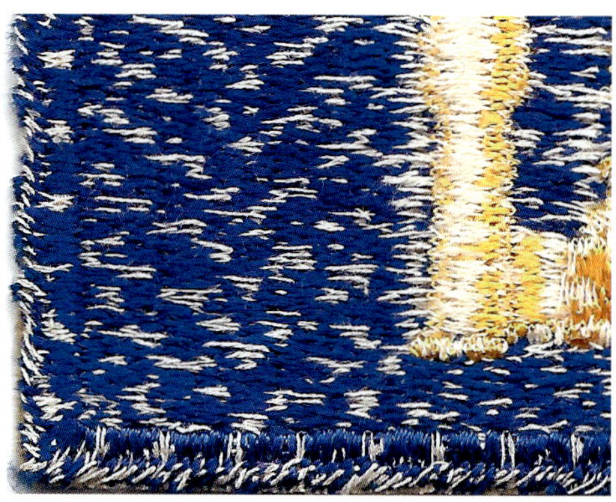

Fig. 03-455: Detail of Fig. 03-453.

NOTES

1 OD backs were also made in the post-WWII era. The general proposition that OD-backed SSI are always early-WWII, which is often found in literature, is wrong! Though keep in mind that the manufacturers of OD back SSI (either WWII or post-WWII) never would have suspected that there would be collectors who would pay a premium for their product in the future. They just used the stock of threads they had available. In that period they used white- and OD-colored back thread without distinction, and the SSI were the same price when sold to the government.

2 The assumption in some literature that post-WWII SSI (and especially the SSI made after 1957, after the introduction of synthetic fibers) should have less or no back thread when compared to their WWII precursors is not always justified. Below is a clear example of a subdued 3rd Armored Div SSI with merrowed edge (made from the late 1960s). The amount of visible back thread will probably again be dependent on the company that manufactured them. It is clear that there is little back thread on the back of the caterpillar threads and on the letters and figure "3," in accordance with the notion that post-war SSI have less visible back thread. Even if some post-1968 SSI continue to have a fair amount of visible back thread, it is true that the majority of post-1968 manufactured patches do not.

Fig. 03-456: Front and back of a post-1968 subdued 3rd Arm Div SSI.

5 | EMBROIDERY STYLES OR PATTERNS

Each company used a particular embroidery technique on the embroidery machine, which resulted in a specific embroidery style or pattern. Very often this may have served as a quality and recognition or identification label of that particular company. The type of embroidery machine also played a major role in the appearance of a certain pattern.

Different kinds of embroidery styles (patterns) appear because of the large number of companies that manufactured the SSI during WWII. The appearances of main thread and back thread are often related to one another.

The different WWII embroidery thread patterns go from irregular and random to very regular, with what appears to be parallel diagonal pattern rows to the embroidery, and from an even embroidered surface to a series of ribs which lie side by side. The following pictures with details of some SSI will illustrate this.

The SSI illustrated below are all genuine and WWII era in manufacture. These are only a sample of all the different kinds of embroidery patterns that have existed during WWII. As a collector, it is not only interesting to have a single SSI of each unit or component in your collection, but also to collect the same patch in all kinds of embroideries and patterns. That way, the collector could easily be busy for many years and could always be looking for another maybe hard to find patch.

On each page a particular embroidery pattern is discussed, illustrated with a front and back scan, as well as detailed scans of the SSI where that pattern was found. This does not mean that these patches were manufactured with the discussed embroidery style alone. Each of these SSI were made in a variety of patterns reflecting the many companies who made them. The following pages will only demonstrate the range of existing embroidery styles and patterns. In most cases the background of the SSI's design is considered, because the little designs and drawings embroidered on this background are mostly of another kind of embroidery technique.

To make it easier for the reader, the different subdivided styles are numbered. Keep in mind that the numbers I am using do not reflect any kind of number designating the different techniques that were in use during that period.

Also, to have a good view of each of the styles, the size of each scanned and shown part of that particular SSI is the same. Every detail of the original patch size is approximately 2.5 cm (1.0 in) wide and 1.2 cm (0.5 in) high. So the size or thickness of the loops, threads, etc., will always be comparable with each other.

REMARKS:

- It is possible that patterns #1 to #4 are of the same kind of style because sometimes a similar back thread pattern can be seen. The degree of the used condition of the SSI could make the difference between these four styles.
- It is also possible that patterns #1 to #7 were common and newer WWII embroidery styles never applied prior to WWII. However, this is just an assumption, because I have not seen such patterns on 1930s-early 1940s SSI, machine-embroidered on felt or OD wool backing material yet.
- Only detailed scans of the embroidery style of the SSI's front are considered, not the back thread pattern. It is always possible that a certain embroidery style could have been used by different manufacturers. To see whether the patches were made by different companies or the same one, it is important to compare the patterns of the back thread of these SSI. The SSI illustrated from Fig. 03-452 to Fig. 03-455 above are a good example of this.

Fig. 03-501

PATTERN #1

Detail of a WWII cut-edge 31st Inf Div SSI. The white background has an irregular and random embroidery pattern. No particular style or pattern can be seen. The patch design's white background feels very even when sliding one's fingers over it.

Fig. 03-502

Fig. 03-503

PATTERN #2

Detail of a WWII cut-edge Tanker Proficiency lozenge patch. The green background has some regularity in its pattern. It is less random than the previous discussed one because now and then what appear to be parallel diagonal pattern rows to the embroidery sloping to the upper right can be seen. The back shows very regular back thread embroidery. The patch design's green background feels very even when sliding one's fingers over it.

Fig. 03-504

Fig. 03-505

PATTERN #3

Detail of a WWII cut-edge 31st Inf Div SSI. The white background has an irregular and random embroidery pattern. No particular style or pattern can be seen. The patch design's white background feels very even when sliding one's fingers over it.

Fig. 03-506

Fig. 03-507

PATTERN #4

Detail of a WWII cut-edge 4th Armored Div SSI with OD back thread (see figure below). The blue/red background shows a very regular pattern. What appear to be parallel diagonal pattern rows to the embroidery, sloping to the upper right, can clearly be seen. The design's yellow, red, or blue background feels very even when sliding fingers over it.

Fig. 03-508

Fig. 03-509

PATTERN #5

Detail of a WWII cut-edge 29th Inf Div SSI. The detail shows a very regular pattern, even more than the previously discussed one. What appear to be parallel diagonal pattern rows to the embroidery, which slope to both the upper right and the upper left, can clearly be seen. The embroidery is so regular that even parallel vertical pattern rows can be seen. Although this feature is visible very clearly in Fig. 03-510 below (front of the patch), this is not a ribbed embroidery style (see further on). The blue or grey background feels very even when sliding one's fingers over it.

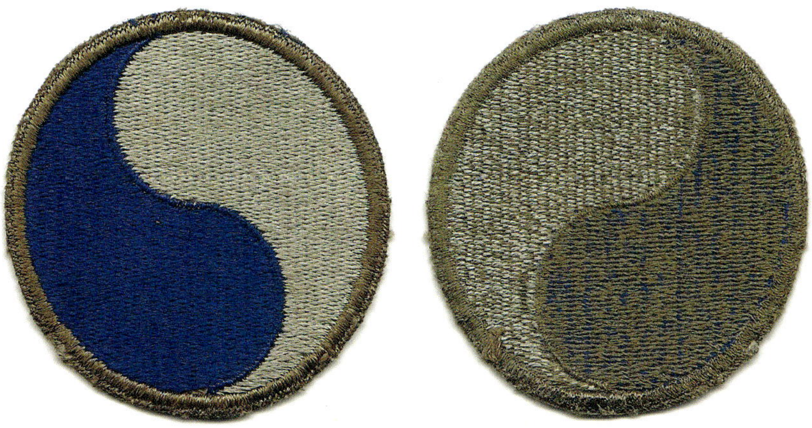

Fig. 03-510

Fig. 03-511

PATTERN #6

Detail of a WWII cut-edge 75th Inf Div SSI. The patch has the same pattern as in pattern #5, but with very small back thread loops. The patch design's red, white, or blue background feels very even when sliding fingers over it.

Fig. 03-512

REMARK REGARDING THE PATTERNS #1 TO #6:

With pattern #1 to #6, looking at the back of the illustrated SSIs, a variety of back thread designs can be found. Except for the last pattern (#6), which has a very small back thread loop, the other embroidery styles all show back thread with a much wider loop, but with differences in density, pattern (in rows, random), etc. It is very difficult, and one might say even impossible, to divide the SSIs with those embroidery styles in subcategories based on the back thread pattern. The variety based on the back thread is even bigger compared to the design thread of those seven patterns.

What follows are a few examples of back thread patterns which also illustrate the different techniques utilized by a certain company and/or embroidery machine as a kind of "signature." They go from little back thread to a completely covered back, from random to regular structured.

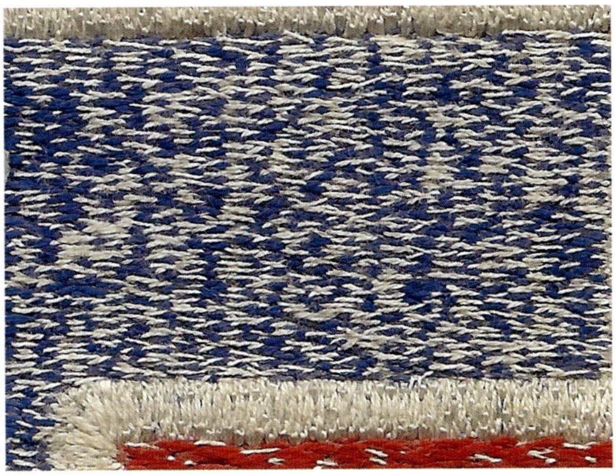
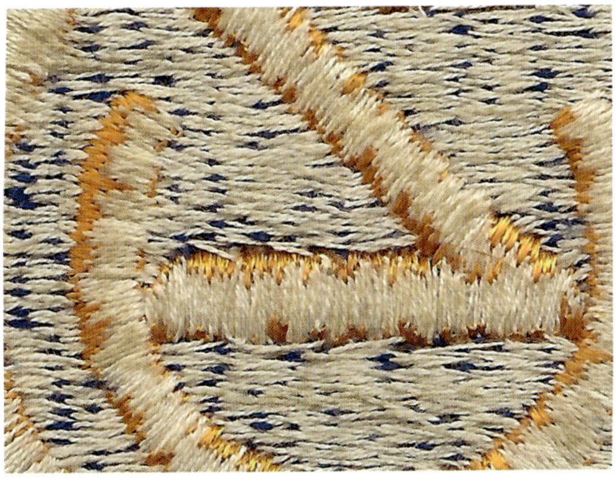

The differences in back thread as a kind of signature of the manufacturer and/or the embroidery machine can be seen very well in Fig. 03-512c below. The patches of the U.S. 87th Inf Div (top row) and those of the U.S. 88th Inf Div (bottom row) have embroidery styles that can be cataloged in one of the patterns #2, #3, or #4, but show many differences looking at the back of the insignia. Not only the back thread pattern of the design's background, but also the details of the design (in particular the acorn design of the 87th Inf Div SSI) show a different technique of embroidery. But from little back thread to lots of it, these are all good, WWII era patches.

This feature is not only seen with white back patches, but also with OD back SSIs or insignia with other back thread colors.

The differently embroidered design details (like the acorns on the shown 87th Inf Div SSIs below) and the differences in back thread also demonstrate that one of these patterns (#2 to #4) was not utilized by one single manufacturer only. As mentioned above, all of the shown SSIs have a design background pattern that can be determined as one of those three embroidery styles. It is very likely that several manufacturers utilized a same kind of technique, certainly if one considers that millions of patches were made during that era.

So besides some specific embroidery styles (see further on in this chapter), it is a good chance that in many cases the back thread pattern was the only "signature" on the patch a manufacturer could have.

Fig. 03-512c

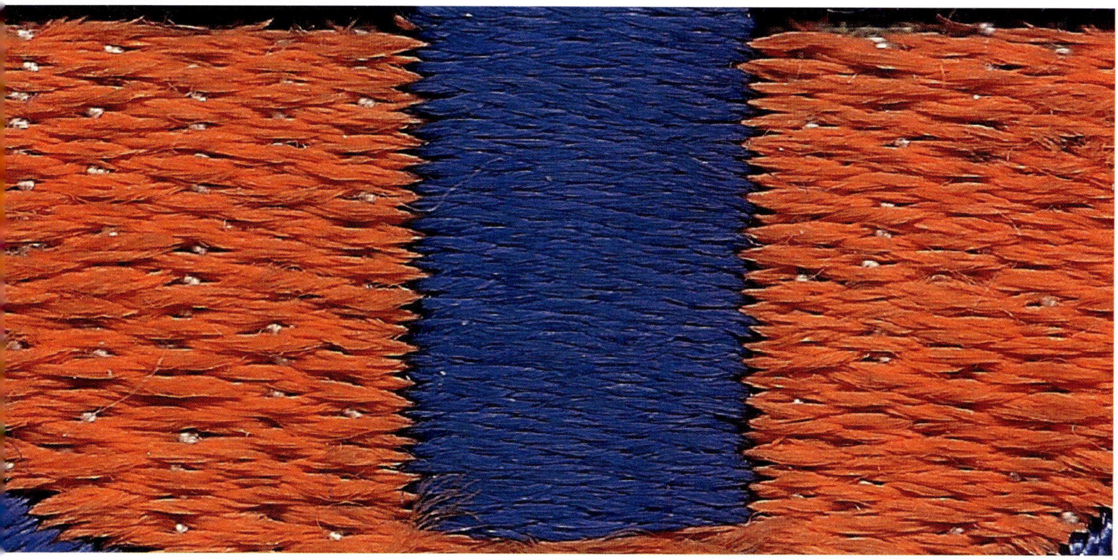

Fig. 03-513

PATTERN #7

Detail of a WWII cut-edge 29th Inf Div SSI. The detail shows a very regular pattern, even more than the previously discussed one. What appear to be parallel diagonal pattern rows to the embroidery, which slope to both the upper right and the upper left, can clearly be seen. The embroidery is so regular that even parallel vertical pattern rows can be seen. Although this feature is visible very clearly in Fig. 03-510 below (front of the patch), this is not a ribbed embroidery style (see further on). The blue or grey background feels very even when sliding one's fingers over it.

Fig. 03-514

Fig. 03-514b

The example of the U.S. 1st Inf Div SSI below shows practically the same embroidery style as pattern #7 (what appear to be parallel diagonal pattern rows to the embroidery, which slope to the upper left), but with a more open and very regular back thread pattern. Here, the same remark as with the previous styles (#1 to #6) about the back thread (different patterns, density, etc.) could thus also be made.

Fig. 03-514c

Fig. 03-515

PATTERN #8

Detail of a WWII cut-edge 9th Inf Div SSI. The embroidery shows a regular pattern. Equally wide, parallel vertical pattern rows can clearly be seen creating flat, very narrow ribs. These ribs do not have a bas relief kind of surface as is common in ribbed embroidery (see further on). Because of the flat and narrow embroidery it is difficult to feel the ribs, but they can be felt as such when sliding very slowly over the patch with one's fingers. The SSI certainly does not feel even as with patterns #1 to #7. Here, we speak of the ribbed embroidery style which can also be seen on the back of the SSI. This style is pre-WWII U.S. made and is discussed further on in this heading after this section with the different patterns.

Fig. 03-516

Fig. 03-517

PATTERN #9

Detail of a WWII cut-edge 88th Inf Div SSI. This is the same (early) WWII style as with pattern #8 above. The vertical manufactured ribs have the same flat appearance as with the previously discussed pattern #8, but are a little bit wider. At the front of the patch these kinds of ribs are again more even than with common ribbed embroidery (see further on), but can be felt as such when sliding over the patch with one's fingers. Although there is not a bas relief-like surface, its feeling is definitely not even as with patterns #1 to #7. This is also an example of a ribbed embroidery style, certainly when one looks at the back of the SSI.

Fig. 03-518

Fig. 03-519

PATTERN #10

Detail of a WWII cut-edge 96th Inf Div SSI. The embroidery shows a regular pattern. Equally wide, parallel diagonal pattern rows can clearly be seen as very pronounced ribs. This bas relief-like surface can also be felt as ribs when sliding over the patch with the fingers. This bas relief-like surface can be seen when one looks over the surface of the patch in the longitudinal direction of the ribs: a wave-like surface. Here we speak of the ribbed embroidery style. This style is also utilized in the U.S. prior to WWII, and is discussed further on in this heading after this section with the different patterns.

Fig. 03-520

Fig. 03-521

PATTERN #11

Detail of a WWII cut-edge 3rd Inf Div SSI. The embroidery shows a regular pattern. Equally wide, parallel diagonal ribs can clearly be seen. These ribs are much wider and are less pronounced than the bas relief-like style of pattern #10, but can be felt as such when sliding over the patch with the fingers. This is also an example of ribbed embroidery.

Fig. 03-522

Fig. 03-523

PATTERN #12

Detail of a WWII cut-edge Western Defense Command SSI. This is a regular pattern. The thread loops are embroidered in vertical pattern rows, even continuing within the different design colors, which create equally wide, parallel vertical ribs. The ribs of both patterns #11 and #12 are equally wide. Although this is a similar ribbed style as the previous discussed pattern #11, the detail picture below demonstrates another used technique. The ribs of this pattern are also less pronounced (flat) than the bas relief-like style of pattern #10, but can easily be felt as such when sliding over the patch with fingers. The surface certainly feels not that even as with patterns #1 to #7. This is another kind of ribbed embroidery, certainly when one looks at the back of the SSI.

Fig. 03-524

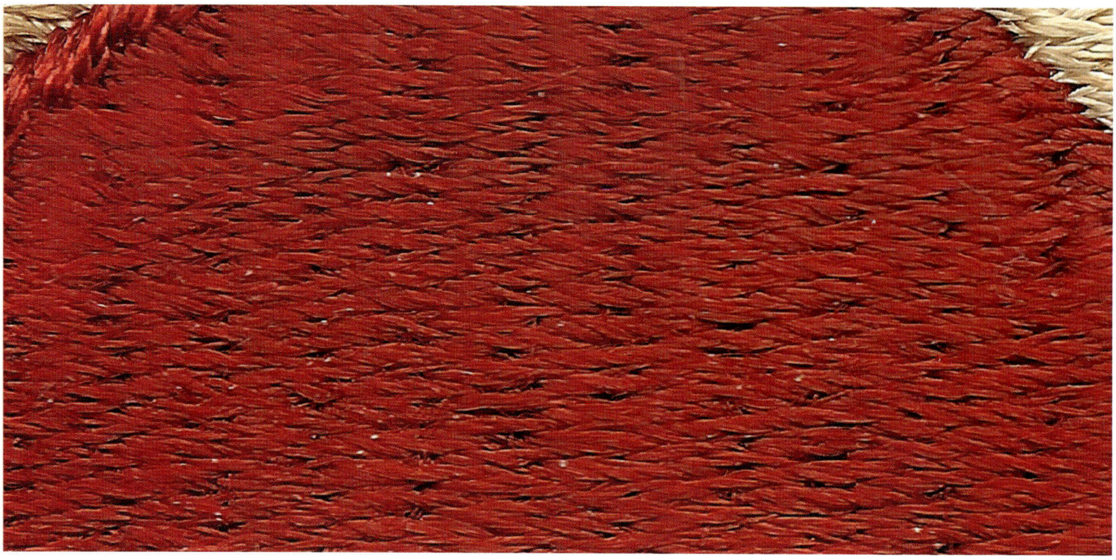

Fig. 03-525

PATTERN #13

Detail of a WWII cut-edge 37th Inf Div SSI. This style can be compared with the patterns #2 to #4 (above) because of what appear to be the parallel diagonal pattern rows to the embroidery sloping to the upper right which can be seen in the detail picture below. But there is a difference with these patterns because of the vertical ribs which can be seen at the red part of the design in Fig. 03-526. This mixed embroidery style shows very narrow, equally wide, parallel vertical ribs. These ribs are also pronounced as a wave-like surface, and can be felt as such when sliding over the patch with the fingers. The feeling of the surface with the patch is certainly not even (bas relief-like surface). This (possibly early) WWII pattern is also a kind of ribbed embroidery style, although the back scan of the SSI below does not demonstrate this feature very clearly.

Fig. 03-526

Fig. 03-527

PATTERN #14

Detail of a WWII cut-edge 38th Inf Div SSI. The detail of the SSI illustrates a similar pattern as the patterns #2 to #4 discussed previously. One can see the same seemingly parallel diagonal pattern rows to the embroidery sloping to the upper right. But also equally wide, vertical ribs (see Fig. 03-528) created by the pattern of the back thread can be seen. These ribs are very wide and pronounced (bas relief-like surface) as with the common ribbed embroidery. These ribs can be felt when sliding over the patch with the fingers. The feeling is definitely not even. This is also an example of a ribbed embroidery style, certainly when one looks at the back of the SSI.

Fig. 03-528

Fig. 03-529

PATTERN #15

Detail of a WWII cut-edge 88th Inf Div SSI. This pattern has the same mixed (likely early) WWII style as with pattern #14 (above). But these ribs are again a little bit wider than the previously discussed pattern. These are again pronounced as a bas relief-like surface, and can be felt as such when sliding over the patch with the fingers. There is certainly a bas relief-like surface, and its feeling is definitely not even. This is also an example of a ribbed embroidery style, when one looks at the back of the SSI.

Fig. 03-530

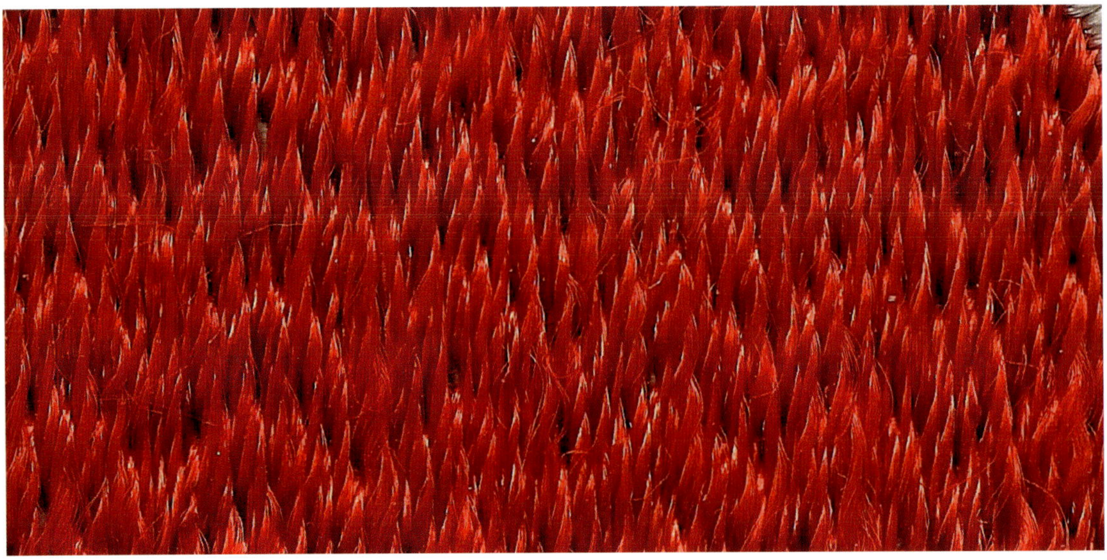

Fig. 03-531

PATTERN #16

Detail of a WWII cut-edge 37th Inf Div SSI. This is also a very regular pattern. The embroidery shows equally wide, parallel horizontal zigzag pattern rows. The surface feels even when sliding over the patch with your finger. Probably this is also an embroidery pattern of one particular manufacturer with which he can be identified, just like the Gemsco embroidery style (see below). This kind of embroidery is rarely seen and can be called the zigzag embroidery style. This style is also utilized in the U.S. prior to WWII, and is discussed further on in this heading after this section with the different patterns.

Fig. 03-532

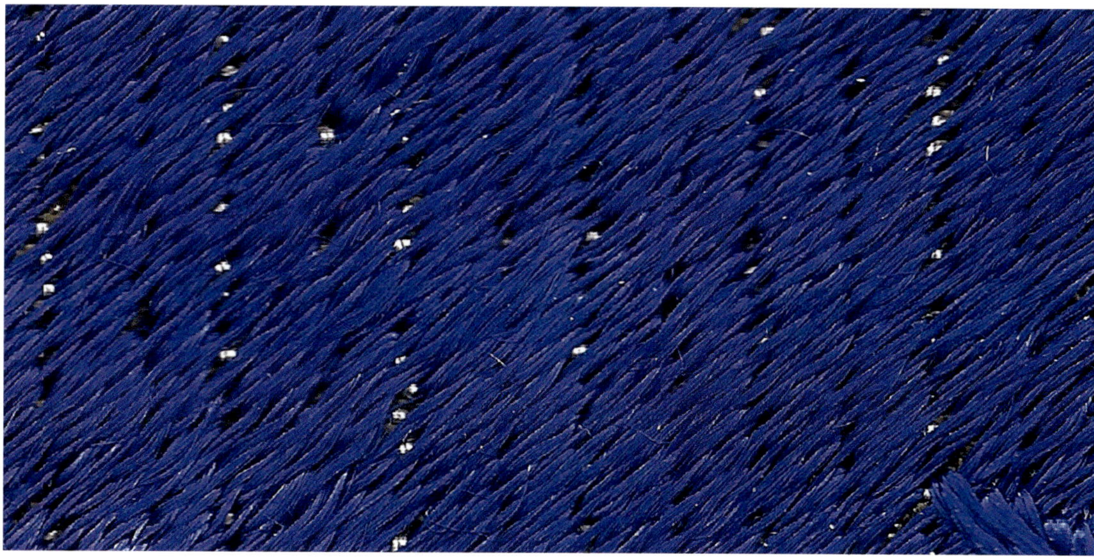

Fig. 03-533

PATTERN #17

Detail of a WWII cut-edge 88th Inf Div SSI. Some regularity in its pattern can be seen. The embroidery is sloping to the upper right. One can also see what appears to be parallel vertical pattern rows in the manufacturer's style. This oblique way of embroidering is discussed further on in this heading after this section with the different patterns.

Fig. 03-534

Fig. 03-535

PATTERN #18

Detail of a WWII cut-edge 104th Inf Div SSI. The embroidery shows a very regular pattern. Parallel horizontal ribs can clearly be seen, alternating with a narrow and wider rib (or pattern row). This is an example of the Gemsco embroidery style and could have been a quality and identification label of that certain company (Gemsco: General Merchandising Company, Milford, CT, U.S.A.). This style is also utilized in the U.S. prior to WWII, and will be discussed further on in this heading after this section with the different patterns.

Fig. 03-536

Fig. 03-537

PATTERN #19

A detail of a (possibly early) WWII cut-edge 8th Inf Div SSI. It has less contiguous embroidery than the common U.S. made SSI, but is very regular in pattern. With each loop a double thread can be seen. This is a pre- and early-WWII U.S. made embroidery style which is discussed further on in this heading after this section with the different patterns.

Fig. 03-538

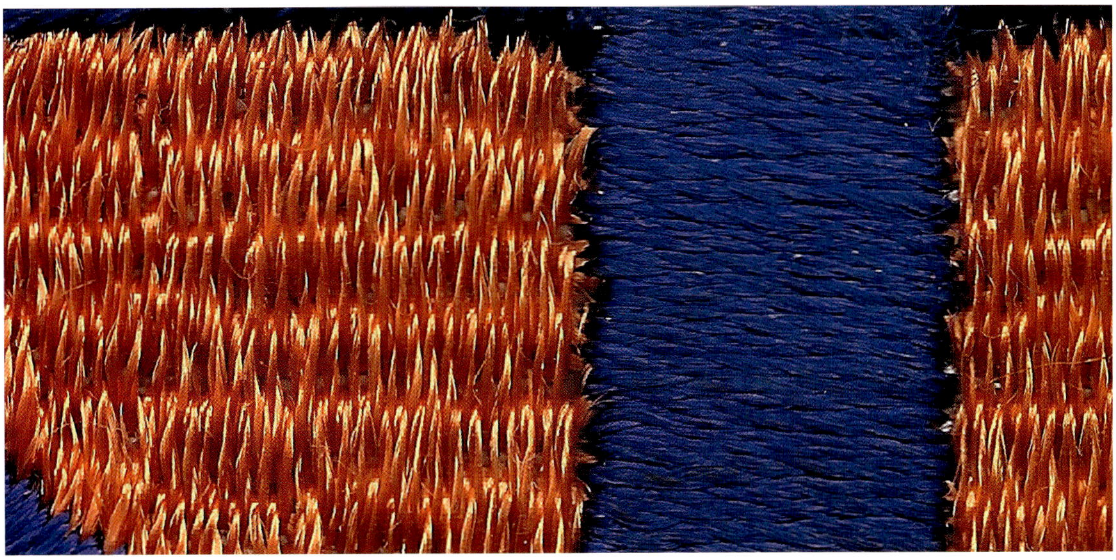

Fig. 03-539

PATTERN #20

A detail of a WWII cut-edge 44th Inf Div SSI. It has practically the same embroidery style as pattern #19 above (see also the back), but with more dense (contiguous) embroidery and another kind of border. It can also be compared with pattern #18 (Gemsco embroidery style), but has equally wide, very narrow embroidery rows instead of the specific alternate narrow and wider pattern rows of the Gemsco embroidery. A bas relief-like surface can be felt as such when sliding over the patch with fingers. The surface of the orange background is definitely not even as with patterns #1 to #7. However, this is not an example of a ribbed embroidery style.

This is likely a pre-WWII embroidery style continued during WWII.

Fig. 03-540

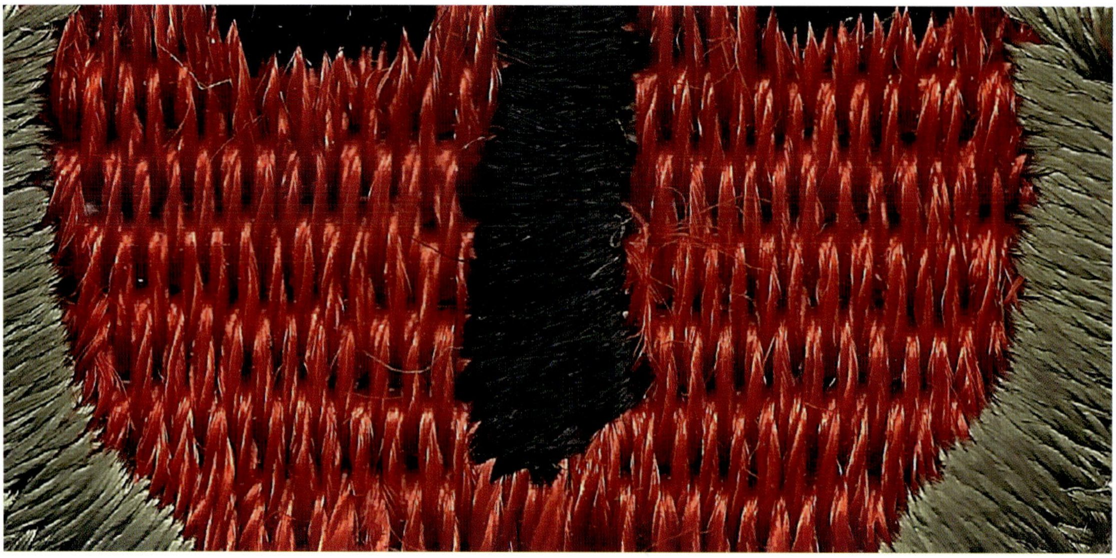

Fig. 03-541

PATTERN #21

A detail of a WWII cut-edge 43rd Inf Div SSI. This embroidery style is almost similar to pattern #19 above, but has a more dense and contiguous embroidery that is not similar to patterns #1 to #6. The small embroidery loops create very narrow parallel ribs, but cannot be considered as such. A big difference between the 8th and 44th Inf Div SSI shown respectively in Fig. 03-538 and Fig. 03-540 above is the pattern of the back thread. The loops of the 43rd Inf Div patch illustrated below are less dense and of another technique. Maybe this is also an early or even pre-WWII embroidery technique utilized in the U.S.

Fig. 03-542

Fig. 03-543

PATTERN #22

A detail of a WWII cut-edge 102nd Inf Div SSI. It is very regular in pattern. As with the 8th Inf Div patch discussed above each loop has a double thread, but the 102nd Inf Div SSI has more contiguous embroidery. This unused and very supple feeling SSI is definitely WWII era made and not of postwar German manufacture, because its embroidery is too similar with some old style (1930s) patches fully machine-embroidered on wool. This subject will be discussed just after this heading's section.

This kind of WWII U.S. made embroidery of the 102nd Inf Div SSI below is not often seen, but the thread loops of this embroidery can be compared with the loops of the zigzag-embroidery (see Fig. 03-531 above). The only difference between these two is the lack of the zigzag embroidery rows with the SSI below.

Fig. 03-544

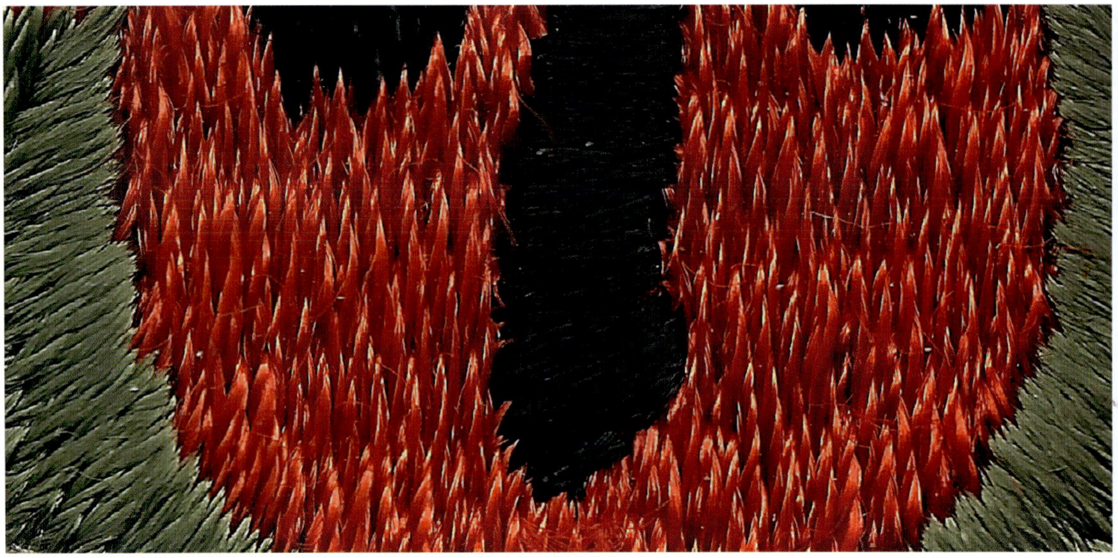

Fig. 03-545

PATTERN #23

A detail of a WWII cut-edge 43rd Inf Div SSI. This embroidery style is similar with pattern #22 above, but has more dense and contiguous embroidery. A big difference from the 102nd Inf Div SSI shown in Fig. 03-544 above is the pattern of the back thread. The 43rd Inf Div patch illustrated below is less dense and of a different technique. The comparison of both SSI's U.S. made styles already utilized prior to WWII are discussed further on in this heading.

Fig. 03-546

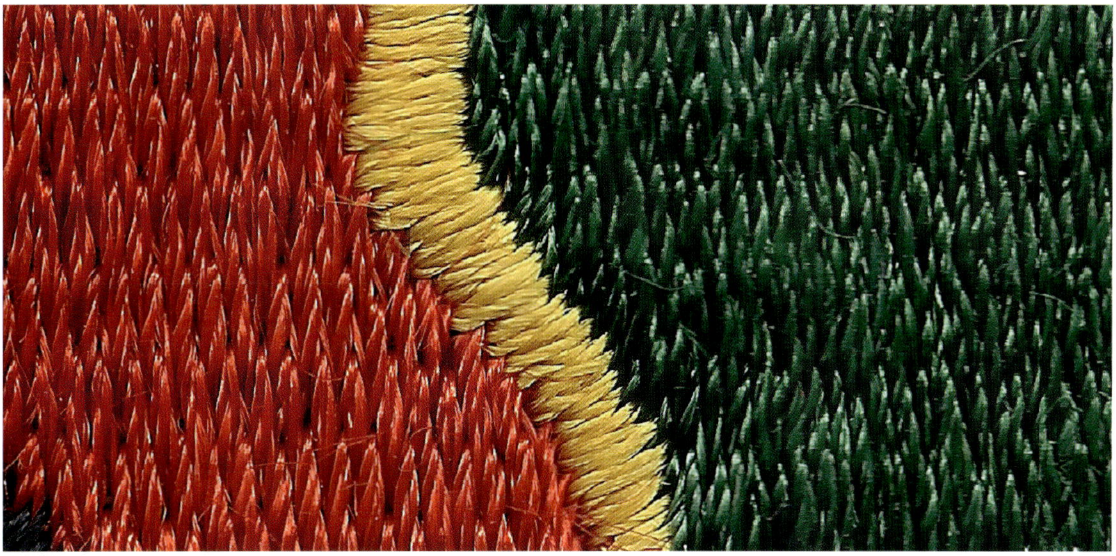

Fig. 03-547

PATTERN #24

A detail of a WWII cut-edge 24th Inf Div SSI with OD back thread. This pattern seems to be similar to the previously discussed styles #22 and #23, with dense and contiguous embroidery (same kind of embroidery loops), but with a different kind of back thread pattern. Although the total image illustrated at Fig. 03-548 shows vertical pattern rows, this is not a ribbed embroidery style. The red background of the design feels even when sliding one's fingers over it. It is certainly not the same style illustrated in patterns #19 to #23.

Because it is difficult to see the back thread in the full size picture of the SSI, a detailed scan of the SSI's back is added on the following page. Here, a different embroidery style can be seen compared with the abovementioned patterns and pictures.

Fig. 03-548

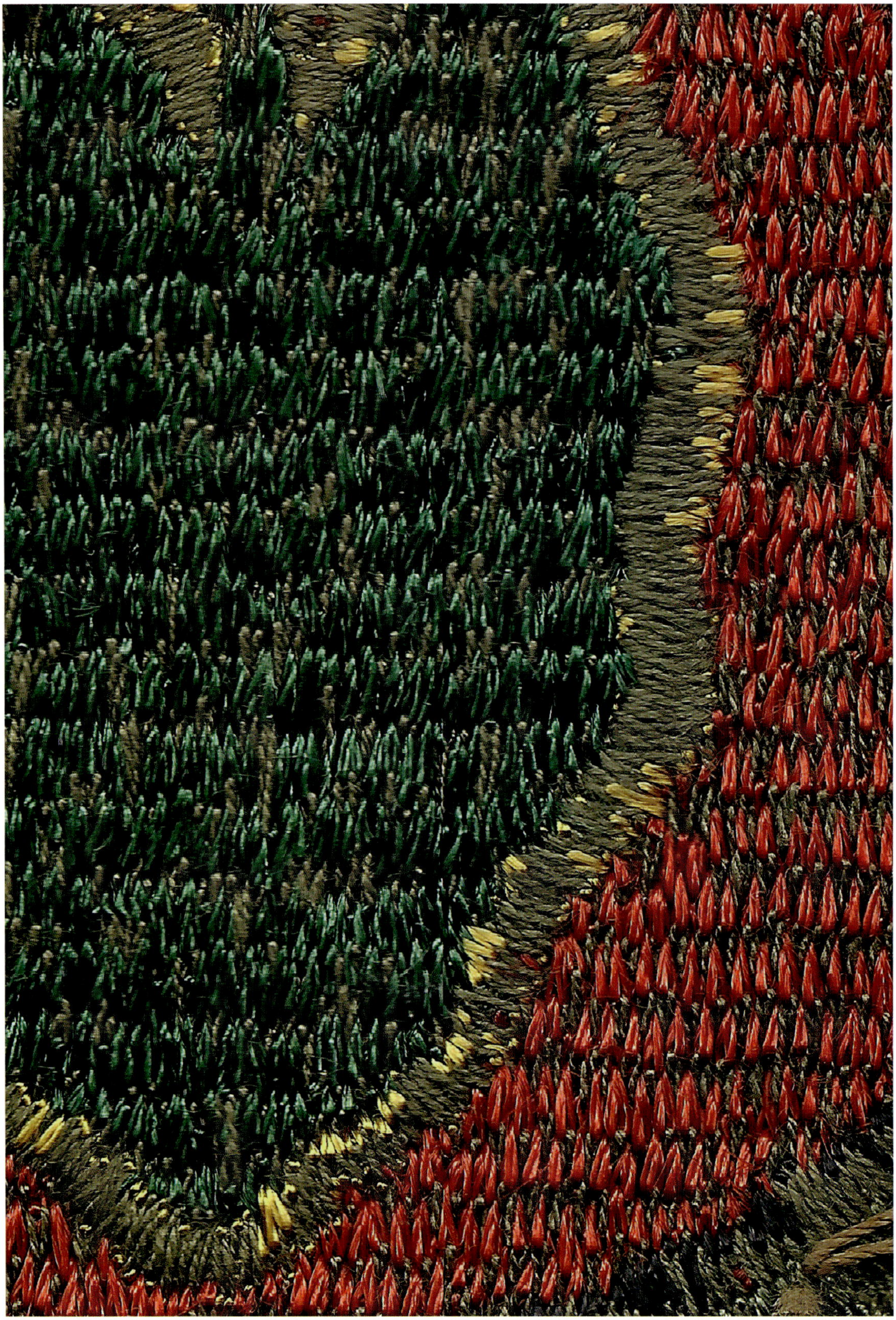

Fig. 03-549: Detail of the back illustrated in Fig. 03-548.

Fig. 03-550

PATTERN #25

A detail of a WWII cut-edge 1st Inf Div SSI with OD back thread. This pattern seems to be similar to the previously discussed styles #22, #23, and #24, with dense and contiguous embroidery (same kind of embroidery loops). Even very narrow horizontal ribs, equally wide as with pattern #9, can be seen and felt as such when sliding fingers over the patch. But it has a bas relief-like surface looking over the front of the patch in the longitudinal direction of the ribs: a wave-like surface, like there is an extra horizontal thread underneath those loops (no flat ribs). It is certainly not the same style illustrated in patterns #19 to #24. Although I could not find a similar and comparable pre-WWII patch, one might be convinced that this also is an older style of embroidery and is not often seen. It has all the characteristics of a WWII U.S. made SSI.

Because it is difficult to see the back thread in the full size picture of the SSI, a detailed scan of the SSI's back is added on the following page. Here also a different embroidery style can be seen compared with the above mentioned patterns and pictures.

Fig. 03-551

Fig. 03-552: Detail of the back illustrated in Fig. 03-551.

Fig. 03-552b

PATTERN #26

Fig. 03-552c

Detail of a WWII cut-edge 1st Inf Div SSI. This style can be compared with pattern #13 (above). The same two features can be seen:

- What appear to be the parallel diagonal pattern rows to the embroidery sloping to the upper right;
- And equally wide, parallel vertical ribs. These ribs are also pronounced as a wave-like surface, and can be felt as such when sliding fingers over the patch. The feeling of the surface with the patch is certainly not even (bas relief-like surface).

The difference with pattern #13 can be seen in the fact that these rows are a bit wider (the thicker of the wave-like rows are further apart from each other).

The back thread also illustrates a specific pattern. It is not that consistent with the ribbed embroideries shown earlier in this book, but is very regularly structured (see Fig. 03-552d on the following page). The back of the patch feels even.

Fig. 03-552d: Detail of the back illustrated in Fig. 03-552c. This very regular structured back thread pattern is not that consistent as with the ribbed embroidery styles shown earlier in this book. When sliding with the fingers over the back, it feels even. This is one of the two differences with pattern #13.

PRE-WWII AND WWII U.S. MADE EMBROIDERY STYLES DISCUSSED.

Some of the embroidery techniques which resulted in certain styles were utilized during WWII. Others already existed before in the 1930s, and were continued during WWII. This was already mentioned in the previous heading of this chapter.

A certain company which used a certain technique would never change its way of manufacturing, or they could have invested in other embroidery machines which had techniques different from their earlier types. Or another reason for a change of the embroidery technique was the change of the patch design (e.g., from a cut-edge SSI with OD border to one without, for reasons explained further on in this book). The latter needed another template or drawing of the patch, sometimes with another stitch order to follow for the operator at the embroidery machine (see earlier). This other stitch order thus resulted in another kind of embroidery pattern. Nevertheless, many companies also continued in their specific known manufacture style as a quality hallmark of their SSI (see below).

Certain pre- or early-WWII SSI on wool, felt, or cotton twill (partially machine-embroidered) base fabric were made according to a specific process. The same way of embroidery was sometimes continued when this company switched to the fully machine-embroidered SSI on cotton twill backing, because the embroidery machines and techniques of that company remained the same. By comparing these types of SSI, the same embroidery pattern will be seen. It may appear that these fully machine-embroidered SSI on cotton base fabric thus were made just after the period of the SSI on wool, felt, or cotton twill. This means early-WWII (beginning 1941). Some of these techniques were even continued during wartime.

Five examples of old style pre-WWII U.S. made embroidery can be seen on the following pages.

The first examples below are two Armored (Arm) SSI compared with the 38th Inf Div SSI. All were utilized with a *ribbed embroidery pattern* (pattern #10), but one is machine-embroidered on OD wool, the other two on cotton twill. All SSI are of U.S. manufacture. The ribs in these examples have a bas relief kind of style (not flat).

Fig. 03-553: An early-WWII OD Wool Arm Forces SSI.

Fig. 03-554: An early-WWII cut-edge 6th Arm Div SSI on cotton twill.

Fig. 03-555: A WWII cut-edge 38th Inf Div SSI, fully machine-embroidered on cotton twill.

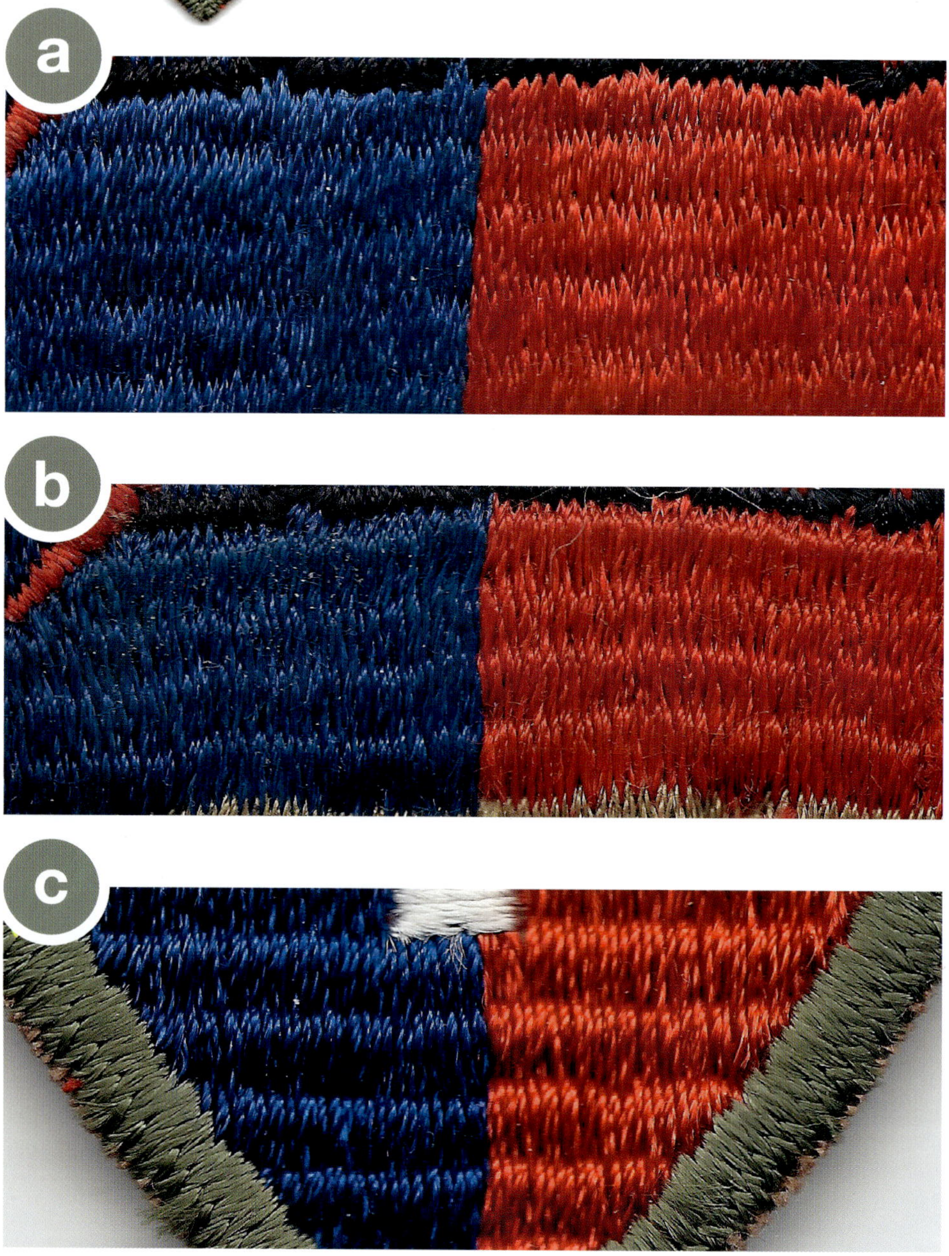

Fig. 03-556:
a Detail of Fig. 03-553
b Detail of Fig. 03-554
c Detail of Fig. 03-555

Fig. 03-557: Back of Fig. 03-553.

Fig. 03-558: Back of Fig. 03-554.

Fig. 03-559: Back of Fig. 03-555.

Even the pre-WWII black back ribbed embroidery was continued during early wartime.

Fig. 03-560: Front and back of a pre-WWII U.S. made 1st Arm Div black back SSI, fully machine-embroidered on OD wool base fabric, with ribbed embroidery pattern.

Fig. 03-561: Front and back of an early-WWII U.S. made, cut-edge 1st Arm Div black back SSI, fully machine-embroidered on cotton twill backing material, applied with the ribbed embroidery style.

Another example of wide flat ribbed embroidery is the WWII cut-edge 9th Inf Div SSI compared with the pre-WWII 9th Inf Div patch on OD wool. Although the ribs are manufactured vertically and horizontally respectively, a similar continued style can be seen.

Fig. 03-562: Front and back of a (likely early-) WWII U.S. made, cut-edge 9th Inf Div black back SSI, fully machine-embroidered on cotton twill backing, with ribbed embroidery. This pattern is similar to pattern #12.

Fig. 03-563: Front and back of a pre-WWII U.S. made 9th Inf Div black back SSI, fully machine-embroidered on OD wool backing material, with ribbed embroidery.

A last example of ribbed embroidery, but with very narrow, flat ribs, is the WWII cut-edge 9th Inf Div SSI compared with the pre-WWII 9th Inf Div patch on OD wool. The WWII cut-edge patch is the same illustrated as in pattern #8. A detail scan of a part of the front of both SSI can be seen on the following page. Again, a similarly continued style can be seen, although a part of the utilized back thread of the pre-WWII SSI is black.

Fig. 03-564: Front and back of a WWII U.S. made, cut-edge 9th Inf Div white back SSI, fully machine-embroidered on cotton twill backing, with ribbed embroidery. This patch is illustrated in pattern #8.

Fig. 03-565: Front and back of a pre-WWII U.S. made 9th Inf Div partial white/black back SSI, fully machine-embroidered on OD wool backing material, reinforced with gauze (as stabilizer) and with ribbed embroidery.

Below is a detail scan of the front of both 9th Inf Div SSI illustrated above. The same style of pattern #8 is demonstrated.

a

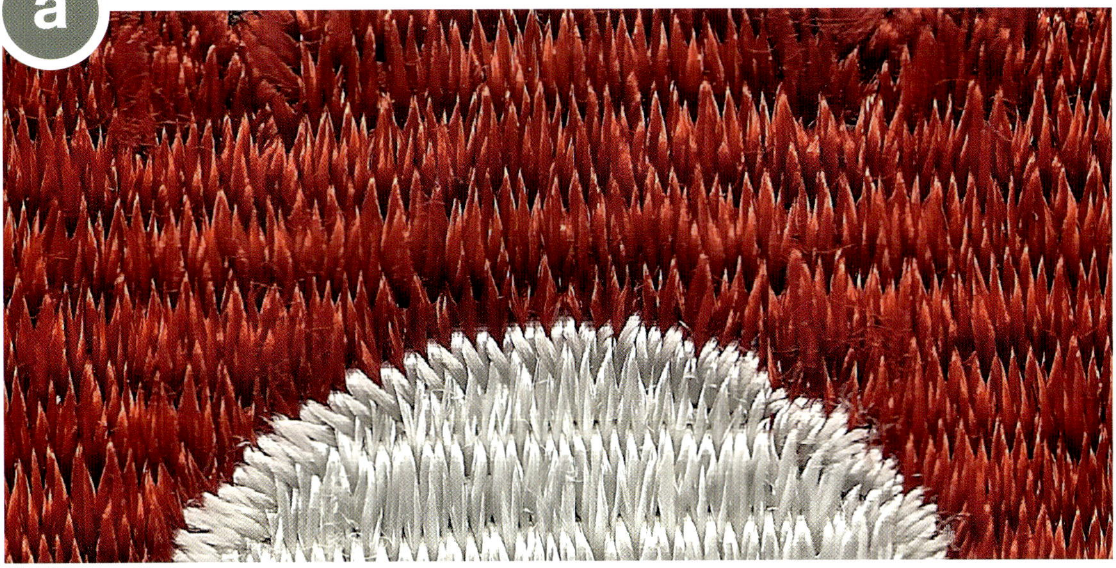

b

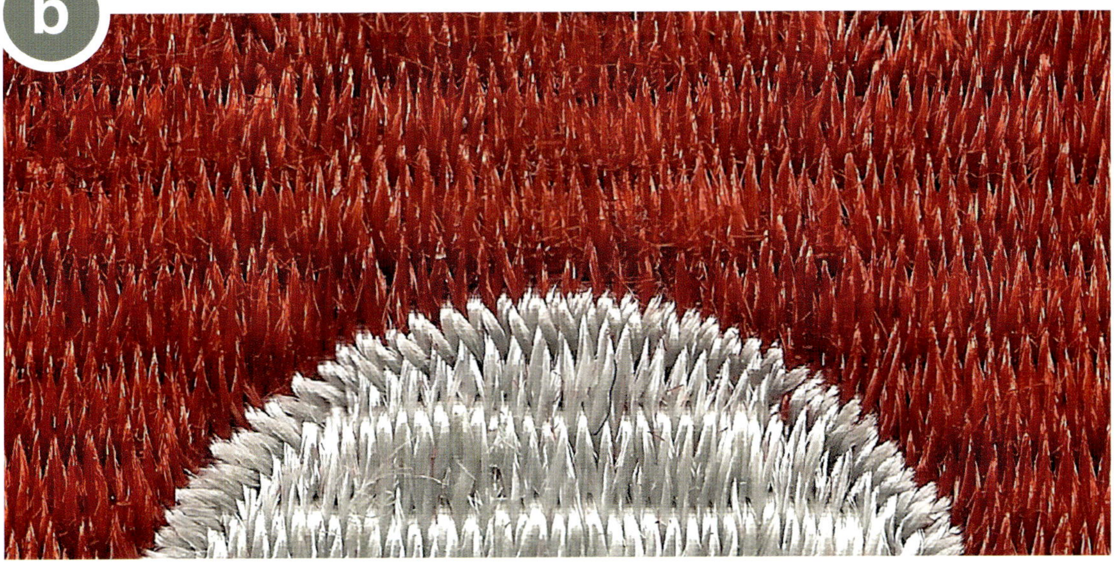

Fig. 03-566: The same embroidery style can be seen on both details.

a Detail of the WWII cut-edge 9th Inf Div SSI illustrated in Fig. 03-564

b Detail of the pre-WWII OD wool 9th Inf Div patch illustrated in Fig. 03-565

A second example of the same manufacture style utilized in the U.S. before and during WWII is the **Gemsco embroidery style**. The 36th Inf Div SSI is pre-WWII era made (1930s). The other two – the 38th and 104th Inf Div patches – are definitely WWII fully machine-embroidered cut-edge SSI. That particular manufacturing style was continued in use from the prewar period into WWII. Earlier it was already mentioned that this embroidery technique could have been a quality and identification label of that certain company. (Note: Gemsco = General Merchandising Co., Milford, CT, U.S.A.)

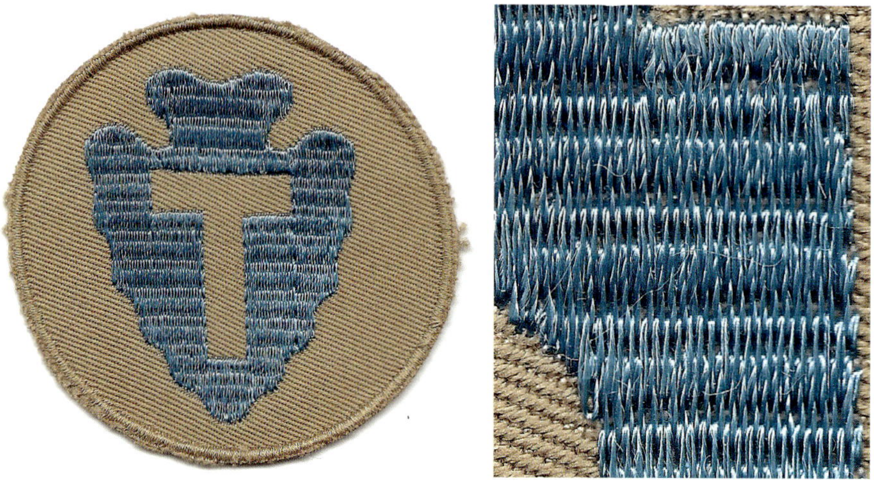

Fig. 03-567: Front of a pre-WWII U.S. made cotton twill 36th Inf Div SSI with detail.

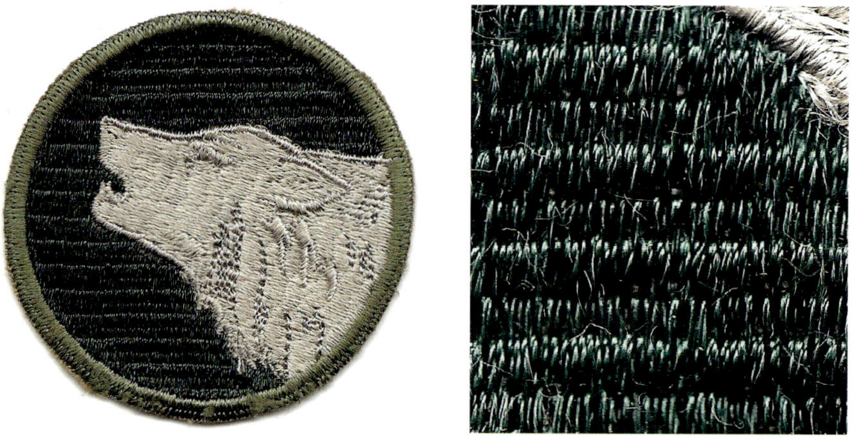

Fig. 03-568: Front of a WWII U.S. made, cut-edge 104th Inf Div SSI with detail.

Fig. 03-569: Front of a WWII U.S. made, cut-edge 38th Inf Div SSI with detail.

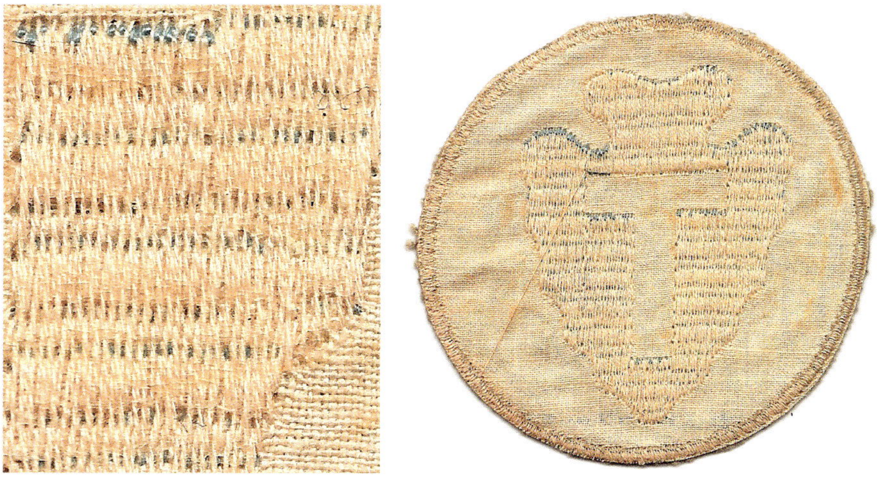

Fig. 03-570: Back of the same pre-WWII cotton twill 36th Inf Div SSI illustrated in Fig. 03-567, with detail.

Fig. 03-571: Back of the same WWII cut-edge 104th Inf Div SSI illustrated in Fig. 03-568, with detail.

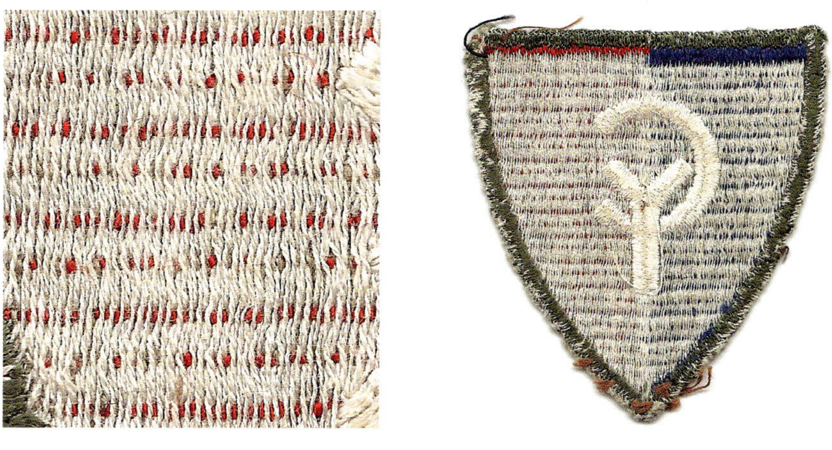

Fig. 03-572: Back of the same WWII cut-edge 38th Inf Div SSI illustrated in Fig. 03-569, with detail.

A third example of old style pre-WWII U.S. made embroidery (below) are two U.S. made 8th Inf Div SSI compared with a post-WWII German made cut-edge 8th Inf Div SSI.

The first two SSI are fully machine-embroidered (one on OD wool and one on cotton twill backing) and are U.S. made, either by a different manufacturer using the same technique, or by one and the same. The latter could be the most likely, because this kind of pattern is rare for a WWII SSI. The blue shield of these two U.S. made SSI are the same size. Even the "8" and the arrow have practically the same appearance. They only have different blue cable colors.

The same specific pattern on both SSI can be seen. For comparison, a detailed scan of the embroidery of both patches is added on the following page. This kind of embroidery has a more open embroidery style (less contiguous threads) than the usual WWII U.S. made embroidery, and with every loop two threads can be seen. A detailed scan of this manufacturing style is also illustrated in Fig. 03-537 and discussed above (pattern #19).

Again, this shows how the backing material of a pre-WWII / early-WWII type SSI (wool) changed into a new type of backing (cotton twill) in the early years of WWII (early 1941), continuing with the same technique and embroidery pattern.

Fig. 03-573: Front and back of a 1930s U.S. made 8th Inf Div SSI, fully machine-embroidered on OD wool.

Fig. 03-574: Front and back of an early-WWII U.S. made, cut-edge 8th Inf Div SSI, fully machine-embroidered on cotton twill with OD border.

Fig. 03-575: Detail of the front of the SSI illustrated in Fig. 03-573 (Pre-WWII U.S. made on OD wool).

Fig. 03-576: Detail of the front of the SSI illustrated in Fig. 03-574 (Early-WWII U.S. made, cut-edge).

Below is a comparison of a detail of the back of the WWII cut-edge U.S. made 8th Inf Div SSI (Fig. 03-574) compared with a detail of the back of the post-WWII German made cut-edge 8th Inf Div SSI (Fig. 03-578 below).

Both were clearly manufactured with a different kind of technique which resulted in different embroidery patterns. Note the horizontal white thread between the white back threads with the U.S. made SSI, which is also seen with the fully machine-embroidered on OD wool 8th Inf Div SSI above (see Fig. 03-573). This feature can not be found on the German made one.

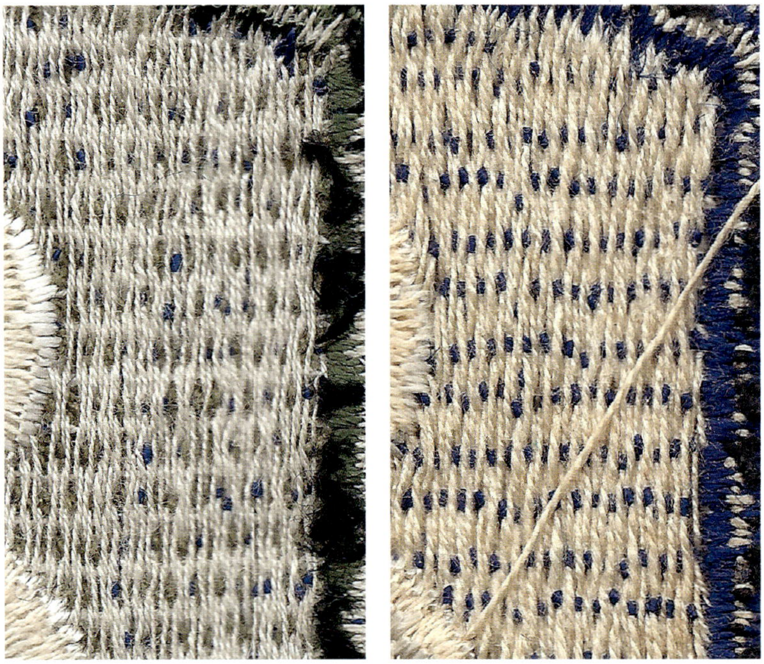

Fig. 03-577: On the left, a detail of the WWII U.S. made, cut-edge 8th Inf Div SSI illustrated on Fig. 03-574 above, and on the right a detail of the post-WWII German made one shown on Fig. 03-578 below.

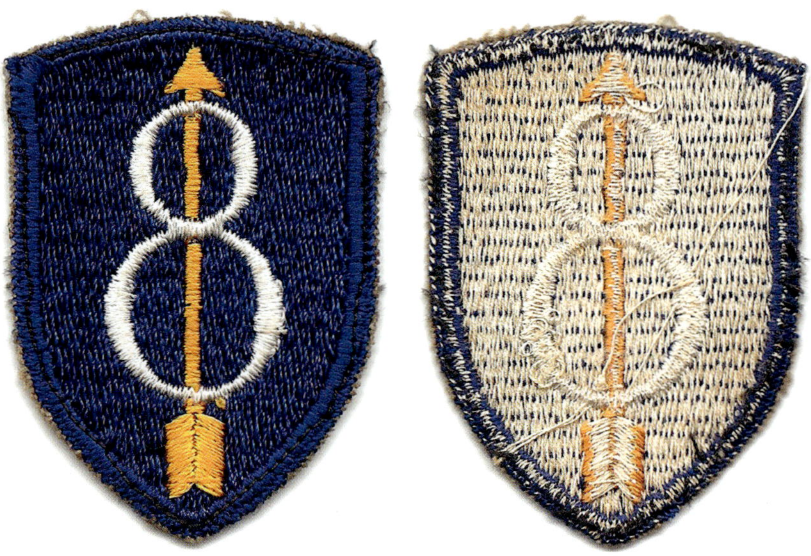

Fig. 03-578: Front and back of a post-WWII German made, cut-edge 8th Inf Div SSI, fully machine-embroidered on cotton twill.

An almost similar embroidery pattern of the WWII cut-edge 8th Inf Div SSI in Fig.03-574 (above) can be seen on the WWII U.S. made cut-edge 44th Inf Div SSI here below, which has pattern #20. The 44th Inf Div SSI has not been manufactured with an OD border. This means that the pre-WWII old style manufacture of SSI was continued during the war, even after changing the design of the SSI by not embroidering the OD border. The fact of omission of the OD border during WWII will be discussed in the following heading.

Fig. 03-579: Front and back of a WWII U.S. made, cut-edge 44th Inf Div SSI, fully machine-embroidered on cotton twill without OD border and applied with pattern #20.

Comparing the SSI above with the 43rd Inf Div patch illustrated below in Fig. 03-580, applied with pattern #21, demonstrates that we have two different embroidery techniques and resulting patterns. The detail pictures of the 44th and 43rd Inf Div patches on the following page will illustrate this very well. Although the detailed pictures of the fronts of both SSI show a similar kind of style, the back thread pattern clearly says otherwise (see Fig. 03-581).

Fig. 03-580: Front and back of a WWII U.S. made, cut-edge 43rd Inf Div SSI, fully machine-embroidered on cotton twill with OD border and applied with pattern #21.

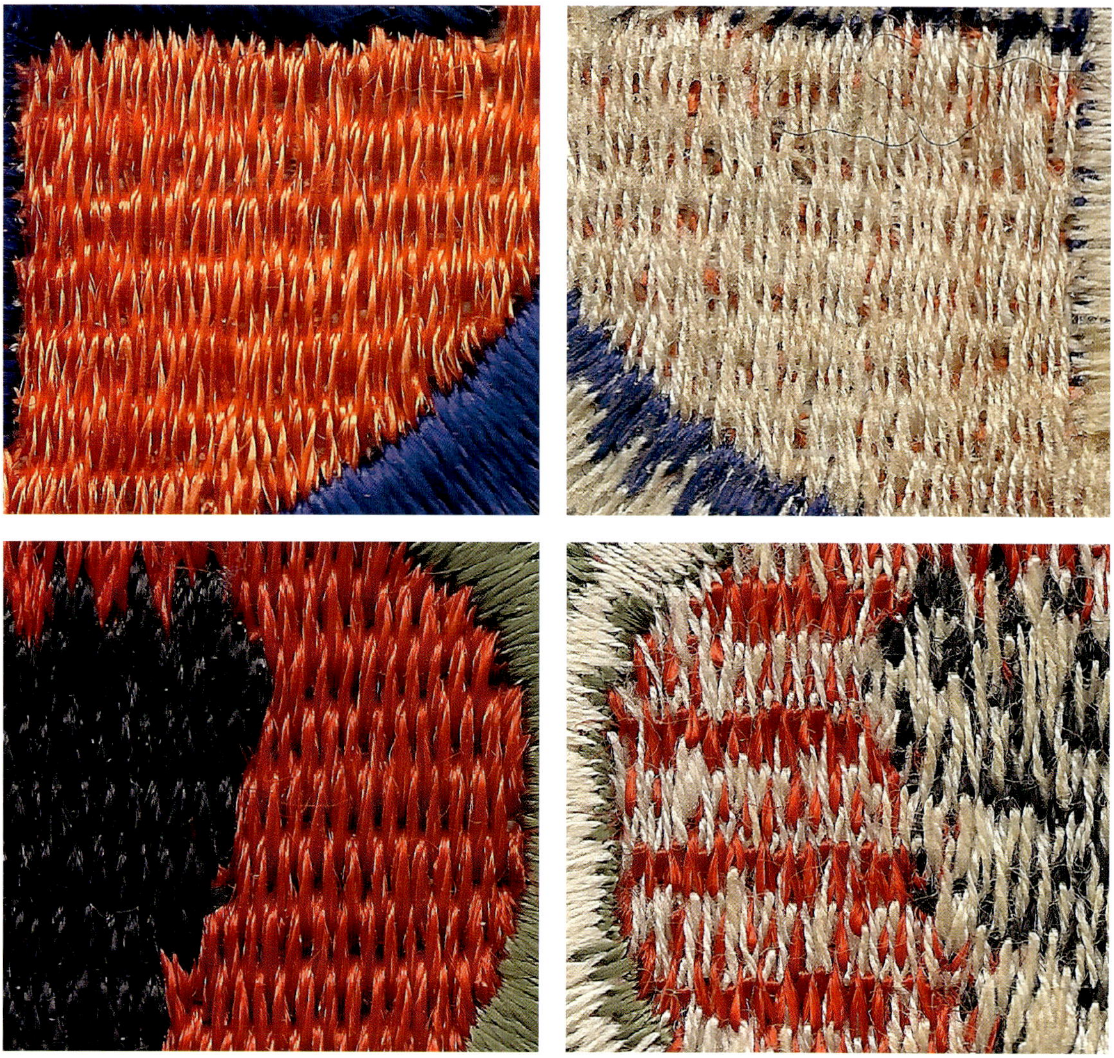

Fig. 03-581: The differences regarding to the back thread can clearly be seen.
Upper pictures: Details of front and back of the 44th Inf Div SSI illustrated in Fig. 03-579 (pattern #20)
Lower pictures: Details of front and back of the 43rd Inf Div SSI illustrated in Fig. 03-580 (pattern #21)

A fourth example of the same manufacture style utilized in the U.S. before and during WWII is the zigzag embroidery style. The first two are both fully machine-embroidered 37th Inf Div SSI on wool base fabric and are pre-WWII era made (1930s). The third 37th Inf Div SSI is a WWII era manufactured on cotton twill backing cut-edge patch. The manufacturer continued with the same embroidery technique. This embroidery style is rarely seen, and could have been an identification means of that particular company. The template on the embroidery machine was most likely drawn with these rows of stitches to be followed by the operator on that machine.

The fact that all these examples below would be of the same manufacturer can be confirmed because all embroidered parts of the SSI are equally large and have the same appearance (if you omit the OD wool border), have also the same technique concerning the back thread, and have the same kind of large white border. There is little doubt that these three were made by the same manufacturer.

Added for comparison is a 1930s U.S. made, partially machine-embroidered on felt, U.S. 4th Army SSI. The zigzag embroidery style was also applied for the leaves of the clover.

Fig. 03-582: Front and back of a 1930s U.S made 37th Inf Div SSI, fully machine-embroidered on OD wool. The special manufacture style can clearly be seen.

Fig. 03-583: Front and back of a 1930s U.S. made 37th Inf Div SSI, fully machine-embroidered on Officer's dark wool elastique.

Fig. 03-584: Front and back of a WWII U.S. made, cut-edge 37th Inf Div SSI, fully machine-embroidered on cotton twill backing material.

Fig. 03-585: Front and back of a 1930s U.S. 4th Army SSI of U.S. manufacture, partially machine-embroidered on red felt base material. The four leaves of the clover are embroidered in the zigzag embroidery style.

The fifth and last example is also pre-WWII U.S. made embroidery. Two patterns, discussed before, are demonstrated and can be seen in Fig. 03-543 (pattern #22) and Fig. 03-545 (pattern #23) with the examples of the WWII U.S. made cut-edge 102nd and 43rd Inf Div SSI (see also the pictures below). Both patterns are very regular and almost equally made. The 43rd Inf Div patch has more dense and contiguous embroidery than the one of the 102nd, but not as much as the newer style, WWII U.S. made SSI. These (likely) newer and more common WWII embroidery styles were discussed above with patterns #1 to #7.

The fact that patterns #22 and #23 are pre-WWII manufacture styles is demonstrated by the pre-WWII 38th Inf Div SSI on OD wool base fabric, which has the same front pattern (e.g., a double thread in each embroidery loop). The detail pictures of all three SSI (both front and back) on the following pages will show this feature. A big difference between the 43rd and 102nd Inf Div SSI is the back thread's pattern. This, of the 43rd Inf Div patch, is comparable to the back thread pattern of the pre-WWII 38th Inf Div SSI (pattern #23), although the latter is more regular. The back thread style of the 102nd Inf Div patch is very much different and not often seen.

Also for comparison, a detail of the post-WWII German made 8th Inf Div SSI (illustrated at Fig. 03-578) is added. This 102nd Inf Div SSI is definitely not German made.

Note that the manufacture style of the SSI embroidered on OD wool is as dense as the cut-edge one, in spite of the use of the unstructured wool backing. This is because of the application of the black mesh as reinforcement (stabilizer) at the back of the patch.

Fig. 03-586: Front and back of a pre-WWII U.S. made 38th Inf Div SSI, fully machine-embroidered on OD wool base cloth and reinforced with black mesh (as stabilizer) at the back (with pattern #23).

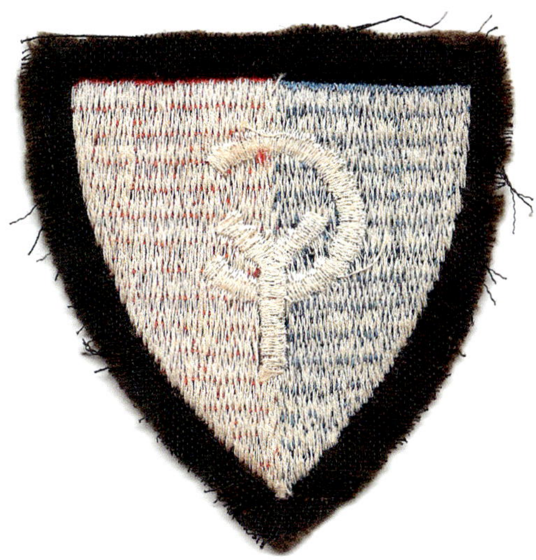

Fig. 03-587: Front and back of a WWII U.S. made, cut-edge 43rd Inf Div SSI, fully machine-embroidered on cotton twill base cloth (applied with pattern #23).

Fig. 03-588: Front and back of a WWII U.S. made, cut-edge 102nd Inf Div SSI, fully machine-embroidered on cotton twill base cloth (applied with pattern #22).

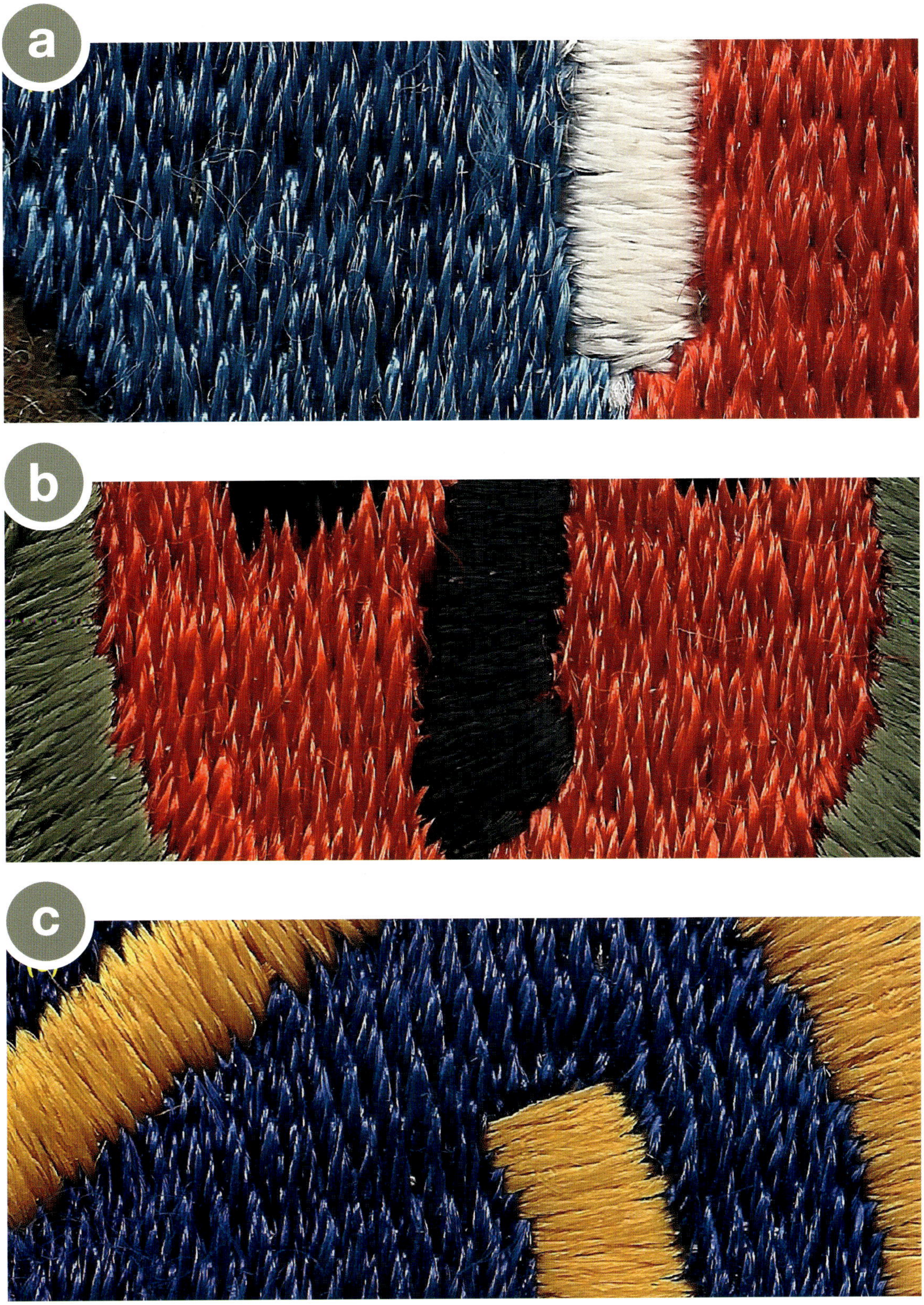

Fig. 03-589: These manufacture styles seem all similar to each other (pattern #23):
a Detail of the front of the pre-WWII 38th Inf Div SSI in Fig. 03-586
b Detail of the front of the WWII cut-edge 43rd Inf Div SSI in Fig. 03-587
c Detail of the front of the WWII cut-edge 102nd Inf Div SSI in Fig. 03-588

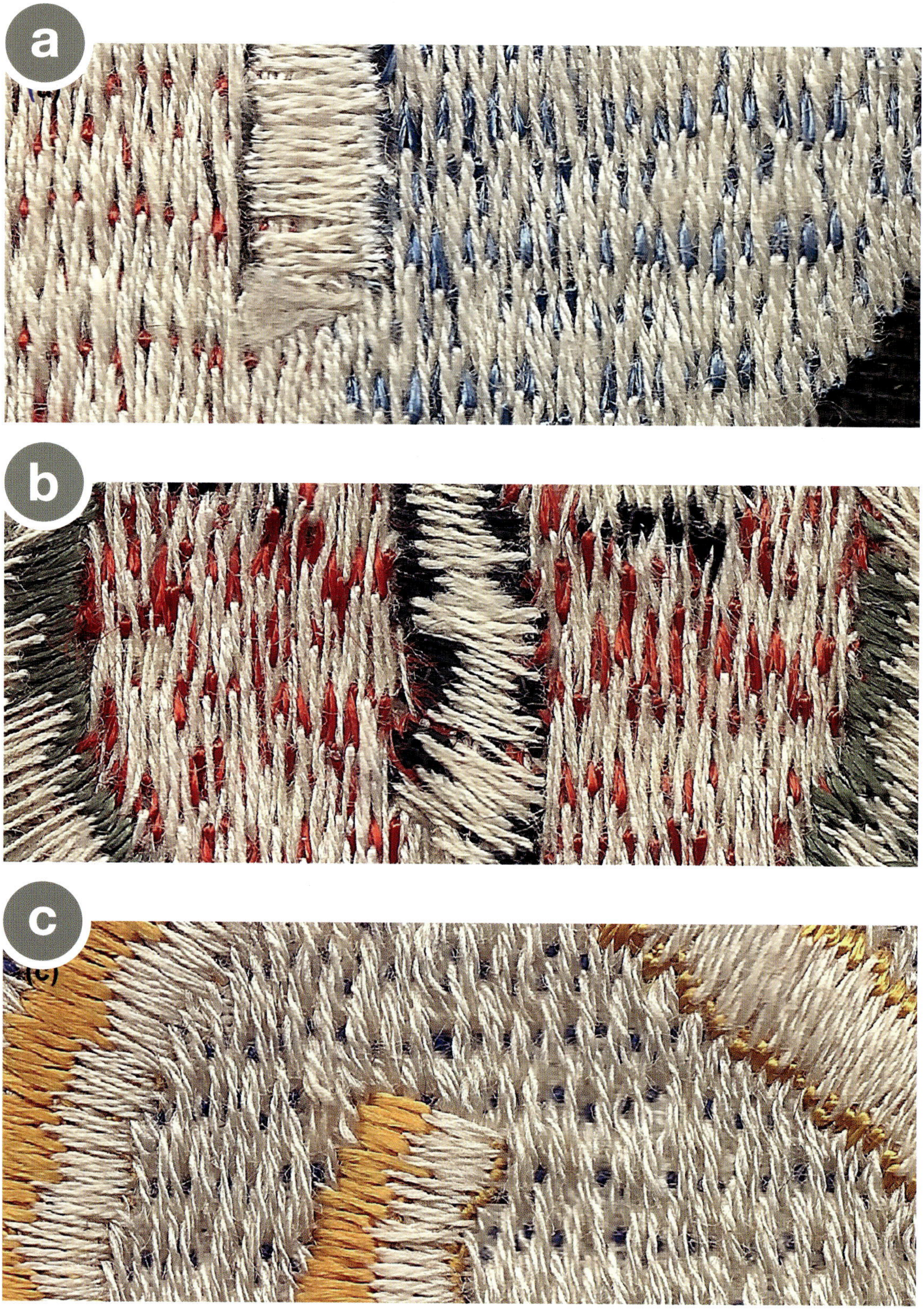

Fig. 03-590: Only (a) and (b) can be considered as the same kind of style (pattern #23):
a Detail of the back of the pre-WWII 38th Inf Div SSI in Fig. 03-586
b Detail of the back of the WWII cut-edge 43rd Inf Div SSI in Fig. 03-587
c Detail of the back of the WWII cut-edge 102nd Inf Div SSI in Fig. 03-588 (pattern #22)

For comparison, notice the details of front and back of the U.S made WWII cut-edge 102nd Inf Div SSI discussed here above and of the post-WWII German made cut-edge 8th Inf Div SSI illustrated in Fig. 03-578. Although very slight, the pattern of the two is different, if one looks very closely at the loops at the front details. While the U.S. made 102nd Inf Div SSI has two threads in each loop (front), the German made SSI shows only a single thread in each loop and has a more regular style than the U.S. made one.

Fig. 03-591: For comparison, the details of front and back of the WWII U.S made, cut-edge 102nd Inf Div SSI discussed here above (top pictures) and of the post-WWII German made, cut-edge 8th Inf Div SSI illustrated in Fig. 03-578 (bottom pictures).

Another example of the embroidery style of pattern #23 that demonstrates its application prior to WWII is the U.S. made 9th Inf Div SSI, fully machine-embroidered on OD wool below. Details of front and back of this patch can be seen on the following page.

Fig. 03-592: Front and back of a WWII U.S. made, cut-edge 9th Inf Div SSI, fully machine-embroidered on cotton twill-base cloth.

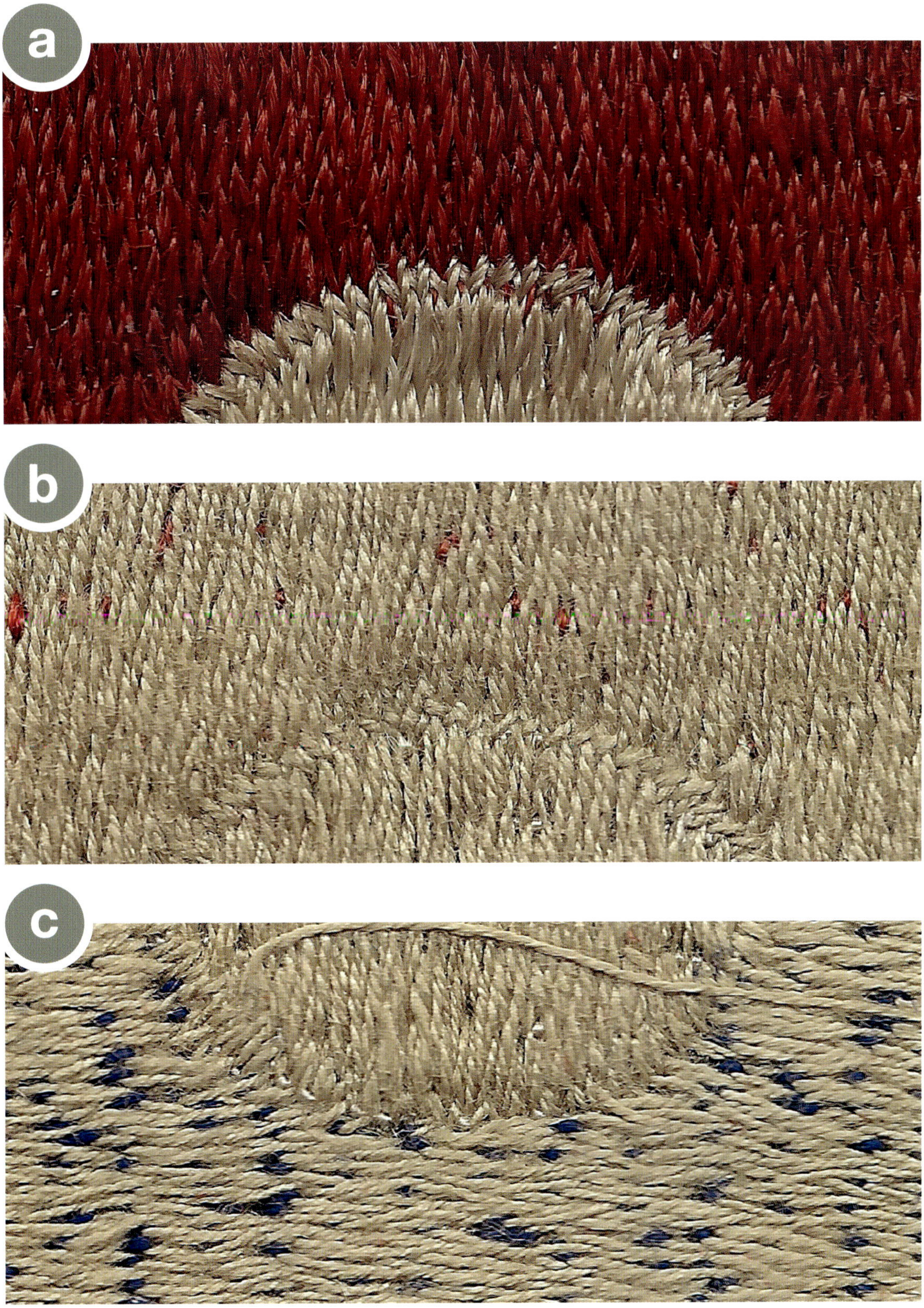

Fig. 03-593: This pre-WWII manufacture style is similar to pattern #23.
a Detail of the front of the pre-WWII 9th Inf Div SSI in Fig. 03-592
b Detail of the upper part of the back of the same SSI
c Detail of the lower part of the back of the same SSI

One last comment: often an oblique embroidery pattern can be seen with certain SSI worn in the usual orientation, more specifically the diamond-shaped ones. The only reason for this kind of pattern is most likely the saving of cotton twill-base fabric. The large roles of backing material consumed by the Schiffli embroidery machine were also valuable during wartime. The cotton backing had to be used as optimal as possible, without too much loss. The manufacture of the diamond-shaped SSI in their usual way for wear did consume too many of the cotton backings after embroidering. The unembroidered part of the base material was cut off afterwards, and this cut part was much less when the SSI was turned with a horizontal base below, instead of a pointed one. During the embroidering, the turned SSI was smaller in height. That way, rows of embroidered SSI could be manufactured closer to one another on that backing, with the saving of cotton twill-base fabric as a final result.

Earlier the use of the Schiffli embroidery machine was explained. Before the actual embroidering, one needed a large-sized drawing with all stitches drawn in by hand. In order for the operator to easily follow the diagrammed stitches they were either vertically or horizontally drawn on that template. When a diamond-shaped SSI needed to be manufactured, often that pre-made template was drawn into a 45° turned position, with all stitches of the patch drawn in that horizontal or vertical direction.

Some of the SSI show a partially oblique embroidery style, with the large background of the SSI vertically or horizontally stitched when turned 45° (to save the backing material), and its smaller design with oblique embroidery (also when turned 45°). This means the design detail shows horizontal or vertical thread loops in the SSI's usual orientation for wear. In all cases, a small design detail was easier to embroider with the direction of the thread loops perpendicular to the longitudinal axis of that detail, even when this detail was turned 45° during the embroidery process, and certainly when this detail only was a thread loop wide.

Or, when the SSI had a larger design detail, this detail often had thread loops with opposite direction than the thread loops of the background on which this detail was embroidered (vertical versus horizontal, when turned 45°). All was dependent on that large template (manufacturer).

In some cases SSI were laid out on backing material in other ways. Some of the diamond-shaped patches still have the horizontal embroidery pattern in their usual diamond orientation for wear. The template diagram of the stitches for that SSI was made and hung up at the embroidery machine in the way the SSI was worn on the sleeve. With no doubt, this particular orientation of that group of SSI on the base fabric resulted in the wastage of more of the base cloth after it was trimmed away. The operator on the embroidery machine always followed the stitches on that template.

The lozenge-shaped SSI (e.g., Rangers patch) and thinner diamonds (e.g., a 5th Inf Div SSI) were never a problem, because they were already flat and thin enough to be manufactured in the usual orientation for wear. The loss of base fabric was probably minimal and negligible compared with the manufacture in a turned position.

Some examples below will clarify this all. This feature can be seen at both pre-WWII and WWII SSI, which means that certain manufacturers were very consciously busy with their commercial business. Of course, there are the usual exceptions as always.

Fig. 03-594: The WWII cut-edge 88th Inf Div SSI.

Fig. 03-595: A WWII cut-edge 1st U.S. Marine Div SSI. The red "1" was embroidered in an oblique way during the manufacturing process because it was only a little part of the SSI and the stitches were drawn on the template that way.

Note that the illustrated 1st U.S. Marine Div SSI worn in the usual orientation (on the left in Fig. 03-395) is not an exact diamond shape. When viewed from the back, the angle on the left side is set slightly lower than that on the right, creating what is in fact a trapezoid, rather than a true diamond. This is for the 45° turned position manufacture and to save cotton twill backing. For a diamond-like shape, this shape of the 1st U.S. Marine Div SSI turned to be the most optimal form for manufacture in a 45°-turned position after the square, with the slightest loss of cotton twill backing. More patches could be placed next to one another on the backing during the embroidery process. Also see the images below.

This series of images below (Fig. 03-596) show the advantages of the turned-position manufacture of an SSI. Starting with a correct sized diamond shape of the 1st U.S. Marine Div [see situation (a)], this shape is placed next to one another in following situation examples.

At situation (b), the SSI are in their usual orientation for wear. Here, one already sees the huge loss of base fabric to be cut off after the SSI's manufacture.

At situation (c), the SSI are placed in a 45° turned position, which shows that there is practically no backing material to be cut after the SSI has finished. Also, the production of the number of SSI has been doubled.

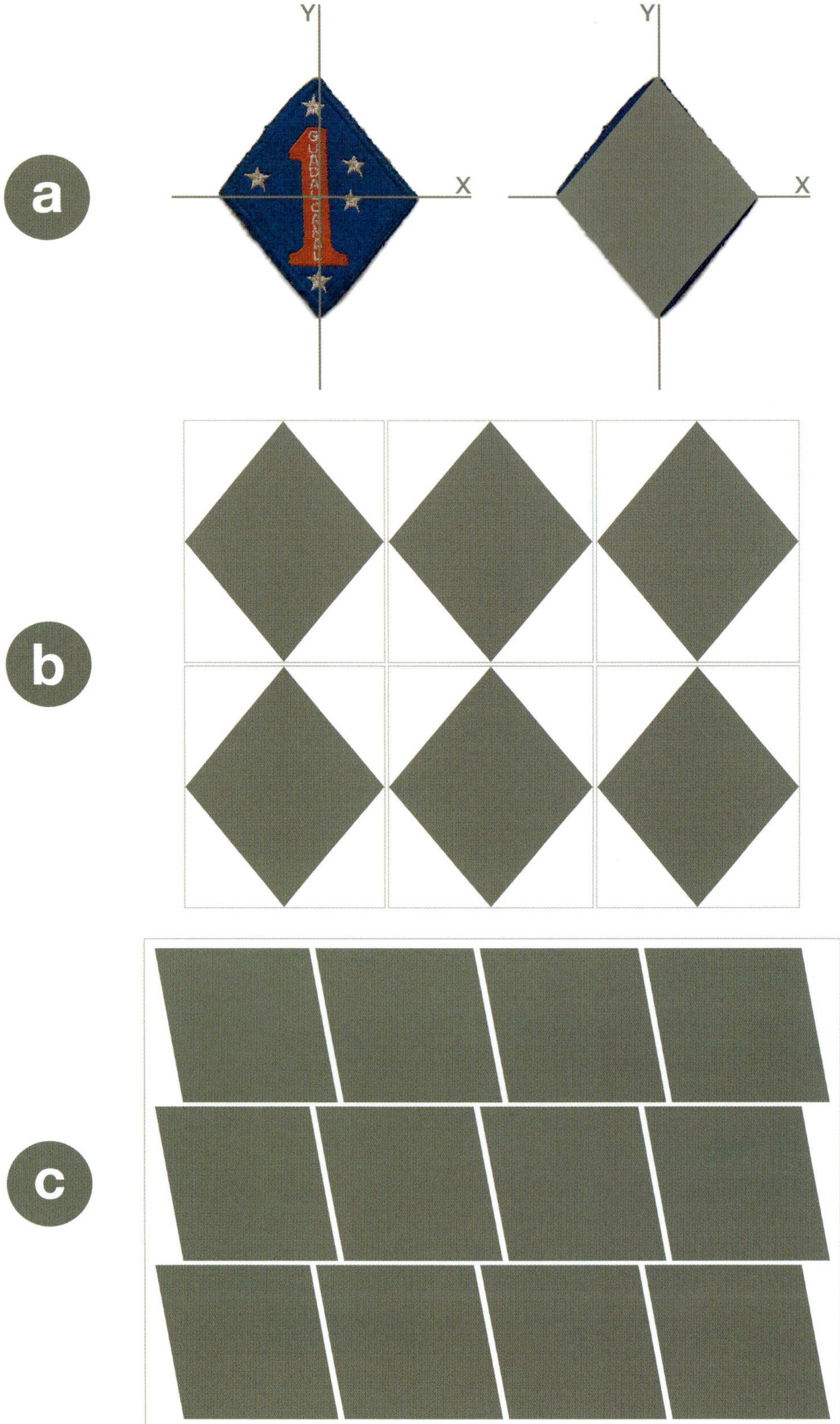

Fig. 03-596: The advantages of a 45°-turned-position manufacture of the SSI.

Fig. 03-597: A WWII cut-edge 45th Inf Div SSI was easier to turn 45° for manufacture because of its square shape. Here a partial oblique embroidery pattern is illustrated. In turned position, horizontal embroidery was applied to the red background as the largest part of the SSI.

Fig. 03-598: A pre-WWII 45th Inf Div SSI with oblique embroidery which demonstrates this method of manufacture was already applied prior to WWII. With the 45°-turned position the embroidery loops of the red background run horizontally, those of the "Thunderbird"-design are vertical. The visible pattern rows are created by the embroidery which is of Gemsco manufacture.

Fig. 03-599: Two WWII cut-edge 45th Inf Div SSI. Not every manufacturer turned in their drawings for the embroidery process. These two patches were made in the normal position for wear.

6 | EXAMPLES OF SSI WITH DIFFERENT EMBROIDERY STYLES

The fact that there are different manufacturers giving their own specific features and characteristics to the SSI is reflected in different types of embroidery styles. An important remark: always keep in mind that certain embroidery styles do not exist for certain SSI.

On the following pages are some examples of original WWII, U.S. made fully machine-embroidered, cut-edge SSI. They are illustrated in pairs, each with different embroidery patterns. Only white backs are illustrated.

Fig. 03-601: A 33rd Inf Div SSI with OD border – Gemsco embroidery style or pattern #18. (Note the repair of the upper section of the yellow cross in both pictures.)

Fig. 03-602: A 33rd Inf Div SSI – Common embroidery. The SSI appears to have pattern #4.

Fig. 03-603: A 28th Inf Div SSI with OD border – Gemsco embroidery style (pattern #18).

Fig. 03-604: A 28th Inf Div SSI with red border – Gemsco embroidery style (pattern #18).

Fig. 03-605: A 30th Inf Div SSI with OD border – This SSI's embroidery style was discussed earlier as pattern #22.

Fig. 03-606: A 30th Inf Div SSI – This patch has embroidery pattern #23.

Fig. 03-607: A 42nd Inf Div SSI – Ribbed embroidery.

Fig. 03-608: A 42nd Inf Div SSI – The patch has embroidery pattern #23.

Fig. 03-609: A 43rd Inf Div SSI with OD border – The patch has embroidery pattern #23.

Fig. 03-610: A 43rd Inf Div SSI with KHAKI border – The patch has embroidery pattern #23 like the one illustrated above in Fig. 03-609.

These two SSI were most likely made by one and the same manufacturer, considering the size and form of the patch, the thickness of the border, the embroidery pattern and back thread, and the size and resemblance of the grape leaf. The upper SSI was worn on the OD-colored uniform; the lower was issued to be sewn on the khaki-colored summer uniform or shirt.

Fig. 03-611: A 75th Inf Div SSI – Common embroidery.

Fig. 03-612: A 75th Inf Div SSI – Common and very regular embroidery (pattern #6). The patch has the same size of embroidery loops (front) as the one above but only the back thread style differs (very small loops).

Looking at the front pictures, both patches have no ribbed bas relief-like embroidery, although one can see vertical rows in their pattern. These pattern rows can certainly not be felt as ribs and are not considered as such.

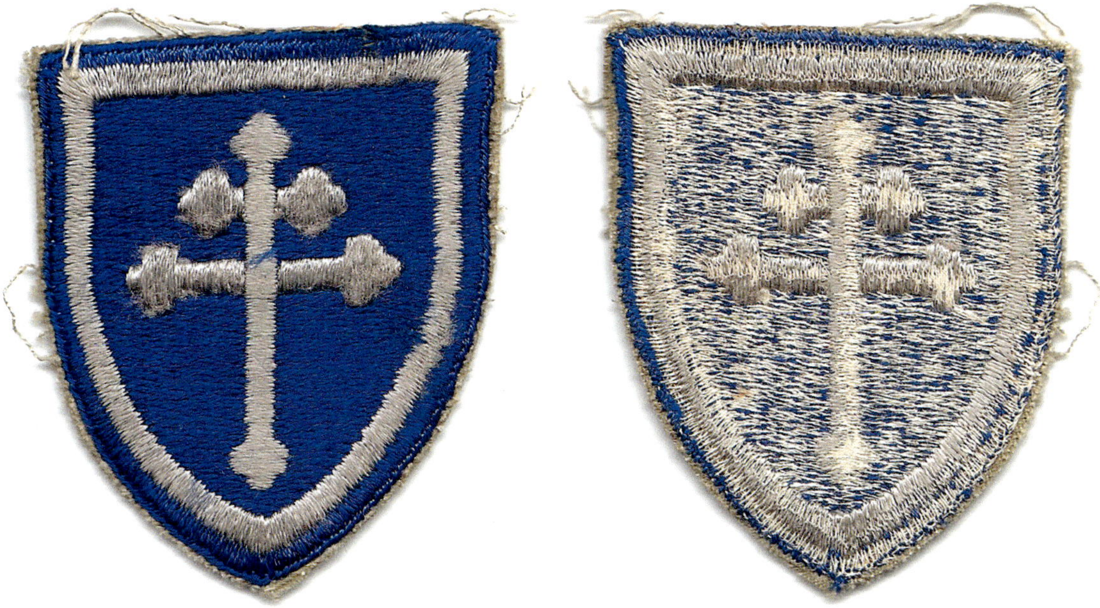

Fig. 03-613: A 79th Inf Div SSI – Common embroidery.

Fig. 03-614: A 79th Inf Div SSI – Ribbed embroidery style.

Fig. 03-615: An 81st Inf Div SSI with the usual black border – Common embroidery.

Fig. 03-616: An 81st Inf Div SSI with the usual black border – Ribbed embroidery.

Fig. 03-617: An 89th Inf Div SSI – Gemsco embroidery and an OD section between the black design and the OD border.

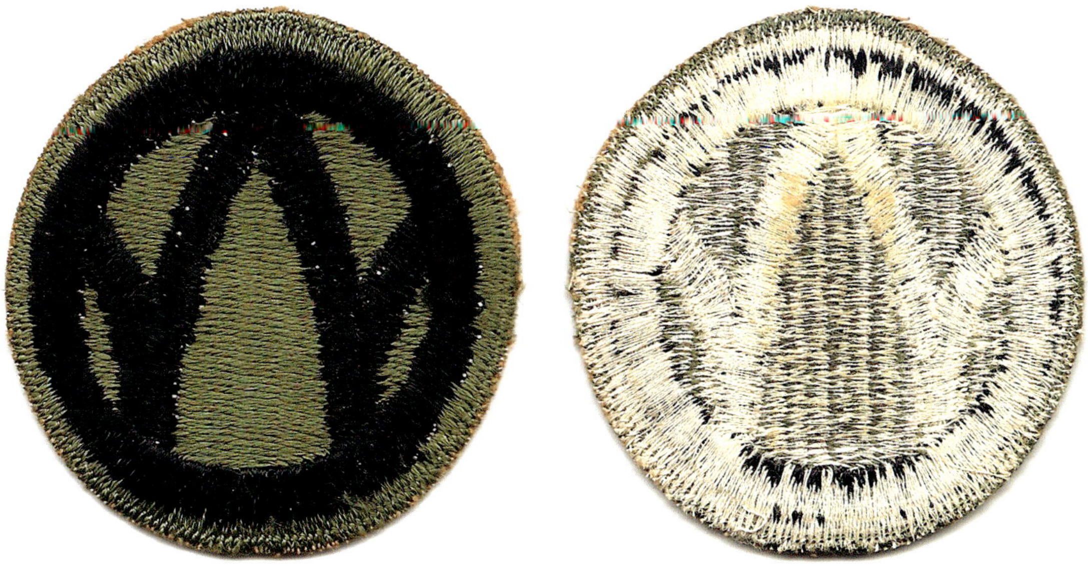

Fig. 03-618: An 89th Inf Div SSI – Common embroidery (pattern #7) and usual manufacture of the design.

Fig. 03-619: A 92nd Inf Div SSI – Common embroidery. At the front picture the bison design seems to have parallel vertical rows in its pattern, but does not have ribbed bas-relief embroidery at all.

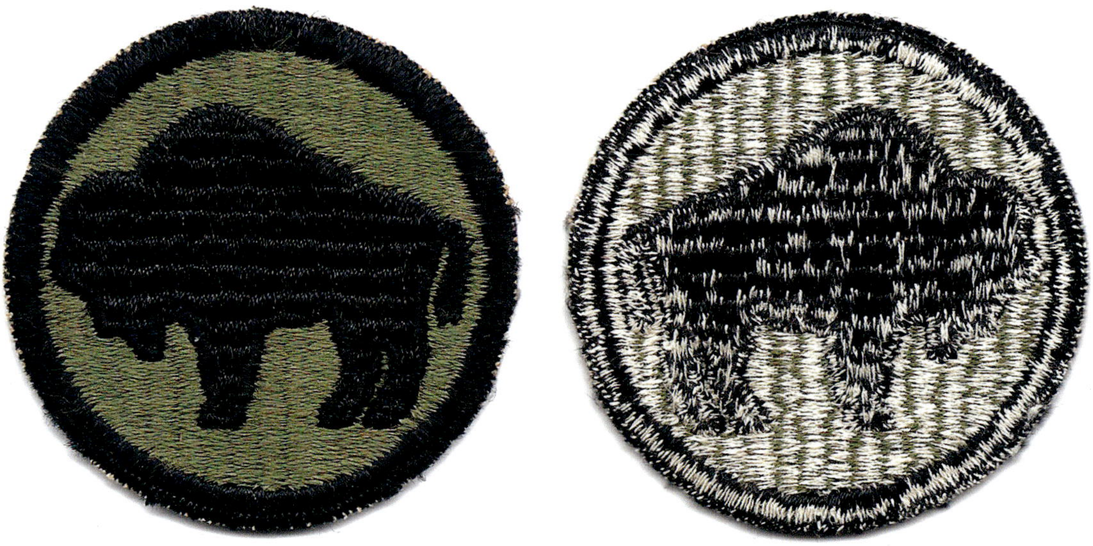

Fig. 03-620: A 92nd Inf Div SSI – Ribbed embroidery (pattern #10).

Fig. 03-621: A 93rd Inf Div SSI – Common embroidery.

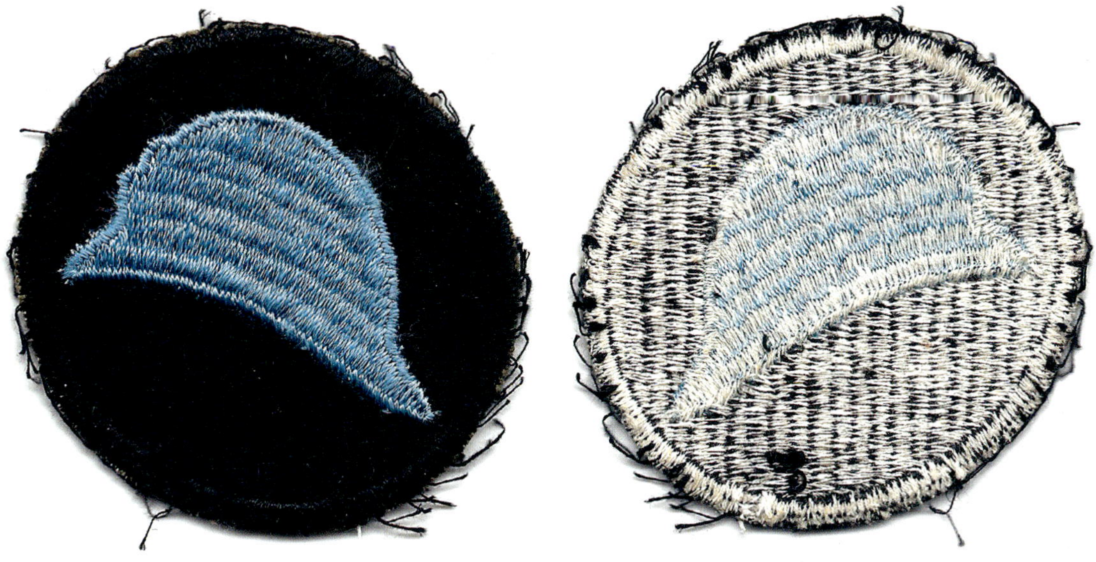

Fig. 03-622: A 93rd Inf Div SSI – Ribbed embroidery (pattern #10).

Fig. 03-623: A U.S. Airborne Command SSI – Common embroidery style.

Fig. 03-624: A U.S. Airborne Command SSI – Gemsco embroidery style.

Fig. 03-625: A 1st U.S. Marine Div SSI – Gemsco embroidery. Note that the SSI has a perfect diamond-shape and was embroidered in the usual worn orientation.

Fig. 03-626: A 1st U.S. Marine Div SSI – Common embroidery. Note that this SSI was manufactured in the turned position. It shows a partial oblique embroidery pattern.

Fig. 03-627: A 1st Marine Amphibious Corps / Raider Battalions SSI – Ribbed embroidery.

Fig. 03-628: A 1st Marine Amphibious Corps / Raider Battalions SSI – Common embroidery.

Fig. 03-629: An 8th Service Command SSI – Ribbed embroidery.

Fig. 03-630: An 8th Service Command SSI – Common embroidery.

Fig. 03-631: An odd 13th Armored Div SSI with vertical and horizontal ribbed embroidery, applied with pattern #9. The red horizontal ribs are slightly smaller than the vertical ones.

Fig. 03-632: An 11th Armored Div SSI – Common embroidery (appears to be pattern #3).

Fig. 03-633: A 3rd U.S. Army SSI with OD border and applied with pattern #9.

Fig. 03-634: Two 3rd U.S. Army SSI without OD border; both applied with common embroidery. SSI (a) is applied with pattern #5 because what appear to be vertical pattern rows to the embroidery can be seen at the front of the SSI. SSI (b) appears to have pattern #3.

7 | OD / BROWN / GREEN BORDER... OR NO BORDER

Another element that can determine the originality of the SSI is the edge or BORDER of the SSI. Every WWII SSI manufactured with the cut-edge principle has an embroidered border.

The border was embroidered around the design and was always focused inward. This means that the thread of the border is always perpendicular to the cut-edge. So this would in effect lock in the embroidery and prevent ravelling of the SSI.

The border of the SSI finished off the SSI. By using these borders, the SSI does not fray and the main and back threads remain nicely together. Try comparing an SSI where the border is broken. The threads next to the broken border will come off a little easier here.

Another feature which is characteristic for a WWII to early 1950s period manufactured border is the **embroidery line** that clearly can be seen near the edge of the border. There appears to be a line of embroidery or a second border along the edge.

A closer look at the border will show that it consists of two parts:

- A wider part of straight single loops which lay next to one another at the inner side of the border;
- And a series of small loops at the outer side of the border as a knot to secure the embroidered border at its edge (see Fig. 03-701).

Fig. 03-701: A detail of the left angled knot loops to secure the border.

The latter is not a second border, but is only part of the embroidery technique to create the border. It is a kind of lock or safety knot to avoid the loops of the border coming loose after the base fabric is cut. That way one can cut very close to the border, even completely cutting the base fabric away next to these knots.

Between these two parts a kind of line is created: the embroidery line. These features can be seen in the detail pictures below.

Often it is stated that the knot loops of this embroidery line (the outer rim of the border) of WWII SSI were more angled than 1950s manufactured SSI. This is not always true. However, it could be possible that many post-WWII patches have wider and straight out knot loops instead of the angled ones, but this is not an exclusive means to exclude a patch from being WWII. Even during WWII there were outer rims with straight out knots. It depended on the embroidery technique manufacturers used on how the borders and their secure knots were made. Below are also some WWII examples with straight out knot loops.

Fig. 03-702: A detail of the border of a WWII 76th Inf Div SSI with to the right angled knot loops to secure the border.

Fig. 03-703: A detail of the border of a WWII 98th Inf Div SSI with to the left angled knot loops to secure the border.

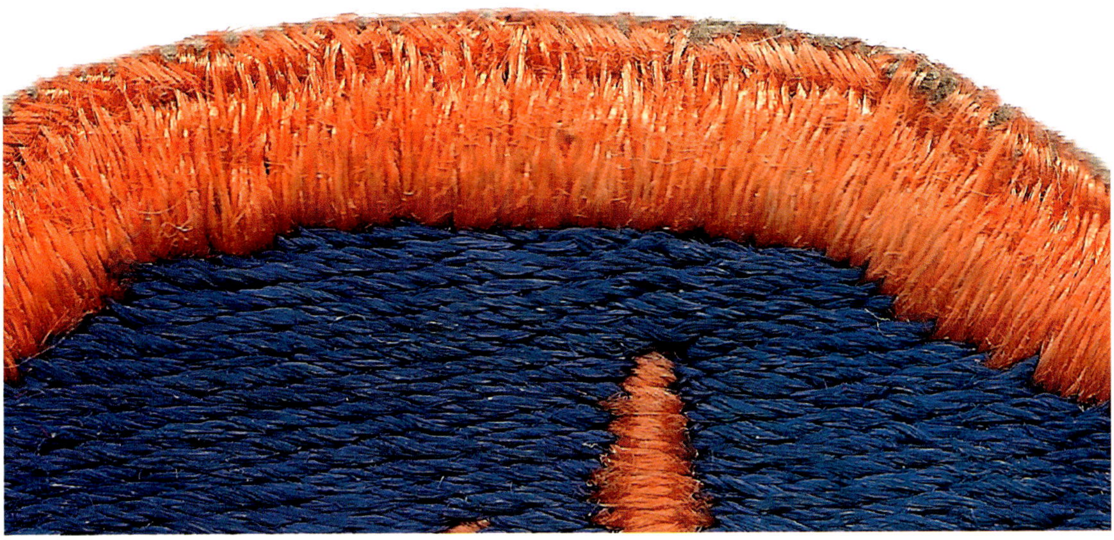

Fig. 03-704: A detail of the OD border of an early-WWII 45th Inf Div SSI with straight knot loops to secure the border.

Fig. 03-705: A detail of the OD border of an early WWII 2nd Inf Div SSI with practically straight knot loops to secure the border.

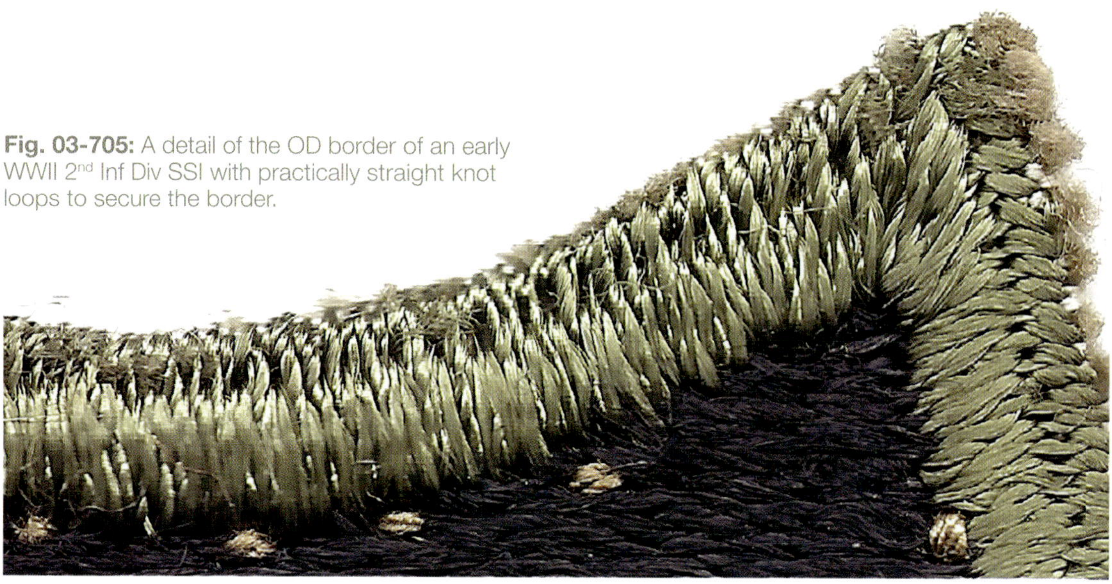

The color of the border depends on:

- The period;
- The SSI of that particular unit (see further on in this book: "The Institute of Heraldry" drawings);
- The company that made them (plus sufficient stock of OD thread).

The **OD border**, **brown border**, and **green border** of fully embroidered cut-edge SSI are a remnant or a simulation of the OD wool edge, which was a feature of the OD wool hand- or machine-embroidered SSI made in the 1920s and '30s.

The use and appearance of OD borders on machine-embroidered SSI is a WWII characteristic. However, it also continued to appear on the SSI of certain units manufactured after WWII.

By means of this border, the SSI on OD wool, as well as the OD-/brown-/green-bordered cut-edge SSI on cotton twill, the SSI could be sewn on the olive drab-colored uniform of the GI with the issued OD-colored cotton sewing thread.

However, during and (certainly) after the war many SSI were sewn on the uniform in all possible ways, in fancy patterns and with various colors of sewing thread (e.g., red sewing thread for U.S. Marine Corps and First Special Service Force patches because of their red borders). This led to ornate SSI on the uniform (e.g., cross-stitch).

In many cases, not only the OD uniform but also shirts had a patch sewn on.

Fig. 03-706: Black thread cross-stitch on a white border – A WWII cut-edge 79th Inf Div SSI.

If it was not the serviceman himself who sewed the patch on his uniform, it could have been either a colleague serviceman who functioned as tailor in the Unit, or a tailor in a nearby town when the serviceman was on leave, or some other person with skills in using a home sewing machine or in hand sewing a patch (such as a relative or friend). They might choose some other colors of sewing thread they believed were correct.

POSSIBLE THEORY: Where did the OD and other colored border come from?

The U.S. Army contracted civilian manufacturers for the production of insignia during WWII to build the necessary stock. It was much easier to turn manufacture over to civilian contractors and monitor their quality.

In the 1930s in the U.S., certain SSI manufacturers made fully machine-embroidered OD wool SSI by specifications and standards received by the government when ordered ("The Institute of Heraldry" Drawings (TIOH Drawings): see chapter 8 heading 1 further on). Those drawings were directives relating to the form, colors, and sizes of the SSI, but made no mention of any border in almost every case. This OD wool border was needed because only a narrow stitched finishing was done around the design, and was not enough to keep the embroidery in place when the wool remnant should have been cut off completely. The wool border partially prevented this ravelling of the embroidery.

Fig. 03-707: Although a WWI period SSI, on the edge the ravelling of the embroidery can clearly be seen as a result of the lack of an OD wool border. The wool base material was cut off too close next to the embroidery which is coming loose on that part of the patch.

Another possible reason for the use of an OD wool border, the SSI could easily be sewn on the OD wool uniform without seeing the – to the GI issued – OD-colored sewing thread. This possibility remains an assumption, however, the SSI with its OD wool border was in fact part of the OD-colored wool uniform.

With these 1930s wool patches, a wide embroidered border was thus not necessary, and only a narrow finishing around the design was done in the same color of that design. After manufacturing the SSI was cut into size and shape, including an OD wool border.

The same pre-WWII companies continued making the SSI on cotton twill-base fabric at the beginning of WWII. The reason for this change of procedure is explained above. This new process utilized the cut-edge principle, where the base fabric was cut off right next to the border. This new kind of SSI needed a specific border to avoid fraying and to increase its durability. Because of the fact that these companies always manufactured SSI with OD wool border, they continued to embroider one in OD-colored thread around the design (instead of using the background color of the design).

This procedure was continued until, somewhere in the course of WWII (probably between the middle and end of 1942), OD-colored rayon thread was more needed for other applications as mentioned above. The manufacturers probably had directives to be thrifty with this kind of thread in their stocks to be used only when necessary (see the U.S. government's specifications in the TIOH drawings). From then on during WWII, for these companies, it could have been difficult to obtain the OD thread because of these other applications. That could explain why some OD-bordered SSI are early-WWII and sometimes hard to find.

This could also explain why SSI of later activated divisions and units (from the period end 1942-beginning 1943) do not have an OD border, but a border in the same color of the background (e.g., a 65th Inf Div SSI).

SSI of the other late formed divisions (end 1942 until 1945), for example the 10th Mountain, 66th, 69th, 71st, 98th, and 106th Inf Div, and many other late organized units (e.g., U.S. Army Groups) have a border either in a color other than the SSI's color(s), or in one of its colors (even a color of a detail on the SSI). With this group, "The Institute of Heraldry" drawings, on which a border probably was mentioned, were followed. They don't exist with OD border.

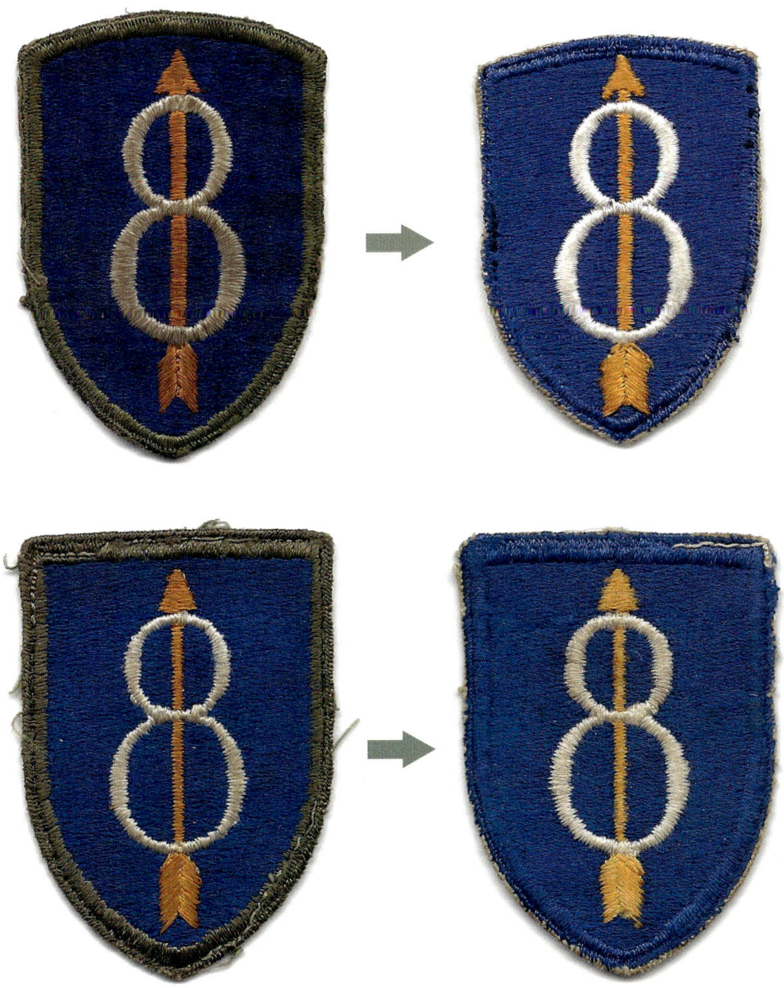

Fig. 03-707a: The common 8th Inf Div SSI (above) and the one with the unusual flat top (below). Both variations are with and without OD border (the OD-bordered flat top 8th Inf Div patch is very rare). Surprisingly, both flat top variations are the same size. Here only the color of the border changed into blue, its background color (same manufacturer?). The common 8th Inf Div patch without OD border is smaller, and fits within the OD border of its counterpart.

It is very likely that there is a connection between the change of OD border to a regular-colored border, with the change from OD back to other colors of back thread (also around end 1942-early 1943). It could have happened in the same period or in successive periods for saving OD-colored thread.

An exception to the theory above is the 89th Inf Div SSI. The WWII TIOH drawing of the patch is foreseen with an OD border (see figure below, at the right), even if it is an October 25, 1918, drawing. It was always manufactured with the OD border in relation to that drawing, even after 1942.

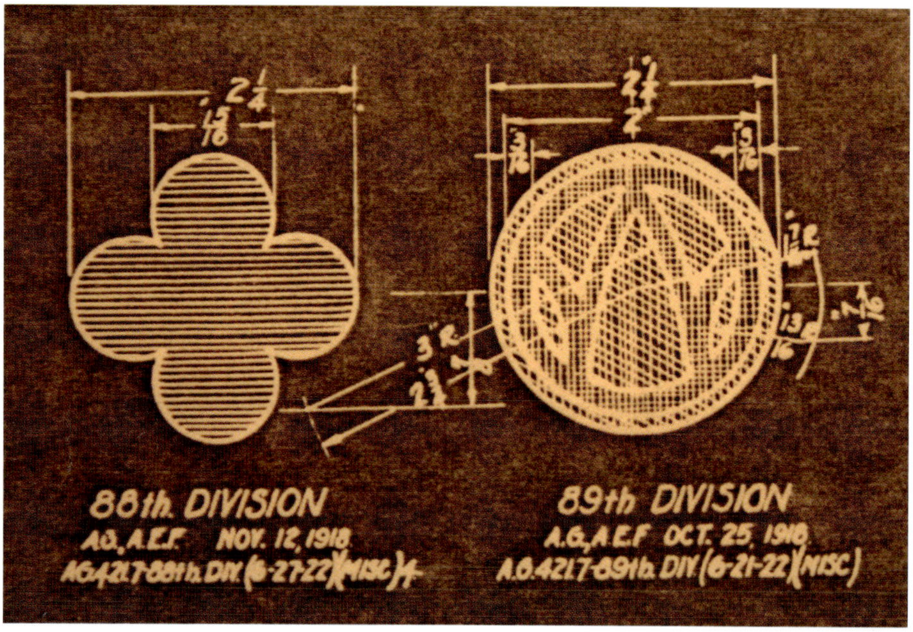

Fig. 03-708: The 1918 dated TIOH-Drawing of the 89th Inf Div SSI at the right was provided with an OD border around the black design. The TIOH-Drawing of the 88th Inf Div SSI at the left was not drawn with one but does exist with OD border. (Courtesy of Craig Pickrall)

Newly contracted WWII manufacturers never saw the use of OD wool and the OD wool border. They only utilized cotton twill-base fabric and followed the directives of "The Institute of Heraldry" drawings received from the government. These companies probably never made SSI with OD border, unless they should have received examples or other directives to embroider one in OD (e.g., the 29th Inf Div SSI, an Armored Div SSI – see paragraph below). That is why SSI without OD border also can be found with the early-WWII OD back thread.

On the other hand, WWII U.S. made fully machine-embroidered, cut-edge Armored Forces, Division, and Battalion SSI were always manufactured with OD

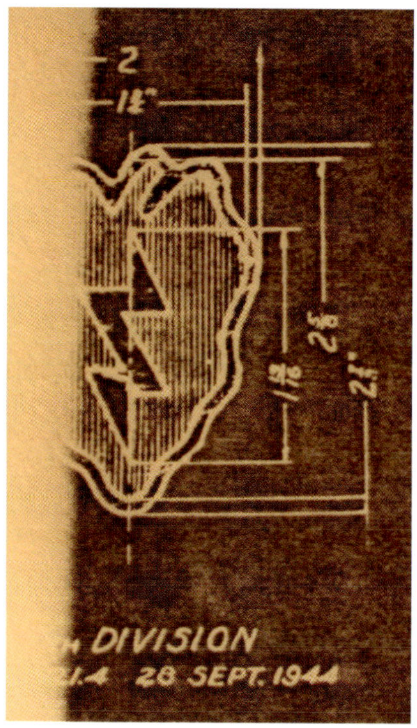

Fig. 03-709: The TIOH-Drawing of the 25th Inf Div SSI was provided with border. The division was activated on October 1, 1941, after the OD wool manufacturing period. Such patch embroidered on OD wool has never been seen. The border was applied in gold-yellow as shown in the drawing, never in OD color. (Courtesy of Craig Pickrall)

border. A reason could be found in the fact that three different colors of thread are used to create the background of the SSI's shield (yellow, red, and blue). Each of these colors touches the edge of the shield on which the border is embroidered.

In the later war period, and following the theory about the omission of the OD border with U.S. made insignia mentioned above, this would mean that the border should be made out of these three colors, with each color next to the same background color. This could have made the manufacturing process more difficult or time consuming (changing of the bobbins on the embroidery machine every time), or could have given cause for more errors.

Another important fact concerning the border is that it should be continuously embroidered out of one single thread to avoid loosening at several points (possible fraying of the multi-colored border of the SSI at the beginning or the end of each used thread).

Probably for one of these aforementioned reasons, the OD border on the U.S. made Armored SSI, and many others, was maintained.

The same can be concluded with the 3rd, 29th, 38th, 41st, 42nd, 75th, 76th, 84th, 94th, 99th, 103rd, and 104th Inf Div patches, the 1st design XI Corps patch, and many other fully machine-embroidered SSI (e.g., the Army Ground Forces SSI) where the background of the shield has more than one color touching the border, and where thus more than one colored thread would be needed for embroidering a border, because here an OD border was already applied or was the best option, and was maintained. Although sometimes a 1st design XI Corps patch with blue border, a 94th Inf Div SSI with grey border, a 99th Inf Div SSI with black border, a 103rd Inf Div SSI with yellow border, a 29th Inf Div SSI with partial blue and grey border, or a 75th Inf Div insignia with a partial blue/white/red border do exist, they are very scarce. Those SSI are certainly not manufacturer's errors. With the example of the 29th Inf Div patch, the color of the border even matches the color of the background: the grey border next to the grey background and the blue border next to the blue background of the shield. The same can be said about the 75th Inf Div SSI, but here with its blue, white, and red part of the shield. Three 75th Inf Div patches, two with and one without OD border, are illustrated below. The most likely reasons why the manufacturer made these rarely seen patches that way (without OD border) were the lack of OD-colored rayon threads in that company's stock or possible directives to be thrifty with this kind of thread.

Fig. 03-709a: Three differently made, original 75th Inf Div patches: two with the usual OD border and one without. The latter is extremely rare, and illustrates even a border could be made out of three colors of threads. Because of the rarity, it is unlikely that more than one company made such insignia.

Below are some examples of these drawings with no mention of any OD or other-colored border, but at the final product an OD border was manufactured.

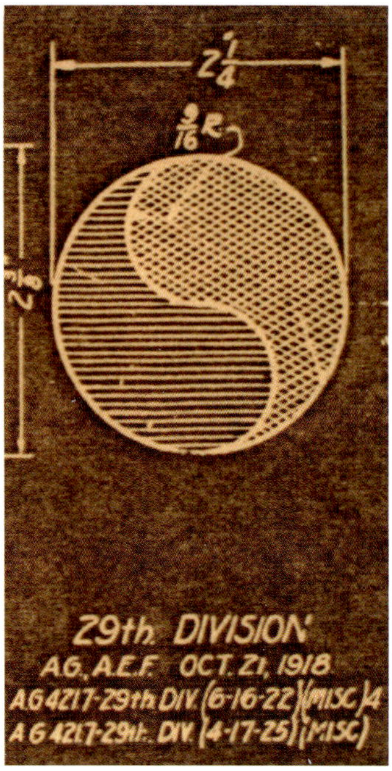

Fig. 03-710: "The Institute of Heraldry"-Drawing of the 29th Inf Div SSI. *(Courtesy of Craig Pickrall)*

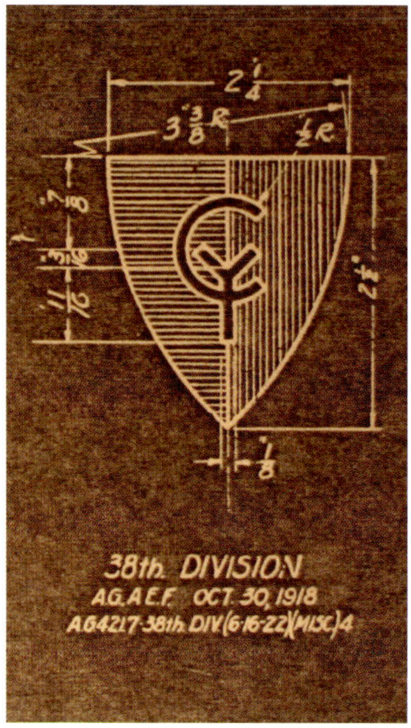

Fig. 03-711: "The Institute of Heraldry"- Drawing of the 38th Inf Div SSI. *(Courtesy of Craig Pickrall)*

Fig. 03-712: This U.S. 4th Army SSI has ribbed embroidery, but has not the usual OD border. This could mean that this SSI was manufactured after 1942 according to TIOH-Drawings and continuing this particular early embroidery style.
Note the repair, done by the manufacturer, on the right side of the patch (front) because of the absence of a part of the ribbed pattern. This feature can also be seen at the back.

The border exists in all colors. When one speaks of NO BORDER, does not mean that the particular SSI does not have one. Every SSI has a machine-embroidered border for the reasons mentioned above. The term NO BORDER indicates that the patch does not have an OD, brown, or green border, but one in another color in conjunction with the background of the shield or the directives of "The Institute of Heraldry" drawings.

This often means that the SSI is smaller in size when the border is of another color than OD/brown/green, which means that the other-colored border not only replaces the one in OD. "The Institute of Heraldry" drawings were always clear about the size of the SSI without OD border, but only for the SSI's shield in a certain background color (which, in most cases, includes the border in that particular background color). For borders with a color other than the shield's background, the "TIOH" drawing of that particular SSI was always the reference.

The 5th and 32nd Inf Div SSI below are very good examples of the difference in size because of the absence of an OD border. A much thinner/smaller variation of these SSI exist because of the skipping of the OD border. "The Institute of Heraldry" drawings are clear about the particular size of the red background or shield of the patch. The manufacturer of the smaller, red-bordered variations included the necessary border within that size.

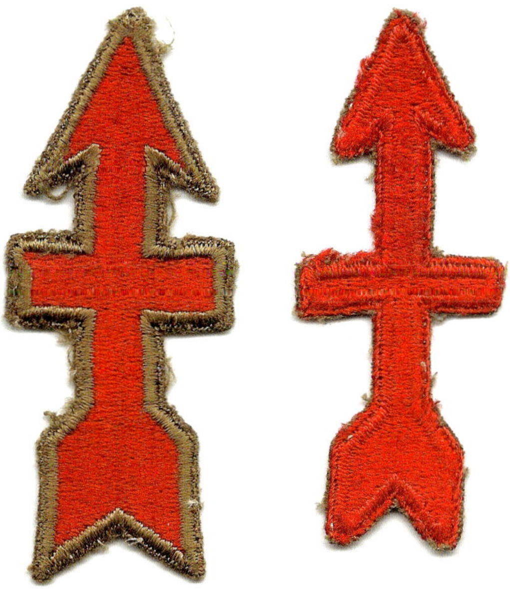

Fig. 03-713: Two 32nd Inf Div SSI: one with OD border and a much thinner variation without (as red border).

Fig. 03-714: Three 5th Inf Div SSI. The one in the middle without OD border is much smaller. The one on the right is oversized. With the latter, either the manufacturer who used to embroider an OD border made the same as the left SSI, but with a red border (lack of OD-colored threads?), or the size at the TIOH-Drawing was interpreted by the manufacturer without border instead of including the border within the size of the patch, in reference to that drawing. The one on the right is definitely a manufacturer's error.

All patches were produced by private manufacturers on government contract and by government specifications ("The Institute of Heraldry" drawings). These drawings specified the final appearance of the SSI, but did allow some discretion by the manufacturer as to just how it would be made. Because so many different manufacturers were involved and the need for SSI was so great, we see all these small variations in the final product.

Fig. 03-715: A 7th Inf Div SSI with OD border.

Fig. 03-716: A 7th Inf Div SSI with brown border.

Fig. 03-717: A less common 7th Inf Div SSI with red border.

Concerning the 7th Inf Div SSI above, it is clear that, depending on the manufacturer and WWII period, an OD border was made or not. The 7th Inf Div SSI without OD border is not so common. That brown or green borders were made suggests that there was not always OD rayon available. The manufacturer therefore used the color closest to OD.

Some SSI have an OD border, while others do not. With the former, an SSI without OD border is rare. With the latter, an OD border is the exception or does not exist.

There were SSI exceptionally or accidentally provided with an OD border during WWII, or (as mentioned above) provided with one in the early-war period, and on which the OD border is rare to very rare.

Fig. 03-718: On the left the usual WWII cut-edge 92nd Inf Div SSI with black border and on the right the WWII era made 92nd Inf Div SSI with rare OD border. Most likely the latter is a manufacture error.

Fig. 03-719: Left: the usual 81st Inf Div SSI with black border; Right: the one with rare OD border. The same remark can be made as with Fig. 03-718 above. Likely the OD border is a manufacturer's error because the 1918 dated TIOH-Drawing illustrated in Fig. 03-720 was provided with a black border.

From a very close look at both OD-bordered patches in Fig. 03-718 and 03-719, one could almost be convinced that both were manufactured by the same manufacturer by seeing practically the same appearance of the embroidery, OD-colored thread, and outlining of the design details.

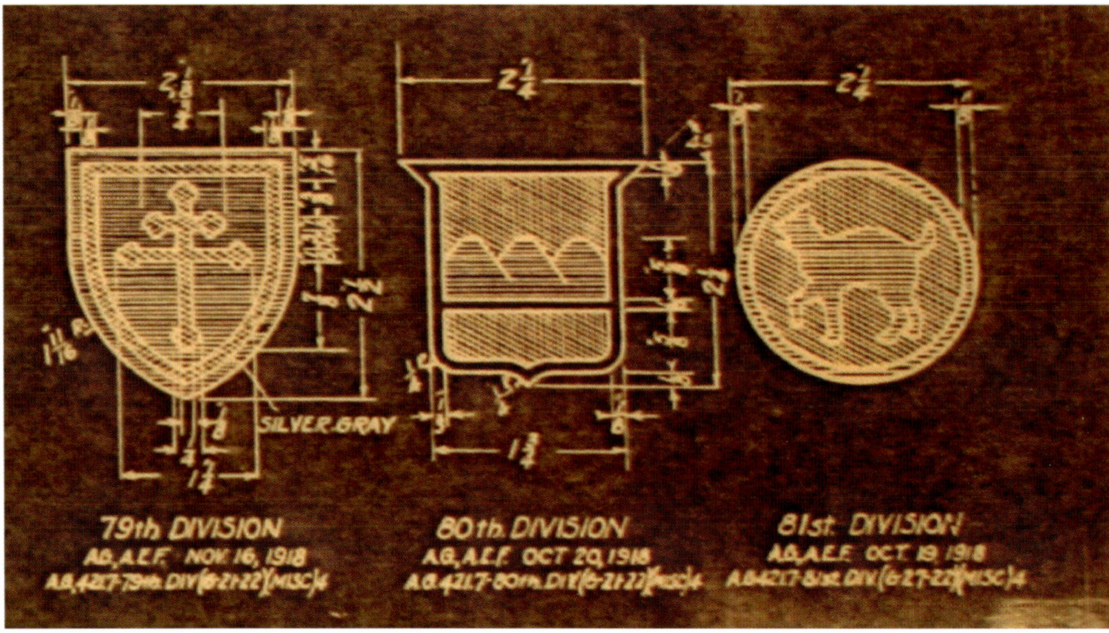

Fig. 03-720: The TIOH-Drawing of the 81st Inf Div SSI on the right, with black border depicted as drawn horizontal lines as with the Wildcat-design. (Courtesy of Craig Pickrall)

Fig. 03-721: On the left the common 83rd Inf Div SSI and on the right the same U.S. made patch but with the harder to find early-WWII OD border.

Fig. 03-722: The usual 88th Inf Div SSI on the left and the rare early-WWII 88th Inf Div SSI with OD border on the right.

Seeing these SSI, one can be certain that the OD border is often only early-WWII, because afterwards the OD border was never seen with these particular U.S.-made SSI. Another good example of such a patch is the 82nd Airborne Div SSI below.

Fig. 03-723: The 82nd AB Div SSI with the usual red border on the left, and the very rare one with OD border on the right.

Some patches can be found more easily, both with and without OD border. A good example is the 27th Inf Div SSI below.

Fig. 03-724: On the left a 27th Inf Div SSI with black border and on the right one with OD border.

Other SSI are never seen or manufactured with an OD border. Here "The Institute of Heraldry" drawings were followed. See some of these SSI below. These are not all of late war activated divisions.

Fig. 03-725: A 66th Inf Div SSI (1st design).

Fig. 03-726: A 66th Inf Div SSI (2nd design).

Fig. 03-727: A 69th Inf Div SSI.

Fig. 03-728: A 79th Inf Div SSI.

Fig. 03-729: A 25th Inf Div SSI.

Fig. 03-730: A 100th Inf Div SSI.

In some cases during WWII, instead of OD borders, KHAKI or TAN borders were made with some of these SSI. The use of tan or khaki borders was for the same reasons as the ones in OD mentioned above. Wartime units assigned to arid, desert, or hot tropical areas were usually issued khaki uniforms. That way, this kind of border color fit much better with the color of the summer uniform. Even in hotter southern regions in the U.S., summer issue khaki uniforms were worn on which the khaki bordered SSI was sewn (just like the pre-WWII partially machine-embroidered khaki cotton twill SSI). The used sewing thread was possibly khaki rayon or cotton thread.

An example of the 43rd Inf Div SSI is illustrated below. Note the different thicknesses of the borders. Depending on the company, these can be embroidered both thick and thin on WWII SSI. Other examples of the 43rd Inf Div SSI can be seen in the previous heading illustrated in Fig. 03-609 and Fig 03-610.

Fig. 03-731: A 43rd Inf Div SSI with a thick OD border.

Often a border is made, for one reason or another, by the serviceman himself [next to other embroidered details (see following chapter)]:

- Either the border, in further cutting off the backing, was damaged or cut through;
- The serviceman found an OD border nicer, and may have thought that it fit more with the issued OD-colored sewing thread to sew on the OD-colored uniform;
- A border in another color than OD was more decorating for the SSI and the service dress uniform of the serviceman;
- Or as a pastime for the serviceman;

The border was made by hand, or with a conventional home sewing machine, or another kind of machine at home or in a workshop to finish textiles and fabrics.

Fig. 03-732: A 43rd Inf Div SSI with a thinner khaki border.

Self-made borders by hand are often characterized by a rather irregular or uneven embroidery style. But, because of the commercial manual work business, sometimes the handiwork of some private people of that era is astonishingly well done, and often there is no difference between machine or handmade. Some people specialized themselves at home in order to make some money domesticallly while helping GIs.

The following example of a special border made by the GI himself is one made with a dog tag chain. This way of finishing did not prevent unravelling of the patch, nor did it protect the border made by the embroidery machine. It had only one goal: to decorate the patch and the uniform where it was sewn on.

This kind of decoration and others added by the serviceman himself will be discussed in the following heading. This 71st Inf Div SSI is one of many examples that show up during and after war. Many WWII era pictures of returning veterans show this way of decorating the SSI and their uniform. These decorations could vary in many ways.

With the example below, the dog tag chain was added after the patch was sewn on the uniform, as noted by the double row of sewing thread. This can be seen in the scan of the back, which shows the piece of fabric of the uniform where the patch was sewn on.

Fig. 03-733: Front of a WWII U.S. made, cut-edge 71st Inf Div SSI decorated with a sewn dogtag chain.

Fig. 03-734: The back of Fig. 03-733, with a part of the uniform – Note the double row of sewing thread (one for the SSI and one for the dogtag chain to attach).

One last important note: over the years a number of WWII veterans were interviewed. If they had shoulder patches during the war that did not have an OD border, they complained that it was difficult to make a neat job of sewing them on their uniforms in the field when they only had OD sewing thread in their repair kit. There were requests made to have OD bordered patches issued at the end of WWII. These SSI could be sewn on their new class A uniforms so they would look neater when they were shipped back home.

In the early years of WWII, when lots of SSI were needed for the newly formed divisions, the Quartermaster Corps (QM) issued them all from the stocks that were made, whether or not they had an OD border. Earlier in this chapter there is mention that in early wartime the OD bordered SSI were not that unusual. The serviceman sewed, probably in most cases, all the issued patches on his uniforms. They received only a couple, just enough to provide the few uniforms with one. The large scale distribution resulted in the fact that the stocks very quickly had a shortage and other SSI had to be made.

Because it was early-WWII, and because of the fact they were all used up, these early OD-bordered SSI are often very rare. But now and then they appear at Internet auctions. They have either an old, used, and dirty appearance from coming off a uniform, or are clean and mint condition.

OD-bordered SSI in clean and mint condition appear more than the used ones. Not being worn or sewn on the uniform, with no needle marks to see, these SSI were sometimes kept aside as a souvenir by the serviceman himself from the moment he was issued the SSI in early wartime.

Nevertheless, it is unlikely that some of these rare SSI were again manufactured in the U.S. in the late-WWII period. "The Institute of Heraldry" drawings and the saving of OD-colored rayon thread by the U.S. civilian manufacturers during WWII say otherwise.

Below are two examples of early-WWII U.S. made, OD bordered SSI in mint condition from the 83rd and 88th Inf Div SSI.

Fig. 03-735: Front and back of an early-WWII U.S. made, cut-edge 83rd Inf Div SSI with OD border.

Fig. 03-736: Front and back of an early-WWII U.S. made, cut-edge 88th Inf Div SSI with OD border.

The request of OD bordered SSI could be a reason why suddenly post-WWII German made machine-embroidered SSI with OD border appeared (such as the OD-bordered 82nd AB Div SSI with complete black back). Patches with OD borders that had existed only at the beginning of WWII were again manufactured (abroad) to be issued to GIs and paratroopers. Civilian companies in the foreign theater were contracted, but only on a small scale. Such SSI were probably not manufactured in large numbers, because these days they are hard to find. These could be one of the orders made by an entire unit (with their own funds) instead of the U.S. Army or U.S. government.

Below is an example of those post-WWII German made machine-embroidered SSI with OD border.

Fig. 03-737: Front and back of a post-WWII German made, cut-edge 2nd Inf Div SSI with OD border and complete OD back.

8 | ELEMENTS OR DETAILS ADDED BY THE SERVICEMAN HIMSELF

Next to the added border (see above in the previous heading), sometimes little details or elements were added afterwards to the patch design by the serviceman himself. These were an improvisation of the GI, paratrooper, or marine, whether or not they were related to the proper design of the patch according to "The Institute of Heraldry" drawings [which are the Government specifications and standards: see chapter 8 heading (1)], or were related to the unit's component:

- A possible example of an improvised detail in unrelated to "The Institute of Heraldry" design is a hand-embroidered red dot (eye) to emphasize the eye of the WWII 45th Inf Division's Thunderbird;
- An example of a detail in relation to "The Institute of Heraldry" design is the pink colored tongue of the Screamin' Eagle of the 101st Airborne Div patch. The tongue was manufactured in white rayon thread at first (manufacturer's error). The paratrooper probably used red ink and it was partially washed away;
- An example of a detail in relation to the unit's component is the embroidered Tank Battalion number with black thread on an Armored Forces SSI.

These details could be either hand-embroidered, added using a conventional home sewing machine, or colored using ink.

Hand-embroidered details distinguish themselves via the irregular embroidery and the absence of back thread at the back of the added detail. Because manual embroidery only needs one needle and thread, the same thread for embroidering the detail can be seen on the back of the SSI.

Home-made machine-embroidered details are sometimes more regular in embroidery. This technique requires two different needles and threads (main thread and catch/back thread – see earlier), and sometimes a different colored back thread, other than the SSI's back thread of the original manufacturer, can be seen in the detail of the back. When the same color of back thread is used (e.g., white), it is not always easy to see if it is a detail added later or not. [Note: Sometimes the original manufacturer also used different colors of back thread (see above). In this case the government specifications and standards displayed via "The Institute of Heraldry" drawings were followed. This does not mean that these elements, which have a back thread of different color, were added afterwards by the serviceman himself.]

In most cases of embroidery, the added detail appears to lie on top of the SSI. The embroidered detail is noticeably thicker than the rest of the patch. Here, the experience of the collector to feel a patch plays a major role.

It is very difficult to distinguish a WWII-added detail from a postwar one. It could be possible that some elements were added afterwards by dealers selling to collectors to upgrade a patch. For example, a certain WWII U.S. Tank Battalion SSI is worth a lot more in value than a common WWII U.S. Armored Forces patch. It is very important for the collector to have the provenance of the SSI and, always interesting to know, to have the veteran's motives for adding the detail.

An example of an added detail can be seen in Fig. 03-801 below.

Fig. 03-801: Front and back of a WWII U.S. made, cut-edge 95th Inf Div SSI with added machine-embroidered outline of the "9".

The example of a WWII cut-edge 95th Inf Div SSI above shows an irregular outline of the "9" in white thread (see front). It is machine-embroidered, because a darker colored back thread can be seen. Because of the irregularity there is a great possibility that the GI or veteran, or a friend or relative, outlined the "9," or modfied it with a private sewing machine.

Points of irregular embroidery are:

- The thread loops are not contiguous;
- Some of the thread loops are more contiguous than the others;
- The outline is not straight (see the outer side of the vertical leg of the "9");
- One outline thread continues over the left leg of the "V" (center of the SSI), while the one above does not;
- In the detail (Fig. 03-802) below, the added outline has a back thread of a whiter shade than the SSI's usual back thread.

Fig. 03-802: Detail of the back of the 95th Inf Div SSI with added outline, illustrated in Fig. 03-801 above.

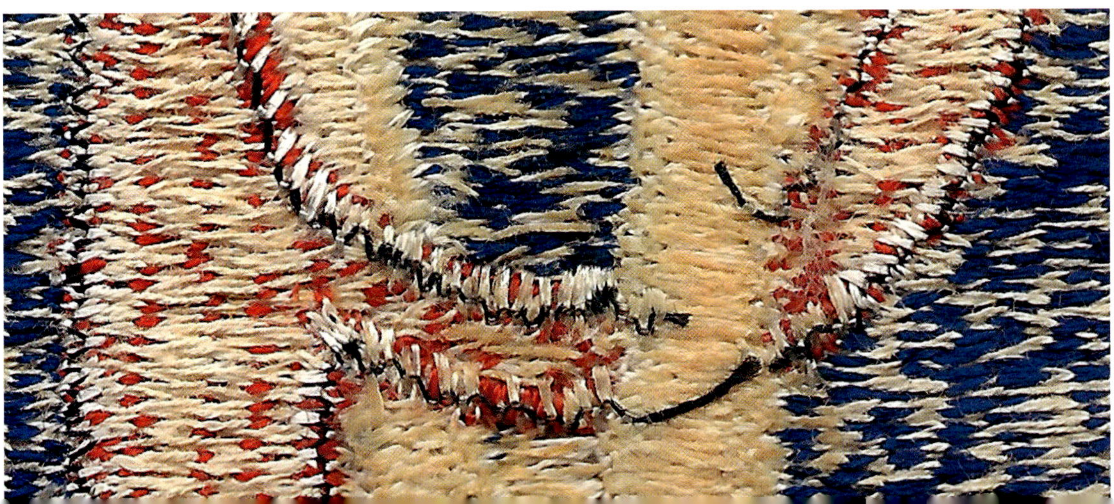

Below are two other U.S.-made WWII 95th Inf Div SSI with outlined "9"s to compare. These both have nice and regular outlines with white back thread and are done by the original manufacturer.

Fig. 03-803: Two WWII U.S. made, cut-edge 95th Inf Div SSI with an original regular machine-embroidered outlined "9".

9 | EXAMPLES OF UNITS AND THEIR SSI WHERE THE PERIOD PLAYS AN IMPORTANT ROLE

Some units either only existed, or were not even activated, during WWII. Therefore, these SSI were made and/or worn only in the WWII time frame. The knowledge of the unit and its SSI is important here. Before buying, the collector needs to do his homework by searching all kinds of information he wants to know on the unit and the SSI.

On the following pages are some examples of U.S. units and their U.S. made SSI where the period plays a major role. Also see Fig. 03-404 to Fig. 03-408 above (heading 4 of this chapter) as examples of post-WWII units.

U.S. Army Group SSI (1st, 6th, 12th, and 15th Army Group) were manufactured and worn between 1943 and 1945. These units were inactivated in 1944 or 1945. 1

Fig. 03-901: Illustrated are three WWII U.S. made, cut-edge Army Group SSI: the 6th (a), the 12th (b) and the 15th Army Group (c).

2

During WWII the U.S. Marine Corps did use SSI, but discontinued their use shortly after (until 1947).

Fig. 03-902: The unauthorized WWII cut-edge first design of the 2nd U.S. Marine Div SSI. From 1943 the patch was manufactured in similarity with the 1st U.S. Marine Div SSI but was changed very quickly into the second design during WWII because of that resemblance. Each unit had to propose their own design.

Fig. 03-903: The authorized WWII cut-edge, second design of the 2nd U.S. Marine Div SSI.

Below are two examples of units with SSI worn only between 1940 and 1945.

Fig. 03-904: Front and back of a WWII cut-edge Armored Forces Demonstration Regiment SSI with OD back thread.

Fig. 03-905: Front and back of a WWII cut-edge Armored School SSI with white back thread.

4

Below is an example of the I Armored Corps SSI. The patch was used from 1940 to 1943. The Corps was reorganized on July 10, 1943, into General Patton's 7th U.S. Army prior to the invasion of Sicily (Operation "Husky") to provide the headquarters for the U.S. forces. The I Armored Corps is definitely a WWII era manufactured patch.

Fig. 03-906: Front and back of a WWII cut-edge I Armored Corps SSI with OD back thread used prior to July 1943.

Fig. 03-907: Front and back of a WWII cut-edge 7th U.S. Army SSI used from July 1943.

5

Below is an example of a unit that existed before and during WWII, but this division was destroyed April 8-10, 1942, in the Philippines by the Japanese 14th Army.

Since this is a cut-edge SSI fully machine-embroidered on a cotton twill backing – meaning the technique used during WWII – and because it also has an OD back and border demonstrates that this is an early-WWII SSI.

Fig. 03-908: Front and back of a WWII cut-edge "Philippine" Division SSI with OD border and OD back thread.

6

Example of the FSSF SSI, worn from September 14, 1942, to January 16, 1945.

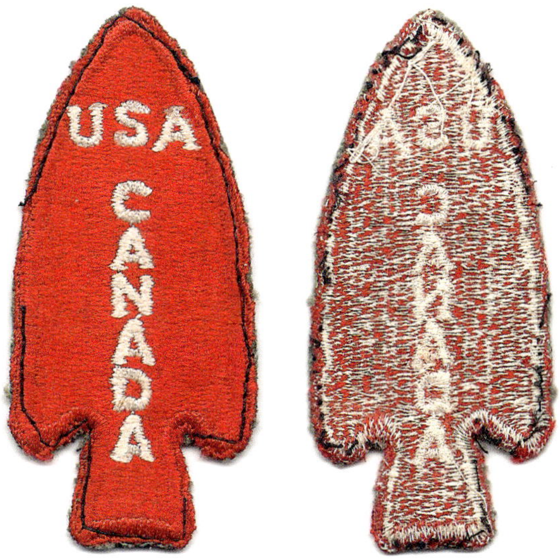

Fig. 03-909: Front and back of a WWII cut-edge 1st Special Service Force SSI.

7 Below is an example of a unit that existed during WWII, but was inactivated soon after. The SSI was worn from May 22, 1941, to July 1, 1946. The OD back of this fully machine-embroidered SSI shows that it is possibly an early-WWII SSI.

Fig. 03-910: Front and back of a WWII cut-edge 1st Coastal Artillery District SSI, fully machine-embroidered on cotton twill with OD back thread.

8 An example of a WWII SSI of the same unit as above, but now as a partially machine-embroidered khaki cotton twill SSI. It was applied with a wider border than the common pre-WWII cotton twill patches, which had a thin stitched border. This patch was made in the early days of WWII for use on the summer uniform (see earlier). Together with the period in which the unit was active, the applied ribbed embroidery pattern, and the more or less used view of the SSI, one can identify this patch as an early-WWII SSI.

Fig. 03-911: Front and back of an early-WWII cut-edge 1st Coastal Artillery District SSI, partially machine-embroidered on khaki cotton base fabric with wide border as a common WWII cut-edge patch.

Below is an example of a unit that existed before, during, and after WWII, but this early draft of the 94th Inf Div SSI was worn from September 6, 1923, to September 5, 1942.

Since this is a cut-edge SSI fully machine-embroidered on a cotton twill backing – meaning the technique used during WWII – and also an OD back and border shows that this is an early-WWII SSI.

Fig. 03-912: Front and back of the early style (first design) 94th Inf Div SSI with OD border and OD back thread.

Fig. 03-913: Front and back of a second design 94th Inf Div SSI with OD border used from 1942.

10 The example of the General HQ South West Pacific Command. A unit that existed during and after WWII, but the version of the SSI during WWII was with the blue flag. Shortly after WWII the flag's color changed to purple.

Fig. 03-914: The WWII SSI with blue flag.

Fig. 03-915: The post-WWII SSI with purple flag design.

11

An example of the 18th Armored Div with partial OD back thread. This unit was never activated before, during, or after WWII, but its SSI was manufactured during WWII in anticipation of its activation.

A little history: The 13th Arm Div was activated on October 15, 1942; the 14th Arm Div was activated on November 15, 1942; the 20th Arm Div was activated on March 15, 1943; and the 16th Arm Div was activated on July 15, 1943. Comparing these activation dates, it is possible that this 18th Arm Div SSI was manufactured somewhere near the end of 1942 or beginning of 1943.

Fig. 03-916: Front and back of a WWII cut-edge 18th Armored Div SSI with partial white and OD back thread.

12 The example below is the first design of the 6th U.S. Army used from January 1927 to January 1945 (illustrated in Fig. 03-917). Because of this, and because of the fact the illustrated patch is a fully machine-embroidered cut-edge SSI on cotton twill, makes this definitely a WWII patch.

Fig. 03-917: The early (first) design of the U.S. 6th Army SSI used prior to January 1945.

Fig. 03-918: The second design of the U.S. 6th Army SSI used from January 1945.

CHAPTER 4
How to Determine When a SSI is Original WWII Era Made?

Method of manufacturing

Besides a few exceptions (see earlier the embroidery styles or patterns), WWII U.S. made SSI do not have loose embroidery, but a nicely close and contiguous main thread. Here one can distinguish either an even and smooth embroidery, or ribbed embroidery; partially or fully machine-embroidered insignia; and utilized base fabric material (or backing) – see earlier.

If necessary, use a magnifying glass and a light to have a clear look at the patch.

Land of manufacturing

For example, German made SSI are mostly post-WWII. However, the (most likely) German made 30th and 76th Inf Div SSI illustrated in chapter 6 (Fig. 06-023 to Fig. 06-025) could be considered as WWII:

1 Because of their manufacture, probably during both Divisions' occupation period in Germany from May to August 1945;

2 And because of the fact that the 30th Inf Div was preparing for action against Japan with reinforcements of the 76th Inf Div, in that same period, prior to their departure to the U.S. just after VJ Day (see further on).

Fig. 04-001: A WWII U.S. made, cut-edge 85th Inf Div SSI.

Embroidery style or pattern

Irregular or regular manufacture style, ribbed embroidery style, Gemsco embroidery style, zigzag embroidery, common WWII style, etc.: see earlier.

Type of backing

Wool – felt – cotton twill: see earlier.

Suppleness

The feeling between the fingers.

A WWII U.S. made, fully machine-embroidered cut-edge SSI feels supple when you let it move between the fingers. Such as, for example, those coming from a uniform and being washed. Here, of course, the experience of the collector plays a major role. Be careful with glue, varnish, or other agents used for SSI to affix in one or another book. This former way of collecting hardened the SSI.

Obviously, an unused mint condition SSI will also be less supple than the used ones, but are certainly not rigid.

Back thread

Both the color (OD, etc.) and the views of this thread (experience) – see earlier.

Also, the use of UV light can determine whether a patch is a post-WWII copy or not. The white colored catch thread utilized during the WWII era has a less bright and more natural dirty-whitish color than white (see chapter 3, heading 4, Fig. 03-441 and Fig. 03-442). This UV light test is discussed further on in this chapter.

Border

OD or another color; merrowed edge versus cut-edge: see earlier.

"Burn" test

When performing this test, cotton and rayon thread, which are natural products, will burn with a flame. Synthetic fibers, such as nylon and polyester, which were utilized in patch manufacture from the late 1960s, will melt with a small plastic-like ball at the end of the test thread, even when the test thread is held only near the flame. Below some tests are illustrated and described with different types of threads: cotton, polyester, silk, and wool.

It is unnecessary and against all rules to fully burn a SSI. There is no benefit to it, and certainly not for the collector. Obviously the seller will never be favorable to let the buyer perform this test as part of a deal. The idea is to get one or more loose threads of the SSI which is to be checked. If not, do not do this test! *In any case do NOT cut the fixed back or main thread.* This does damage the SSI and does separate the threads of the backing.

It is not always possible to test *all* threads of an SSI because there are not always loose threads available (see also different colors of main thread, backing, back thread, border, etc.), so this test cannot guarantee 100% certainty.

FIBER #1: Cotton and rayon

The base material or backing of WWII U.S. made cut-edge SSI is cotton twill fabric, but the embroidery is of rayon threads.

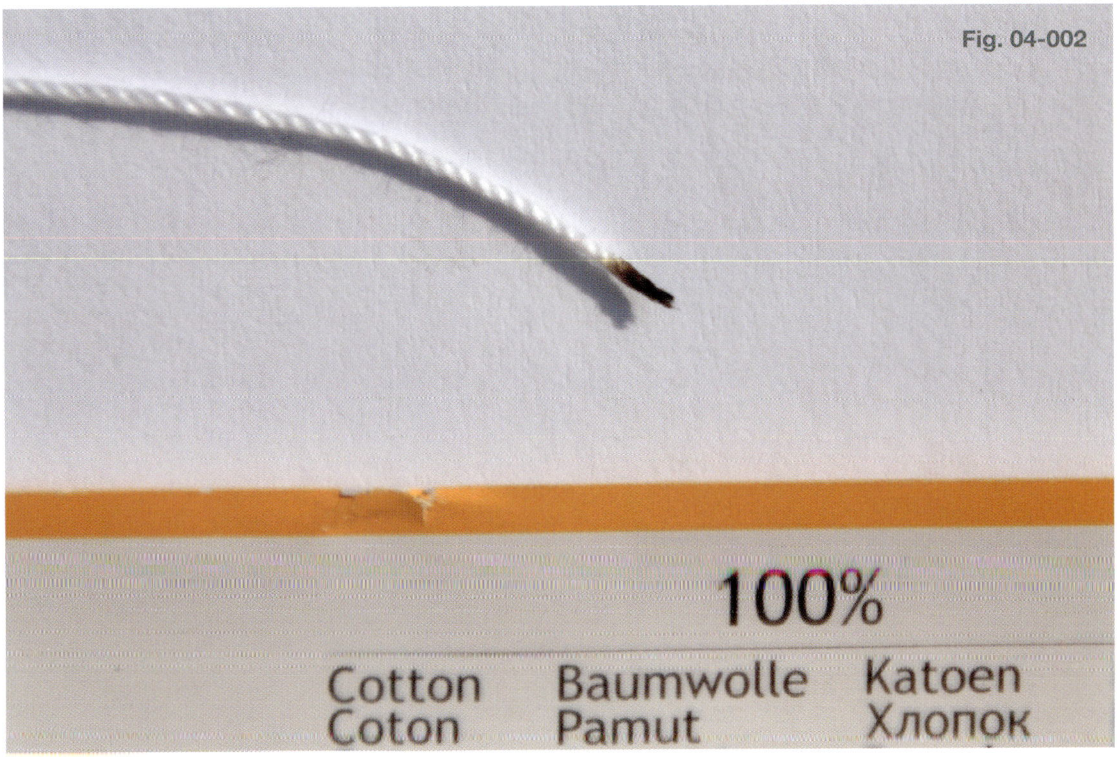

Fig. 04-002

When approaching a flame, the cotton/rayon thread does not shrink from it. In the flame the thread will burn, leaving little or no ash. When removed from the flame it can continue to burn with a flame, or will self-extinguish with some afterglow. The smell of the smoke is like burning paper.

Because rayon is a cellulose-based fiber, it will burn in the same manner as cotton.

Fig. 04-003

Cotton / Rayon

FIBER #2: Synthetic threads (nylon, polyester, etc.)

Fig. 04-004

When approaching a flame the polyester thread melts and pulls away from the flame. Held in the flame, the thread will continue melting and will even burn with a flame. When removed from the flame, the thread may self-extinguish or continue burning until it extinguishes. A hard dark brown- to black-colored plastic-like little ball or bead is left at the end of the thread (see below Fig. 04-005), which can not be crushed or which can hardly be removed.

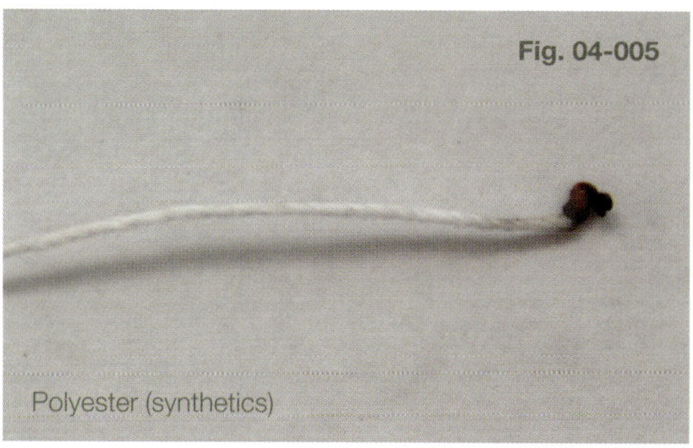
Fig. 04-005

Polyester (synthetics)

FIBER #3: Silk

When approaching a flame the end of the thread starts to burn very slowly and curls away from it. Held in the flame, the silk thread burns slowly. When removed from the flame, the thread may continue burning with a little flame and/or will self-extinguish, leaving a black ball of ash at the end of the test thread (Fig. 04-006). This ball of ash can be removed from the test thread and crushed into little pieces very easily (see below Fig. 04-007). The smell of the smoke is like burning hair because of the animal nature of the silk.

Fig. 04-006a

Fig. 04-006b

Fig. 04-007

FIBER #4: Wool

Wool will react the same way as silk because it is also of a natural animal nature (such as our hair), with the same kind of smell when burning. See the description of silk above.

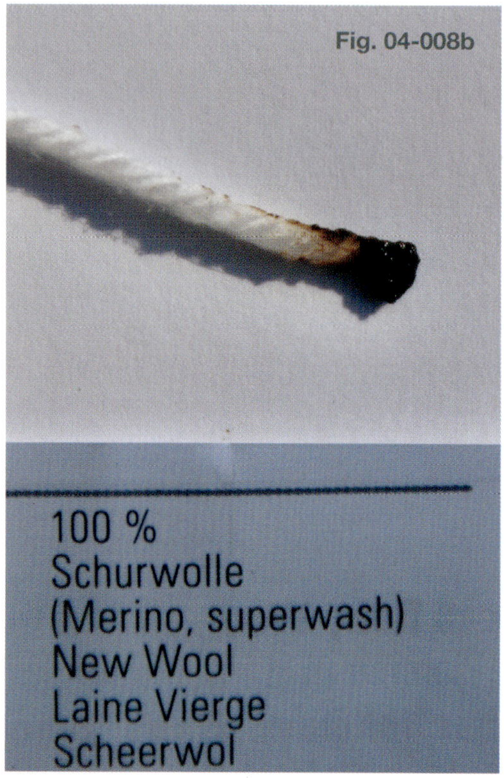

Fig. 04-010

"Black light" or Ultraviolet (UV) light test

Normally, a WWII rayon thread (for the embroidery of the SSI) or cotton thread (for the backing material) does not respond to this kind of light, and thus the patch does not light.

The following guidelines are needed for a successful test:

- This test is best performed in a dark room or place with the SSI on a dark piece of paper, fabric, or any other kind of dark background to see the possible glow (even to see the possible glow of the backing on the edge of the SSI's border);
- Next to the tested patch lies a white handkerchief or white piece of paper for comparison, so as to clearly see the difference in the glow;
- The UV light is being held about 15 to 20 cm (6 to 8 in) above the patch;
- Not necessarily a condition with the test, but it can always be interesting to also have a SSI of which you have no doubt as to being original WWII next to the tested patch.

If the patch lightens or, as collectors would say, glows, the patch is in most occasions not WWII era made, but a post-WWII copy.

IMPORTANT REMARK: Detergent powders for washing have a blue pigment in their composition. When white laundry is washed the blue pigment attaches to the white fibers to make the laundry appear whiter in sunlight than before because of the high bluish appearance. "Washing whiter than white" is often used in those powders' commercials. The use of these powders can leave this particular substance on the threads of the SSI or cause a chemical reaction similar to the white laundry. The white back thread will appear whiter than before, and the patch could glow with UV light, even original WWII SSI. This could happen with SSI coming from a patch blanket that has hung on a wall and which was washed several times over the years. Here it is important to look at other points which are consistent with a WWII SSI. The following pictures will demonstrate this. The 101st AB Div SSI on the right has a glowing "Airborne" tab, although I am 100% certain it is genuine. Front and back of the SSI are also illustrated below to show a good view. The unattached tab came together with the shield.

Fig. 04-011: The glow of the WWII "Airborne"-tab indicates that it was likely washed with detergent powders. Although certain copies will glow similarly, the illustrated SSI is 100% genuine and original WWII.

Fig. 04-012: Front and back of the same WWII U.S. made, cut-edge 101st AB Div SSI illustrated on the right in Fig. 04-011.

Also mentioned in chapter 3, heading 4, if one looks very closely at the back of a WWII-period manufactured patch with a large portion of white design, one can see that the white catch or back thread has a different kind of white than the white design thread when the latter appears at the back. So the white back thread is in fact not white at all. It has more or less a bright and non-colored-like, "natural" dirty-white impression. This rayon fiber appears to have come directly from the production line without being colored. This important feature can also be seen above in Fig. 03-441 and Fig. 03-442.

Under UV light, the WWII (and even pre-WWII) rayon fiber does not react (glow), however, the white design thread will appear whiter than the dirty-white colored back thread. This feature is demonstrated in the two pictures below (see Fig. 04-013 and Fig. 04-014). This reaction of the white rayon threads to the UV light is certainly nothing compared to the glow illustrated above with the example of the detergent powders.

In the following chapter, a copy of the 135th AB "Phantom" Div SSI is discussed. Pictures of this copy illustrate this particular feature mentioned above (Fig. 05-009 and Fig. 05-010). When a patch has such white back threads, together with other mentioned reasons in that chapter, it is clearly a copy. After testing dozens of genuine SSI and comparing them to this copied 135th AB "Phantom" patch, there is no doubt.

It could happen that a genuine SSI reacts under UV light, as it should have white back threads. Either way, it is important to have the results of several of these tests before making conclusions.

Fig. 04-013. Difference in reaction between white design threads and dirty white back threads. These back threads react less bright with UV light. However, WWII white design threads do certainly not have that kind of reaction as a white piece of paper (the glowing strip on the right side of the picture).

Fig. 04-014: When looking very closely to the XXIV Corps SSI (on the right), with UV light the white design threads appear as little shiny spots between the mat and un-reacting back threads.

Evidence of use – Signs of wear and age

Worn and used SSI: the presence of remnants of cut sewing thread on the border of a patch which came from a uniform; traces of a tightly sewn thread on the border of the patch; or needle or thread marks (holes) from being sewn on a uniform; or the presence of a pleat on the patch because of the ironed crease into the sleeve of the uniform (together with needle marks).

Fig. 04-015: A mint unused SSI versus a SSI in used condition.

Fig. 04-016: A First Special Service Force SSI in used condition with remnants of white and red sewing thread. The white thread has been sewn at first because on some places one can see the red thread being sewn over it.

Recognition of a SSI in an original WWII photo

The period of the unit's existence

This is the knowledge and research of the collector: see earlier. The collector needs to do his homework to know that certain time frame of existence.

The provenance of the SSI (either mint or used condition)

This is the most reliable of all check points, if you know for 100% the SSI comes from a WWII veteran and has been worn on a uniform during WWII.

CONCLUSION

This above list is not exhaustive. Perhaps there may still be elements that can show that a SSI is original WWII or not that the author is not aware of. Some other important features to distinguish WWII from copies and reproductions are also mentioned and discussed in the following chapter.

Experience and knowledge play a major role. A single test will never give full guaranteed designation that a SSI is an original WWII. On the other hand, it is also true that a negative result of one of the above-mentioned tests does not exclude a SSI from being WWII. It is important that the collector looks at and feels the SSI very well, and takes into account several of these tests.

When one buys a SSI via the Internet, make sure that there are very clear and detailed photographs (if necessary at your own request). If not, it is better to refrain from buying.

If several of these points above satisfy, one can almost be convinced of the originality of the WWII SSI.

IMPORTANT REMARKS:

1 *Labels on backsides*

Labels on backsides of SSI are not always a proof of originality. These are very easy to reproduce and to age.

2 *Sizing*

Sizing is used to strengthen the cotton twill backing to avoid fraying at the edges even more. It is a waxy- or varnish-like product that was sprayed or brushed on the backing. This can be seen as:

- Either small glistening dots on the back of the SSI and right next to the border on the backing when the SSI is held into the light;
- Or a thin, whitish substance, just next to the border on the backing (to see on the complete backing edge, where it is not cut close enough to the border). This can be seen in the picture of the 6th Army Group patch below. Only during WWII (1943-1945) were the Army Groups active and their SSI manufactured.

In literature on SSI, it is often stated that sizing would be only post-WWII. After WWII it was probably used more and more, but a few sources in the U.S. have confirmed that they have had SSI which were still wrapped up and which had a date stamp on the packaging indicating manufacture during WWII.

The evidence suggests that this technique was utilized rather late in WWII, and/or by specific manufacturers during the war.

Fig. 04-017: The white-colored sizing can be seen on the top and the bottom of the WWII U.S. made, cut-edge 6th Army Group SSI.

Fig. 04-018: Detail of the top of the 6th Army Group SSI illustrated in Fig. 04-017 above.

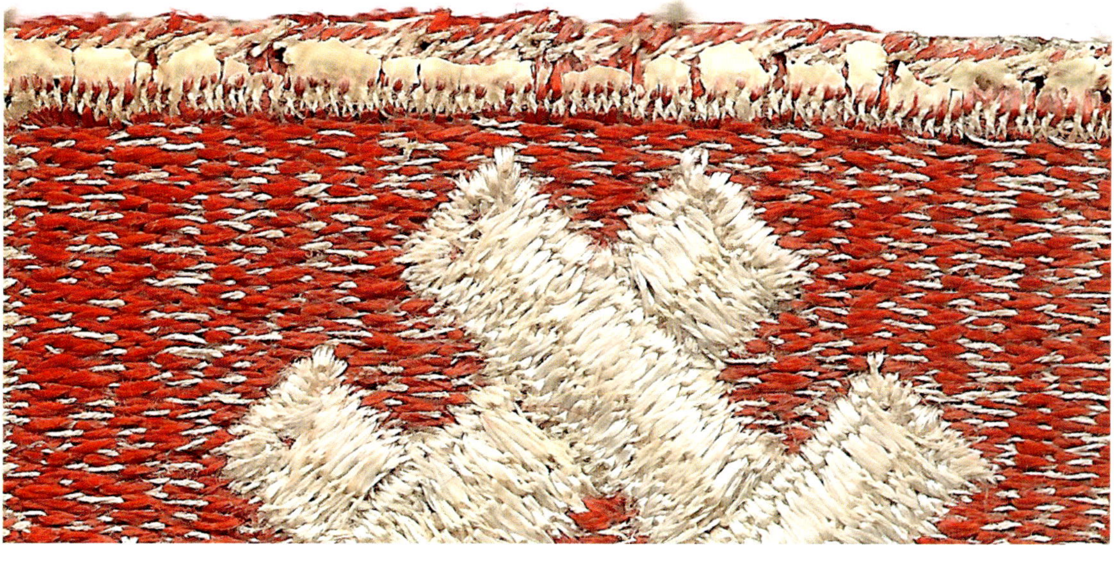

CHAPTER 5
Reproductions and Copies

Before discussing the reproductions, copies, or fakes, it should be mentioned that we are not speaking of the post-WWII SSI that were made for the U.S. military by the different contractors, even abroad. Manufacturing methods and the fibers utilized changed and improved over the years; however, the purpose of the U.S. government contracts still remained the same: to provide patches to the U.S. military to be worn by the troops.

Militaria of every time period have had copies made of artefacts. After a particular event has occurred all kinds of objects in this regard have been reproduced, not just to hand out (e.g., for veterans to hand out at reunions), but also to sell for profit.

With these sales, if it is acknowledged that they are copies, it will never pose a problem for the purchaser.

Unfortunately, the opposite is mostly true. In many cases, copies are sold as original period pieces, with exorbitant prices and profits for the seller as a result. These copies, sold as original pieces, are sometimes also called fakes by collectors. This situation is no different when considering WWI, Interwar, and WWII SSI and other material, all of which have been the subject of reproductions or copies.

WWII SSI were manufactured well after the war (as late as 1952) to fulfill U.S. Government contracts. The manufacturers had no duplicity in mind at that time, but this changed when some people saw a living in this business.

All of this said, this discussion will now move to the issue of how to distinguish a copy from an original WWII-period insignia, which is the purpose of this book. In many cases it is possible to make this distinction, but here it should be noted that with today's technology one can produce very good copies. Even for a trained eye it is not always easy to make this distinction.

The advice still stands:

- To have large, detailed, and clear pictures of both the front and back of the insignia with a good description. If needed request them from the seller. If one does not get them, refrain from the deal;
- Always hold the SSI in your hands (if possible), to study it well and perhaps ask the seller questions about its origin (also see the points in the previous chapter);
- Search in advance for information concerning the SSI and the unit, with all kinds of documentation, before one buys.

However, a collector may be uncertain regarding a particular SSI. In this case the rule will always apply: IF YOU DOUBT, DON'T BUY IT!

As will be seen, not everything is a copy. Presumably, during the WWII era and certainly shortly afterwards many versions of SSI designs for units which were already obsolete by WWII were reproduced (e.g., old style WWI and 1920s SSI). These were then, shortly after the war, sold to collectors at modest prices. Today they are sometimes sold for a lot of money as WWI, PRE-WWII, WWII, and GENUINE. This group is further discussed in this chapter, and can be considered REPRODUCTIONS or, as collectors sometimes call them, REPROS.

Some WWII SSI were also reproduced after WWII (e.g., Special U.S. units, such as the Rangers SSI).

All these were either fully machine-embroidered on cotton twill-base fabric or partially machine-embroidered on felt or wool, sometimes with a slight difference from the original (a smaller size, another shade of the original color, etc.). Also, some of these companies reproduced WWI or 1920s patches in the old way: felt on felt, or felt on wool.

Unlike the many poor quality copies, well made reproductions may be desired by some collectors for SSI they would like to add to their collection. It is up to each collector personally to decide whether or not to include a copy in their collection. For the collector, a reproduction or, in some exceptional cases when well made and known as such, a copy can possibly fill an empty place (or "hole") in their collection. Expensive pieces that would be beyond the collector's budget can thus be replaced. Provided, of course, that these "replacement" SSI were described as reproductions or copies and will be continued to be classified as such. When selling them, the collector should also not misrepresent them.

Below is a good example of a post-WWII copy of the 95th Inf Div. This SSI, with the two legs of the "V" on top of the "9," is a manufacturer's error and is scarce. These days, such SSI are very much reproduced because of their increasing value. This particular one below was sold on the Internet as genuine and as original WWII era made.

For comparison, an original WWII SSI of the 95th Inf Div is added below.

Fig. 05-001: Front and back of a post-WWII copy of the 95th Inf Div SSI.

Fig. 05-002: To compare with the one illustrated above, the front and back of the same type of 95th Inf Div SSI, but original WWII era manufactured.

Although the copy is very well made, the difference between the copy and the original SSI is good to see and to feel. Under a UV light the copy *does not* glow.

Some other findings:

1 With the copy, a ribbed embroidery style is imitated, but some individual ribs run into another. This feature can be seen at the back of the copy (Fig. 05-001), at the inner side of the vertical leg of the "9" at the beginning of the upwards curve. A WWII period ribbed embroidery construction has no such characteristic;

2 The copy is much thinner than the original one, and likely to have that certain suppleness as an original WWII SSI should be. The thinner the patch is, the more supple it will be;

3 The back of the copy feels very rough (like sandpaper);

4 The machine-embroidery pattern of the white back thread of the post-WWII copy is very irregular (see Fig. 05-001 and Fig. 05-004);

5 A detailed scan of the copy (below) shows an open embroidery style which is inconsistent with the theory on the WWII U.S. made, fully machine-embroidered, cut-edge SSI. Even the blue cotton twill can be seen between the threads;

Fig. 05-003: Location of the detail illustrated on the following page.

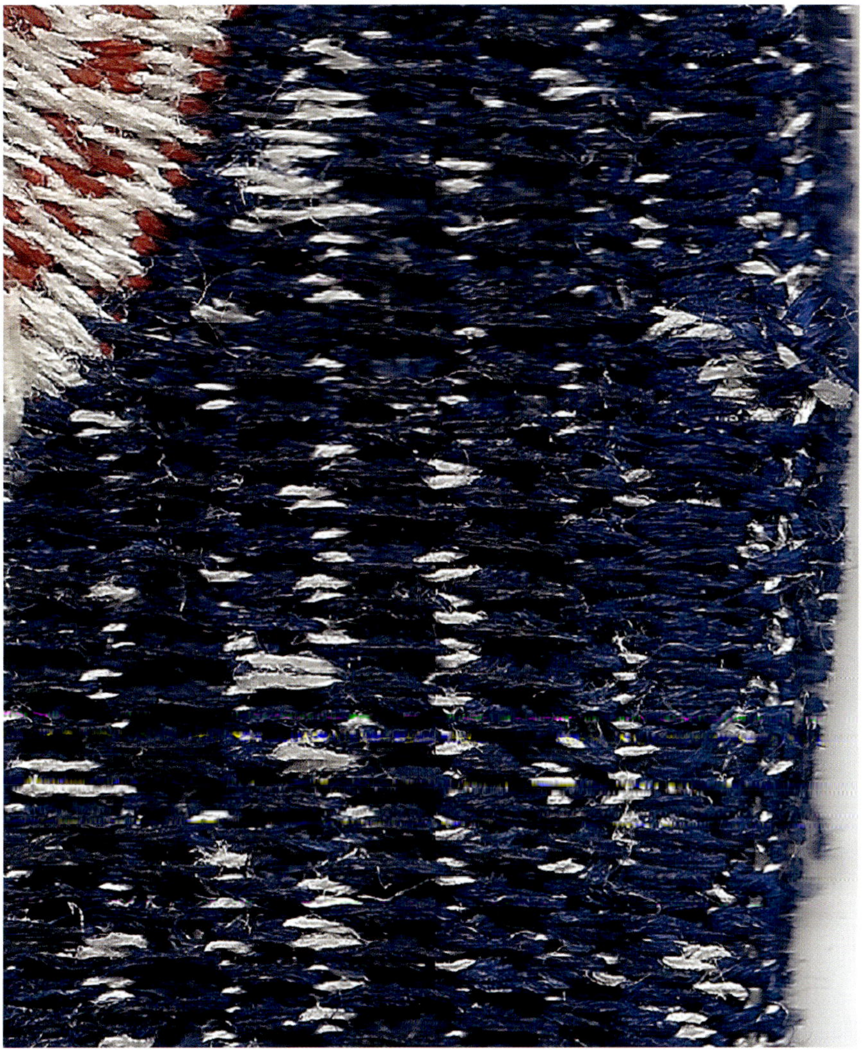

Fig. 05-004: Detail scan of the part shown in Fig. 05-003.

Below is another example of a copy: the 135th AB "Phantom" Div patch (Fig. 05-005). The irregular pattern of the back thread demonstrates this. Rows of back thread are converging at the bottom part of the patch, which is not a WWII era characteristic, and can only be of a copy. Also the patch is not supple and flexible at all compared to its original WWII counterpart, although no glue or wax can be found at the back. Even the wavy border is very unusual for a WWII SSI.

The next feature that indicates the patch is a copy is the "AIRBORNE" tab. It is too irregularly manufactured, so that the collector already should have doubts at first sight. The space between "AIR" and "BORNE" is unseen on genuine WWII "Airborne" SSI, and the different sizes of all letters on the tab is unusual to WWII manufacture. Also in this example we can mention that this patch NEVER has been seen with an attached "Airborne" tab yet.

Nevertheless, this is a very well made copy. For comparison, an example of a genuine WWII cut-edge 135th AB "Phantom" Div SSI is added below (see Fig. 05-006). Here it is clear that more differences can be seen. The design of the spider (particularly the body) of the copy differs very much from the original WWII SSI. The latter has a better detailed spider design.

Fig. 05-005: Front and back of a well made copy of the 135th AB 'Phantom' Div SSI.

Fig. 05-006: Front and back of an original WWII U.S. made, cut-edge 135th AB 'Phantom' Div SSI.

To demonstrate how well made that copy was, detailed pictures of both the copy and original WWII SSI are illustrated.

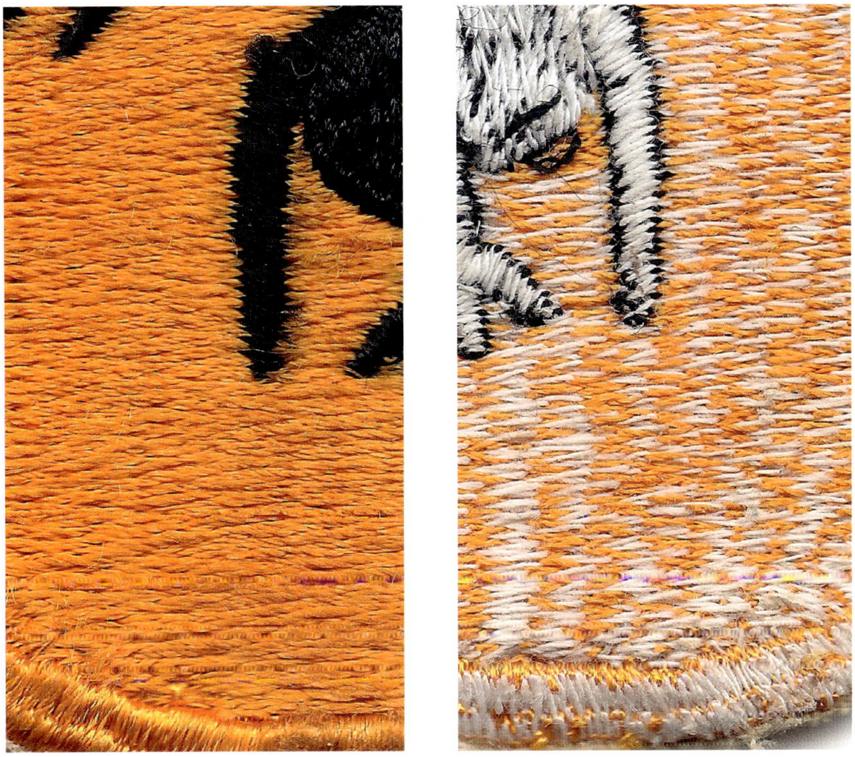

Fig. 05-007: Details of front and back of the copied 135th AB "Phantom" Div SSI illustrated here above in Fig. 05-005. At the back the converging rows of back thread can clearly be seen.

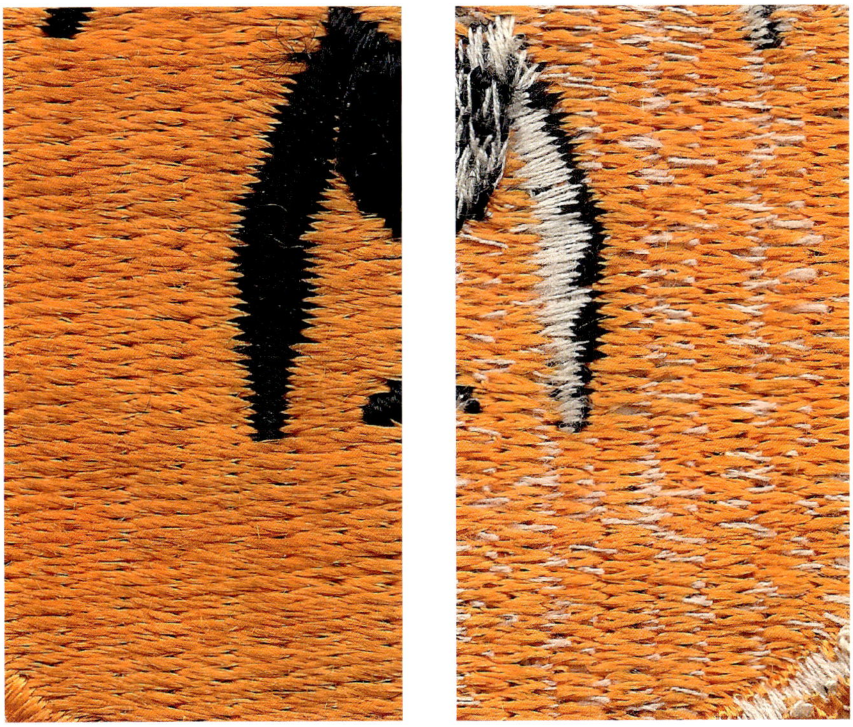

Fig. 05-008: Details of front and back of the original WWII U.S. made, cut-edge 135th AB "Phantom" Div SSI illustrated in Fig. 05-006.

A last possible method to determine whether the 135th AB "Phantom" Div patch illustrated in Fig. 05-005 is a copy or not is the UV light test. The patch does not react to the UV light as one would think a copy should do. This can be seen in Fig 05-009 below, where the difference of reaction to the UV light with the piece of white paper is too significant (see the glowing strip on the right side of the picture). Also, the white shine of the copy's white back threads is nothing compared to the glow of the "Airborne" tab in Fig. 04-011, in the previous chapter. However, when looking very well at the pictures below, one can see that the white back threads have a whiter appearance than those of the WWII cut-edge 101st AB Div SSI that is used for comparison. The white design threads appearing as little shiny spots at the back of the XXIV Corps patch are similar in reaction to the UV light to the copy's catch threads. In fact, the back thread of the copied 135th AB "Phantom" Div patch has a real white color instead of the uncolored dirty-whitish impression of the rayon back threads utilized prior to and during WWII (see chapter 4).

When a patch has such white back threads, together with the other above-mentioned reasons, it is clearly a copy. After testing dozens of genuine SSI and comparing them to this copied 135th AB "Phantom" patch, there is no doubt.

Fig. 05-009: The difference between the utilized back threads. On genuine WWII patches these back threads can never be white-colored.

Fig. 05-010: All white threads on both patches are clearly distinguishable from the utilized back thread of the XXIV Corps SSI (on the left).

The last example of a post-WWII copy is not fully, but partially machine-embroidered on yellow felt. The illustrated 103rd Inf Div patch was sold on the Internet as pre-WWII-1930s. When holding the patch between the fingers, the felt base fabric is too thin to be original. During the 1930s, if felt backing material was used, and although felt is very fleeting, the felt fabric of genuine pre-WWII SSI is thicker, and is of a better quality than that illustrated below.

Fig. 05-011: Front and back of a copy of a 1930s felt 103rd Inf Div SSI which was sold as genuine.

It is not because of the poor quality base fabric that this 103rd Inf Div is added. However, it is a good example of how irregular the embroidery of a copy or reproduction could be.

Another issue posing doubts to its originality is the UV light test. The patch does not glow, but its back threads give the appearance which real white threads have in reaction to the light. This feature is discussed earlier in this and the previous chapter.

When one takes a closer look at the detailed scans of the embroidery below a very irregular embroidery style can be seen. Often the direction of the tread loops change from sloping to the upper right, to horizontal, to sloping to the bottom right. Some parts have contiguous embroidery, while other parts even show holes in the manufacturing style. Sometimes diagonal pattern rows to the embroidery can be seen, which indicates machine embroidery.

It is unlikely that WWII manufacturers or even those in the 1930s, and with the use of the commercial embroidery machine, made such bad quality SSI for the U.S. military. For comparison, two original early 1930s felt SSI (a 2nd and 40th Inf Div SSI, both partially machine-embroidered and not reinforced on the back) are added below. See the nice dense embroidery of those two, even for that early period prior to WWII. The difference in the embroidery's quality between the two and the 103rd Inf Div patch is too big, even without reinforcement (also called stabilizer). Also, their felt base material is twice as thick than the felt of the 103rd Inf Div patch.

It is very important for the collector to hold the SSI between your fingers and to take a very close look at the manufacturing style. A magnifying glass is always helpful. Otherwise, large clear pictures of the SSI and a good description are also a big help.

Fig. 05-012: Detail scan of the front of the felt 103rd Inf Div SSI. Different kinds of embroidery styles can be seen (open / contiguous).

Fig. 05-013: Two original early 1930s felt SSI of the 2nd and 40th Inf Div to compare, both partially machine-embroidered without reinforcement (or stabilizer) on the back.

Fig. 05-014: The backs of the two SSI illustrated here above at Fig 05-013.

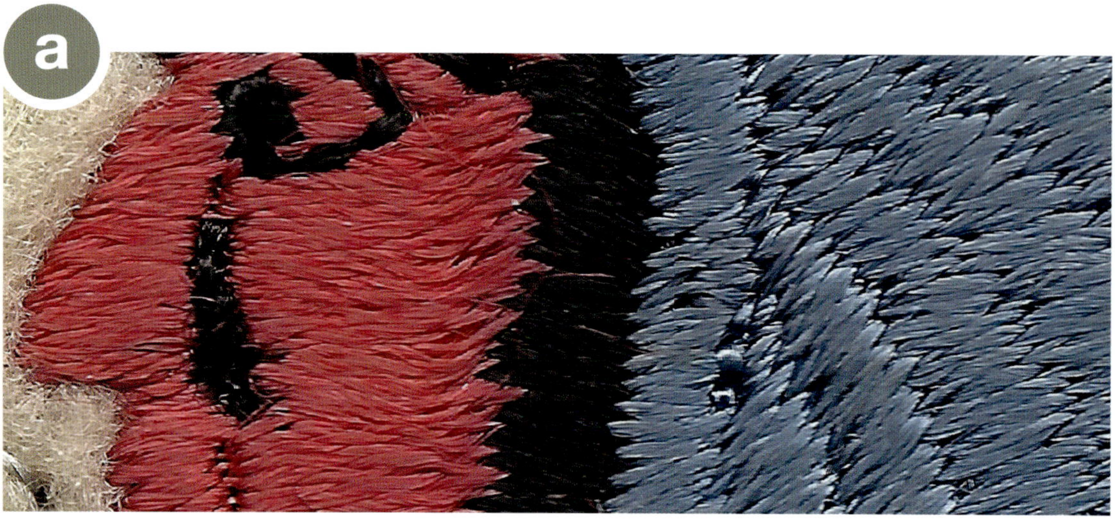

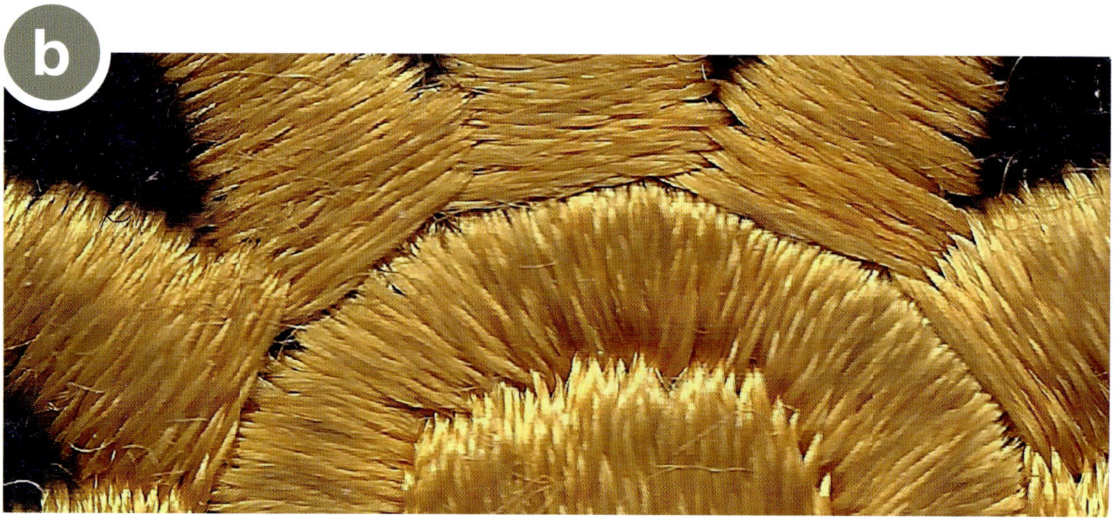

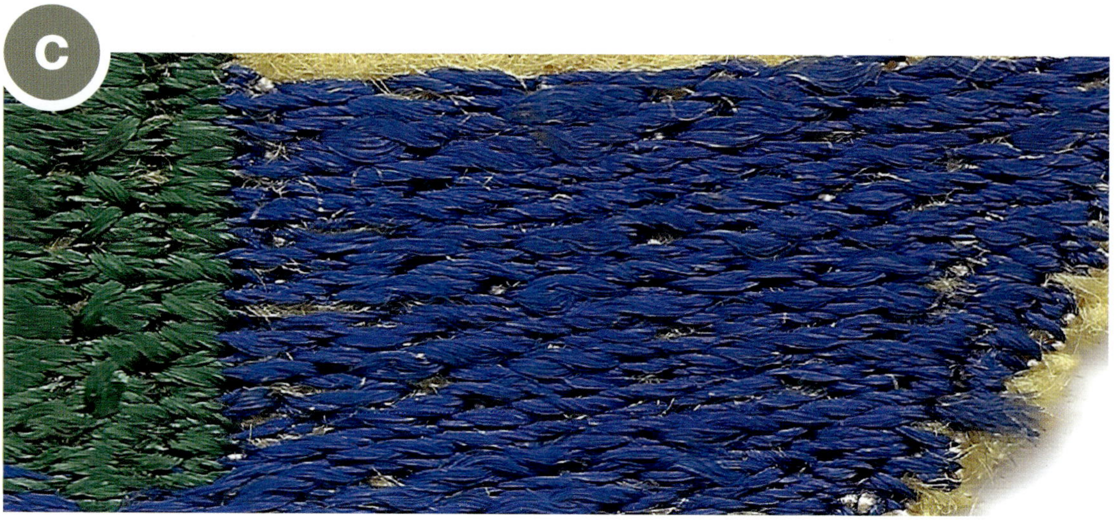

Fig. 05-015: Compare the difference in embroidery. Even without reinforcement (or stabilizer) on the back the upper two styles [(a) and (b)] are very much of a better quality.
a and **b** are details of the machine embroidery of the two genuine SSI illustrated in Fig. 05-013.
c is a detail of the machine embroidery of the copied 103rd Inf Div patch illustrated in Fig. 05-011.

Next to the characteristics to determine whether a patch is genuine WWII or not (see previous chapter), a lot more features are mentioned in this chapter to see if a patch is a copy/reproduction or not, such as the use of synthetic fibers, white catch thread and/or unusual embroidery styles, or manufactured patches of particular WWI units, etc.

If possible, it is always interesting to compare the patch you see with other patches of the same kind (unit) to see the differences. Laying next to each other, both patches can provide an amount of information to determine if the desired patch is a genuine one or not. The knowledge of this unit's patch and of how it should look is very important. Before even considering buying a patch on the Internet, look up the same patch on different sites and compare them with each other. If necessary ask other people's opinions, and not only those of the dealer.

When buying the patch at a show or a shop, be aware that copies and reproductions could always be in front of you. At that moment the experienced collector, with his greater experience, will have the greater advantage in deciding if they are original or copy. However, even a veteran collector can not know every detail and may need to research details of the particular SSI in question. Also, be aware that there are some tools, such as a magnifying glass or a little UV light (on batteries), that you might use.

Below are some other interesting features to take into account:

- WWII or other genuine SSI have often more defined details and designs. The details of some copies and reproductions are often manufactured more crudely;
- WWII have no plastic cover or protection at their back;
- The details on WWII fully machine-embroidered, cut-edge SSI are not reinforced with gauze on their back. Often copies and reproductions have this particular feature at the back of a certain numerical designation;
- WWII SSI have no catch thread with a synthetic thread like appearance (such as a fishing line). Often the copies/reproductions have a thinner nylon- or polyester-looking back thread. See the example of the 1st Filipino Unit patches below: the copy is on the left, the original SSI on the right;
- The designs of copies and reproductions often show other colors, or sharper and brighter colors. The WWI-style 10th Inf Div patch below is a good example of another used color. The reproduction has a light blue background, while the original WWI SSI has dark blue felt backing material. An example of a sharper color is the 1st Filipino Unit below. With the original SSI (on the right) golden-yellow/orange design thread is used versus the bright yellow of the copy/reproduction (on the left). This is also the case with the Rangers SSI, where usually the golden-yellow-colored design thread is used for the letters and border. On the other hand, original WWII Armored triangles with lemon-yellow apex do exist;
- Specific WWII tabs or patches often have a particular shape and size. Often copies/reproductions differ too much;
- The specific appearance of particular letters, figures, etc., could be a method to distinguish real SSI from copies/reproductions;
- When U.S.-made, the SSI show a specific embroidery style. When computer designed and manufactured, often the copies/reproductions show other styles and patterns. Most of the WWII patterns are shown and discussed in chapter 3, heading 5;

An example: A 1st Philippine Regiment patch, also known as the 1st Filipino Unit. The reproduction/copy is illustrated on the left, the WWII SSI on the right. A few visible features:

- The reproduction/copy has another color (yellow) than the original SSI (golden-yellow/orange);
- The lava flow is better detailed on the WWII SSI;
- The back of the reproduction/copy shows back thread with a synthetic fishing line appearance.

Fig. 05-016: The fronts of two cut-edge 1st Filipino Unit patches: the one on the left is a reproduction; the one on the right is genuine WWII. *(Courtesy of Eric Czerwinski)*

Fig. 05-017: The backs of the same 1st Filipino Unit patches illustrated in Fig. 05-016. Again, the one on the left is a reproduction; the one on the right is genuine WWII. *(Courtesy of Eric Czerwinski)*

As mentioned above, at the end of WWII and shortly after (1945-early 1950s) certain companies that were also SSI manufacturers for the U.S. military during WWII could continue their livelihood by further manufacturing certain patches which were then sold to the public. They could continue this manufacture utilizing their own embroidery machines and work force. Those companies focussed on collectors who, after the victory of the U.S. Armed Forces, were looking for a lasting keepsake of these historic events, and for the U.S. collector at the time they were absolutely magnificent. A list of some of these manufacturers is added further on.

The SSI of units that were newly manufactured were either reproductions of old patches of WWI units that no longer existed (e.g., 10th and 11th Inf Div – see pictures below, 14th Inf Div, etc.), or reproductions from units that had existed during the interwar period (e.g., Cavalry Divisions – only the 1st and 2nd Cav Div were active during WWII and used U.S. made cut-edge SSI; the other Cavalry Div had authorized insignia but were not activated). Also, insignia of special and rare WWII units were made (e.g., Ranger Scrolls, First Special Service Force patches, etc.).

These kinds of insignia were:

- Either partially machine-embroidered on felt, with the color of the felt as the main color of the SSI. But this color often differed from that of the original SSI;
- Or partially machine-embroidered on wool;
- Or fully machine-embroidered on a cotton twill-base fabric with the cut-edge principle. These reproductions did not differ in manufacturing method from the original WWII cut-edge insignia, and sometimes it will be very difficult to distinguish them from each other. Often their background color differed from this of the original SSI;
- Or sometimes composed of felt on felt, or felt on wool.

See the examples of post-WWII made WWI patches below. The real WWI 10th Inf Div SSI had a dark blue background, not light blue.

Fig. 05-018: Front and back of a partially machine-embroidered, WWI-style 10th Inf Div reproduction on felt.

Fig. 05-019: Front of a post-WWII U.S. made fully machine-embroidered, cut-edge WWI-style 10th Inf Div reproduction. The patch has the same light blue background color as the felt one, instead of the usual dark blue of the original WWI SSI. *(Courtesy of Eric Czerwinski)*

Fig. 05-020: Front of a post-WWII U.S. made WWI-style 11th Inf Div reproduction, partially machine-embroidered on felt, reinforced with gauze (also called stabilizer). *(Courtesy of Eric Czerwinski)*

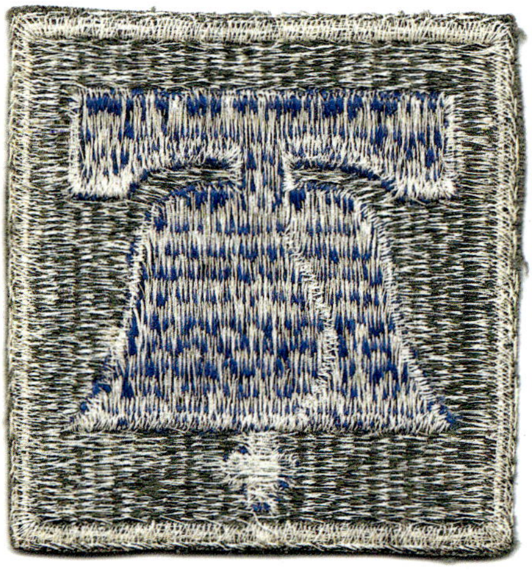

Fig. 05-021: Front and back of a post-WWII U.S. made fully machine-embroidered, cut-edge WWI-style 76th Inf Div reproduction. Although this design was never used during WWII., its manufacture did not differ in any way of the WWII cut-edge insignia.

The U.S. made partially or fully machine-embroidered SSI above are all original and reproductions, but certainly not WWII or PRE-WWII. The collector needs to have or needs to look up the knowledge in connection with these units and their correct insignia and design.

Also, the surplus stocks of WWII SSI of other companies were bought up by these firms to continue selling to collectors, even into the 1950s. That way, and replenished with their own reproductions, they had a large offering of patches for sale to collectors.

These companies were, among others (including their old addresses):

- **The Patch King** (P.O. Box 101, Madison Square Station, New York 10, N.Y. – Owners: Sol Marks and Al Maller);
- **Springers** (617 N. Stanton Street, El Paso, Texas 79901 or P.O. Box 577, El Paso, Texas, 79944);
- **Hobby Guild of America** (New York);
- **Roy Paris** (1314 Main Street, Dallas, Texas);
- **Wolf Appleton** (566 Broadway, New York 12, N.Y.);
- **The Insignia Mart** (703 Broadway, New York 3, N.Y.);
- **H. J. Saunders** (since 1968 – P.O. Box 414, Vermilion, Ohio, 44089-0414).

For a small amount, one could order a patch or a group of patches in one of their catalogues and paste it/them in a special collector's book. Some examples of such available catalogues, provided with prices, can be seen on the following pages (Fig 05-024 to Fig 05-028).

Fig. 05-022: Front and back of a post-WWII U.S. made, partially machine-embroidered 80th Inf Div reproduction on felt.

Fig. 05-023: Example of a post-WWII era made reproduction of a WWI or Interwar 88th Inf Div patch. Such kind of SSI appears in the 1945 catalogue "Shoulder Patch Insignia of the U.S. Armed Forces" compiled by Wolf Appleton, New York.

Fig. 05-024: The Patch King advertisement.

On the following pages:
Fig. 05-025 to Fig 05-027: Different pages of The Patch King Catalogue.

THE PATCH KING

in answer to your many requests, now offers you a group of 10 different assortments. If you will check the prices against our regular price list you will note savings of up to 50%. ACT NOW!

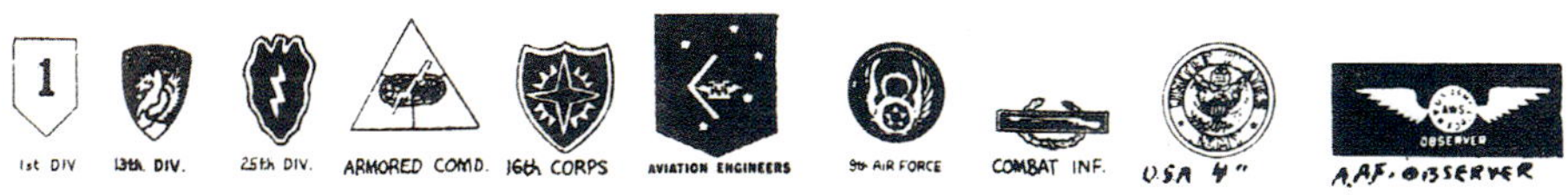

ASSORTMENT 101. Contains 10 authentic embroidered regulation size patches (illustration for identification purposes only). Regular price $2.43. Our New Low price **$1.00.**

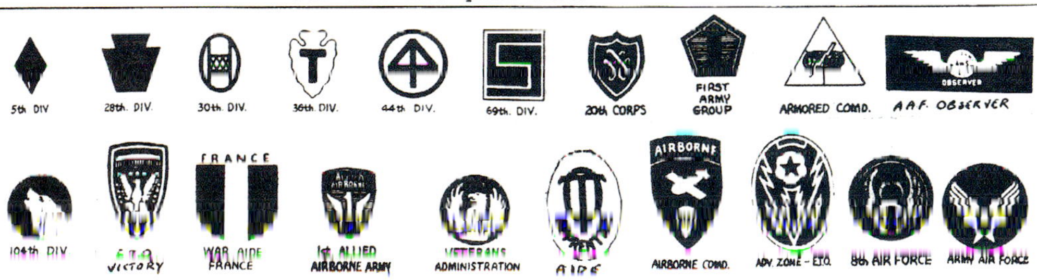

ASSORTMENT 102. Contains 20 authentic embroidered regulation size patches (illustration for identification purposes only). Regular price $4.94. Our New Low price **$2.00.**

ASSORTMENT 104. Contains the complete set of 16 authentic embroidered regulation size Air Force Patches (illustration for identification purposes only). Regular Price $3.74. Our New Low price **$2.75.**

THE PATCH KING

P.O. BOX 101. MADISON SQUARE STATION NEW YORK 10. N. Y.

Fig. 05-025: Page of The Patch King Catalogue.

ASSORTMENT 103. Contains 50 authentic embroidered regulation size patches (illustration for identification purposes only). Regular price $10.70. Our New Low price **$5.00.**

ASSORTMENT 105. Contains the complete set of 15 authentic embroidered regulation size R.A.F. and R.C.A.F. Wings. Regular Price $5.25. Our New Low price **$3.00.**

ASSORTMENT 106
10 assorted Civil Air Patrol and Air Warden Patches. Regular Price $3.50. Our New Low Price **$1.50.**

ASSORTMENT 107
10 Metal Collar Insignia. Regular Price $3.50. Our New Low Price **$1.00.**

ASSORTMENT 108
Contains 20 authentic embroidered World War I Regulation size Patches. Value up to $5.00. Our New Low Price **$2.50.**

ASSORTMENT 109 and 110
We have been bombarded with requests for Campaign Ribbons and Decorations. The PATCH KING now offers these original colorful campaign ribbons to add to your collection. We have prepared a group of these bars (our selection) and have priced them at a new low to introduce this fascinating hobby. Assortment 109 — 6 Bars 50c. Assortment 110 — 15 Bars $1.00.

Send 25 cents for Our Illustrated Catalogue and Sample Patch

Fig. 05-026: Page of The Patch King Catalogue.

The new U.S. embroidered insignia album containing 439 of the most up to date patches. This album contains 3[illegible] pages of actual size embroidered shoulder insignia, plus 9 additional blank pages so that you might add those patches that are not shown. This album is loose leaf and made so that you can easily add extra pages.*
The size is $11\frac{1}{2}$ x 15. OUR LOW Price (complete with actual patches) **$69.50.**
Based on our low prices that appear in our price list, the value of the patches only without the album would be **$88.00.** ACT NOW — SAVE MONEY & HAVE A NEAT COLLECTION.

We have the same album (as above) empty without patches. The patches can be inserted at will. The album has 36 pages with the actual illustration and titles, plus 9 **extra blank** pages.* Even without inserting patches, this album can be used as an illustrated guide.

OUR LOW PRICE **$9.00.**

*Additional blank pages for these albums can be had at $.75 dozen.

Our smaller album, also loose leaf, contains 147 actual size embroidered shoulder patches covering 11 pages plus 2 extra blank pages.* The size is $11\frac{1}{2}$ x 15.
OUR LOW PRICE (complete with actual patches) **$19.50.**
Based on our low prices that appear in our price list, the value of the patches only without the album would be **$25.00.** ACT NOW — SAVE MONEY & HAVE A NEAT COLLECTION.

We have the same album (as above) empty without patches. These patches can be inserted at will. The album has 11 pages with printed titles, plus 2 extra blank pages*

OUR LOW PRICE **$3.75.**

*Additional blank pages for these albums can be had at $.75 dozen.

ORDER BLANK

THE PATCH KING — Dept. 347
P. O. Box 101, Madison Square Station, New York 10, N. Y.

☐ I am enclosing $...................please send me the following items I have circled.
You may send the balance of $...................C.O.D.

Asst. No.	101	102	103	104	105
	106	107	108	109	110

Album No. 1944 Complete with Patches. 1944 Empty.
1945 Complete with Patches. 1945 Empty.

Deposit required on all orders.

(Please print)

Name__________ Address __________ City __________ Zone ____ State __________

THE PATCH KING

P.O. BOX 101. MADISON SQUARE STATION NEW YORK 10. N. Y.

Fig. 05-027: Page of The Patch King Catalogue.

Fig. 05-028: The Wolf Appleton catalogue.

As one can read on one of The Patch King's catalogue pages, not only separate patches could be bought. Even complete bound insignia albums could be ordered with a large number of patches already pasted in, together with some extra blank pages for additional patches. All these patches were the company's own reproductions or bought up stock of original WWII SSI. Below are some pictures of such an album, including the title page and one of the pages with pasted Corps patches.

Fig. 05-029: One of those insignia albums collectors could buy. The patches were already pasted in. *(Courtesy of Eric Czerwinski)*

Fig. 05-030: One page of the insignia album illustrated in Fig. 05-029. The patches were already pasted in. *(Courtesy of Eric Czerwinski)*

Also, in close collaboration and through contracts with those companies, producers of food products put patches sealed in a cellophane wrapper in boxes of food as a publicity stunt (e.g., cereal boxes). When buying these boxes, collectors were therefore encouraged to continue to collect the SSI.

Below is an example of a 94th Inf Div SSI with a flaw in the embroidery. This patch is the property of Dr. Howard Lanham and came from Patch King when he was a child. They had some introductory deals, and for a small amount of money they sold the collector a pile of insignia. These must have been overruns and rejects (flawed patches) from a WWII period manufacturer. As mentioned above, firms such as Patch King bought up a lot of surplus stock from other people in the trade after the war.

This patch allows you to see the backing material where the embroidery machine failed to sew (khaki cotton twill-base fabric).

Fig. 05-031: Front and back of a flawed 94th Inf Div SSI. *(Courtesy of Howard G. Lanham)*

The collecting business covers all time periods. Even prior to WWII certain companies made reproductions for collectors. Below are examples of typical pre-WWII Studley insignia (Interwar period). In the 1920s-1930s, the Studley company also manufactured reproduction WWI unit SSI for collectors during that period. These insignia are also much smaller in size and design than the usual embroidered WWII counterparts.

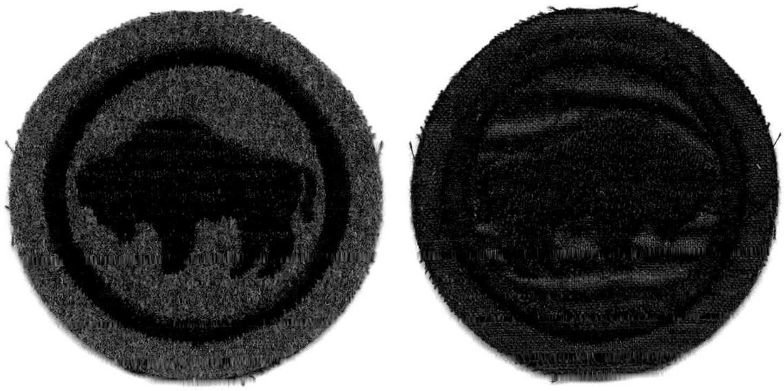

Fig. 05-032: Front and back of a pre-WWII made Studley 92nd Inf Div patch, partially machine-embroidered on OD wool and cut to shape, made for collectors.

Fig. 05-033: The original size (100%) of the Studley patch versus the original size (100%) of the genuine WWII SSI.

Another example of a 1920s-1930s Studley patch is the one of the 38th Inf Div below. It is also illustrated next to its original WWII counterpart to compare the size, which is clearly different.

A very striking feature to see is the ribbed embroidery style of the Studley patch, which is inconsistent with one of the early manufacturing styles applied during the Interwar and early-WWII period. This confirms again what is written in chapter 3, heading 5.

Fig. 05-034: Front and back of a pre-WWII made Studley 38th Inf Div patch, partially machine-embroidered on OD wool and cut to shape, made for collectors. The Studley patch is illustrated in its 100% size, like the added WWII U.S. made cut-edge 38th Inf Div SSI.

CHAPTER 6

Comparison with the Post-WWII German Made, Fully Machine-Embroidered, Cut-Edge SSI for U.S. Units

An important detail in the recognition of the originality of WWII U.S. made, machine-embroidered SSI is the difference from the post-WWII SSI made in Germany. This manufacturing style is similar to the style of the U.S. made SSI, but the German machine embroidery technique has a more open embroidery style in 90% of the cases. It is a less consecutive embroidery pattern and has a distinctive look. In collector terminology and in lectures it is called a "salt and pepper" look because of the open embroidery texture. This can clearly be seen on the front and back of the U.S. 6th Army SSI illustrated below (and details).

Fig. 06-001: Front and back of a post-WWII German made, cut-edge 6th U.S. Army SSI.

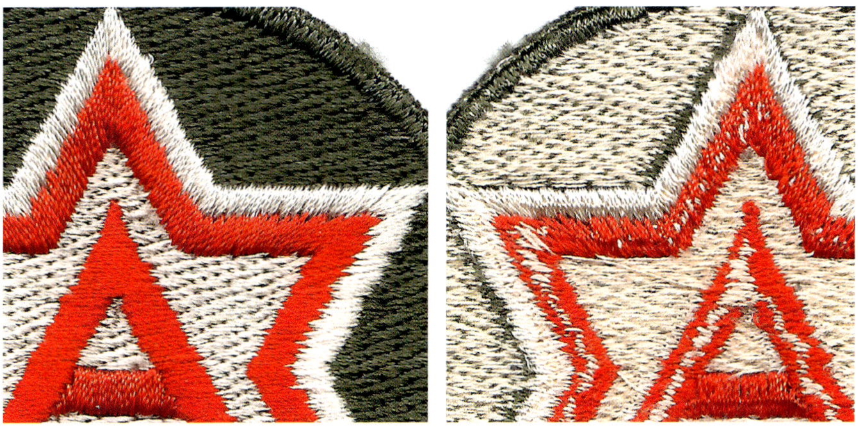

Fig. 06-002: Details of front and back of the SSI illustrated in Fig. 06-001.

Like the U.S. made SSI, these German made ones were also fully machine-embroidered on a cotton twill-base fabric and then individually cut. Here, the same cut-edge principle was also applied.

On the following pages are some examples of patches with post-WWII German open embroidery texture.

Fig. 06-003: Above: Front and back of a post-WWII German made, cut-edge 7th U.S. Army SSI; Below: its original and common WWII U.S. made counterpart for comparison which is smaller in size.

Fig. 06-004: Front and back of a post-WWII German made, cut-edge X Corps SSI.

Fig. 06-005: Front and back of a post-WWII German made, cut-edge 43rd Inf Div SSI with white back thread.

Fig. 06-006: Front and back of a post-WWII German made, cut-edge 43rd Inf Div SSI with black back thread. Even the blue cotton twill backing material is visible on the edge.

Fig. 06-007: Front and back of a post-WWII German made, cut-edge 3rd Inf Div SSI with white back thread.

Fig. 06-008: Front and back of a post-WWII German made, cut-edge 25th Inf Div SSI.

One should not be mistaken with the German made WOVEN SSI, which have a different appearance than the German embroidered ones. These can wrongly be seen as U.S. made. See the example below, on the right, next to the two German made fully machine-embroidered cut-edge SSI. All three are of post-WWII manufacture. An important feature of a woven SSI is the fact that thc back has reversed colors from the front and its even appearance (see earlier in chapter 3, heading 1).

Fig. 06-009: The fronts of three post-WWII German made 1st Inf Div SSI. The one on the right is woven, the other two are fully machine-embroidered cut-edge patches. *(Courtesy of L. Kleine)*

Fig. 06-010: The back of the SSI illustrated in Fig.06-009. The woven SSI on the right is reinforced with khaki cotton twill on the back which was often utilized. Because of the cotton twill, the reversed colors cannot be seen. *(Courtesy of L. Kleine)*

Often SSI of U.S. units that have not been engaged in the European theater during WWII appear in a manufacture style of a country from this theater (German, British, etc. manufacture). Those SSI were manufactured and used as a former combat patch for wear on the right shoulder when authorized.

Below are post-WWII German made, cut-edge examples of the 40th Inf Div, 2nd U.S. Army, and 4th U.S. Army. The two Armies never even left the U.S., as they were training armies.

Fig. 06-011: A post-WWII cut-edge 40th Inf Div SSI of German manufacture.

Fig. 06-012: Detail scan of the back of the German made, cut-edge 40th Inf Div SSI illustrated in Fig. 06-011 above.

Fig. 06-013: A post-WWII German made cut-edge 4th U.S. Army SSI.

Fig. 06-014: A post-WWII German made cut-edge 2nd U.S. Army SSI.

For the sake of comparison the following details are provided. In the first picture (Fig. 06-015), one can see detail (a) of the early-WWII U.S. made cut-edge 8th Inf Div SSI of Fig. 03-574 compared with detail (b) of the post-WWII German made 2nd U.S. Army SSI illustrated here above. Both have similar open embroidery, however, the German made one has a more regular texture.

On the following page, the details of their backs are illustrated in Fig. 06-016. Here the differences between those two SSI [details (a) and (c) of the figure] are very clear. Also for comparison detail (b) is added in this picture, and is of the post-WWII German made 8th Inf Div SSI of Fig. 03-578.

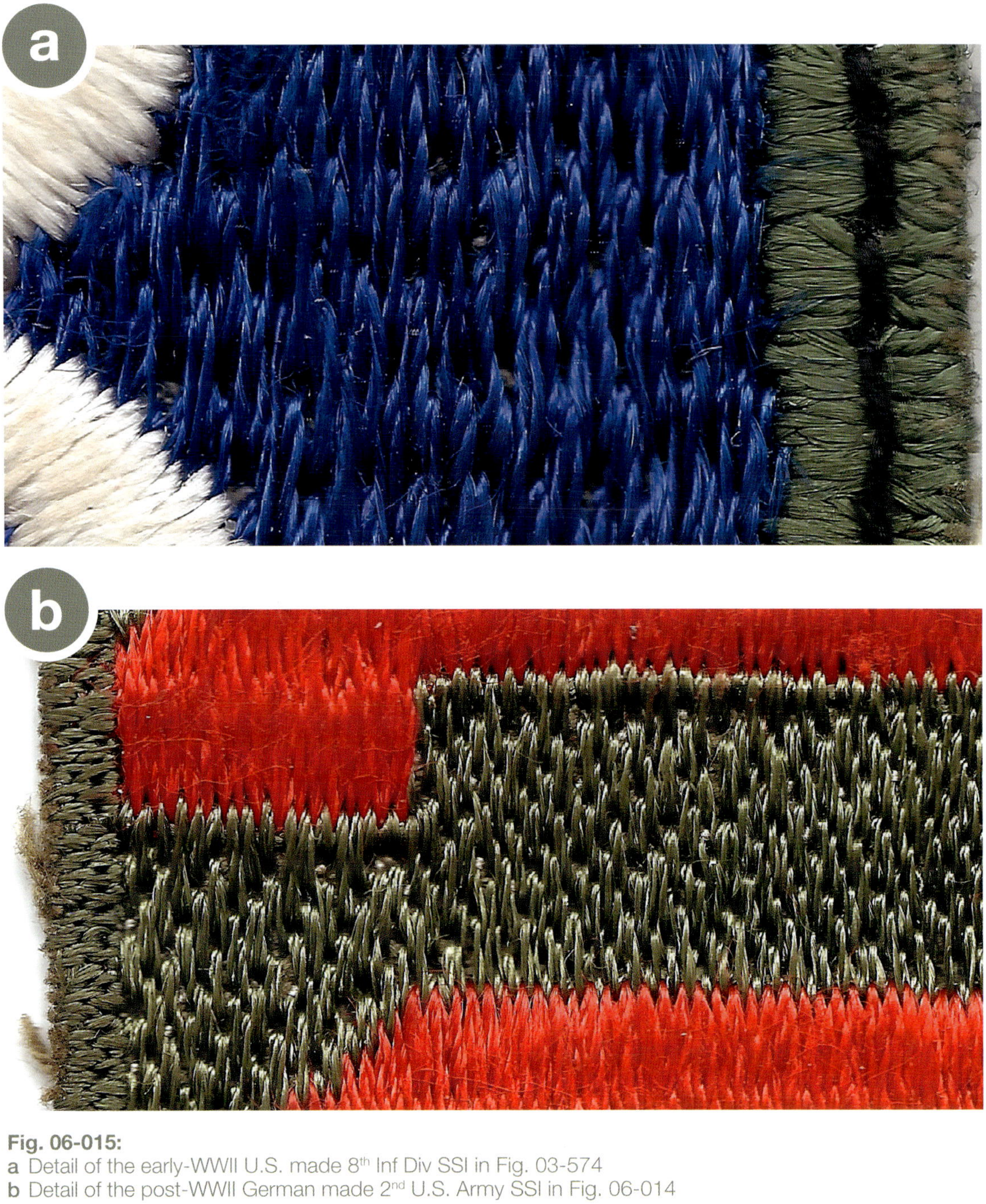

Fig. 06-015:
a Detail of the early-WWII U.S. made 8th Inf Div SSI in Fig. 03-574
b Detail of the post-WWII German made 2nd U.S. Army SSI in Fig. 06-014

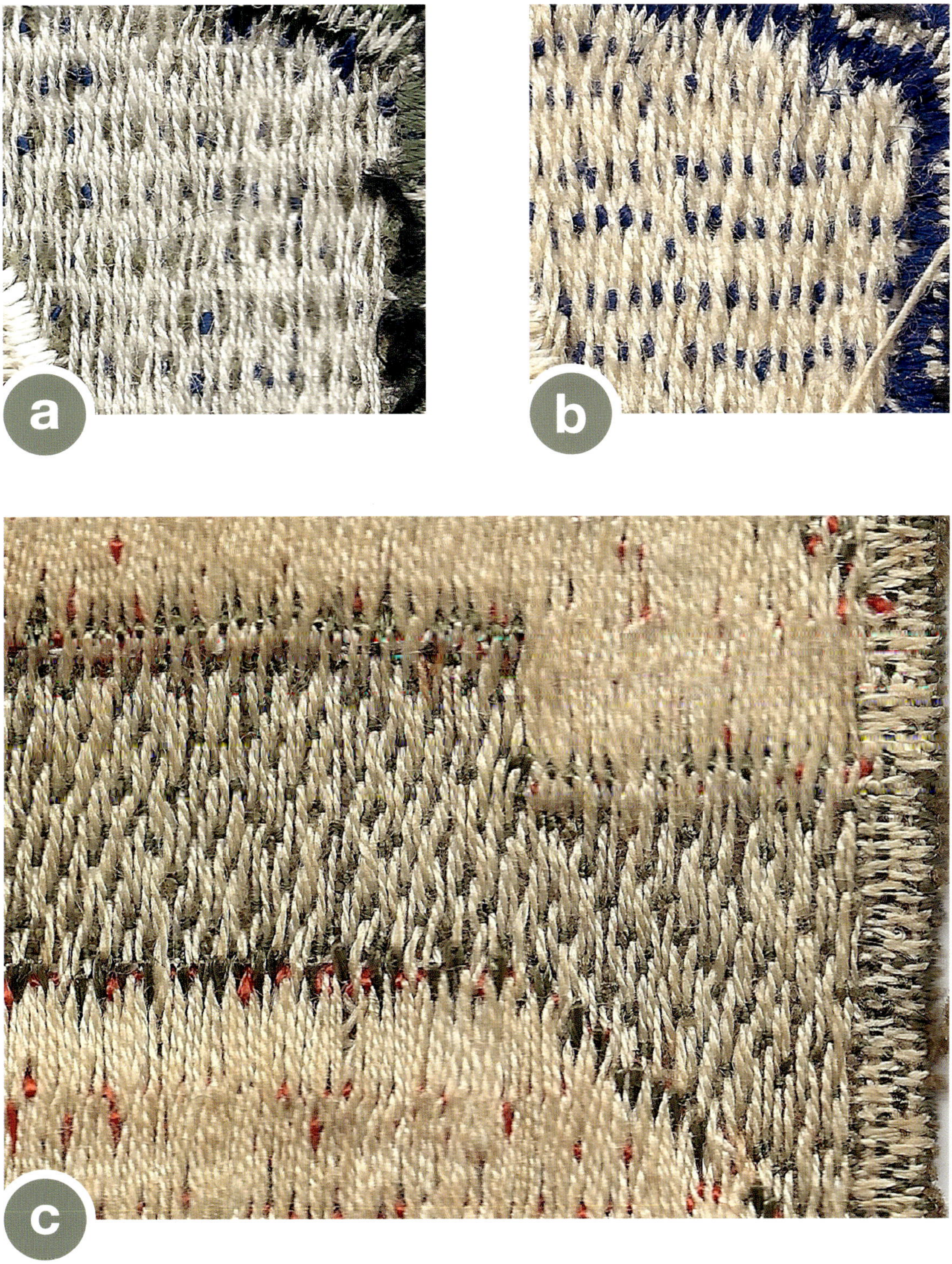

Fig. 06-016:
a Detail of the early-WWII U.S. made, cut-edge 8th Inf Div SSI in Fig. 03-574
b Detail of the post-WWII German made 8th Inf Div SSI illustrated in Fig. 03-578
c Detail of the post-WWII German made 2nd U.S. Army SSI in Fig. 06-014
Both (b) and (c) are almost similar styles and are of German manufacture.

In some cases, the German machine-embroidered SSI are very difficult to distinguish from their U.S. counterparts (nicely close and contiguous embroidery style – see the examples below). In this matter, the experience of the collector also plays a large role, because these manufacturing styles often come back and are at the time recognizable.

Fig. 06-017: Above: the fronts of post-WWII German made, cut-edge SSI of the 1st and 2nd Armored Div; Below: the fronts of their WWII U.S. made, cut-edge counterparts.

Fig. 06-018: Above: the backs of the post-WWII German made SSI of the 1st and 2nd Arm Div illustrated in Fig. 06-017. Below: the backs of the WWII U.S. made counterparts at the same figure. All patches are very nice OD backs, but the German made ones have a particular style.

Fig. 06-019: Front and back of a post-WWII German made, cut-edge 2nd Inf Div SSI with complete OD back.

Fig. 06-020: Front and back of a WWII U.S. made, cut-edge 2nd Inf Div SSI with complete white back.

Fig. 06-021: Details of the 2nd Inf Div SSI previously shown: The details above are those of the German made, cut-edge 2nd Inf Div SSI illustrated in Fig. 06-019; the details below are of the U.S. made, cut-edge 2nd Inf Div SSI of Fig. 06-020.

Fig. 06-022: Front and back of a post-WWII German made, cut-edge 2nd Inf Div SSI with another kind of embroidery style, with complete white back.

Fig. 06-023: An unusual fully machine-embroidered, black backed, cut-edge 30th Inf Div SSI as the one illustrated here. This kind of patch is very thin and supple in comparison with all other machine-embroidered insignia.

At Internet auctions and in literature, many assumptions and opinions have been made and written down regarding the following SSI of the 30th and 76th Inf Div. These SSI have an unusual embroidery pattern, and are very thin and supple in comparison with all other fully machine-embroidered SSI (U.S. and foreign theater made). The following is a study on these particular shoulder patches.

The route of the 30th Inf Div through Europe during WWII is illustrated in Fig. 06-028 below, and ended in Germany, as many other U.S. Divisions did at the end of the war. The Division met the Russians in the Magdeburg area and did some occupation duties until that area was given to the Russians for further occupation some time after. Afterwards the Division went to the German/Czech border for further occupation duties, near Possneck (Germany), in the neighborhood of the 76th Inf Div. The latter was also in the European Theater of Operations and ended in the Chemnitz area in Germany, also near the German/Czech border (Div HQ stayed in Limbach-Oberfrohna). The 76th Inf Division's way through Europe can be seen on the same map illustrated in Fig. 06-028 below.

In June 1945, the 30th Inf Div was alerted for deployment for action in the Pacific and probably needed more troops. These likely came from the nearby 76th Inf Div, because in the months after VE-Day, many troops were transferred from the 76th Inf Div to the 30th Inf Div to prepare to go fight against the Japanese. Of the fact of these transfers at the end of the war, I have seen uniforms of veterans who served in the 76th Inf Div during WWII with the same aforementioned 30th Inf Div patch on the uniform's sleeve.

In the following months (June to August 1945), the 30th Inf Div continued their work near the German/Czech border, and likely trained for future actions in Japan. Because of the end of all WWII hostilities in early August 1945, the 30th Inf Div never departed for Japan. The Division made the trip through France, was shipped aboard the Queen Mary, and returned to the U.S., where it arrived in New York on August 21, 1945. The 76th Inf Div was inactivated on August 31, 1945, in Germany (Limbach-Oberfrohna).

This unusual fully machine-embroidered, black backed 30th Inf Div SSI, such as the one illustrated in Fig. 06-023 above, is clearly not of U.S. manufacture. Although the patch was applied with the "cut-edge" principle, it has a very regular pattern and less dense embroidery than U.S. made ones, and is very thin and supple. It also has a particular horizontal embroidered bas relief-like surface (in the normal position for wear).

The 76th Inf Div SSI also exists with this kind of unusual pattern, with black back thread, and also very thin manufactured and supple. Two examples of this SSI are illustrated here below. Both patches have more dense embroidery than the 30th Inf Div patch and have the same appearance (border, utilized colors of threads, etc.). However, looking at the red and blue part of the design, there is a visible difference between those two 76th Inf Div insignia: the one in Fig. 06-024 has an even surface (no bas relief); the second in Fig. 06-025 has a ribbed kind of embroidery.

Detailed scans of both the front and back of these three SSI are illustrated in Fig. 06-026 and Fig 06-027.

Fig. 06-024: An unusual fully machine-embroidered, black backed, cut-edge 76th Inf Div SSI. At first sight this patch has no similar embroidery pattern as the 30th Inf Div SSI illustrated in Fig. 06-023. Only the detail scans of both patches below reveal an almost similar style with certain parts.

Fig. 06-025: Another 76th Inf Div SSI of the same kind as the one illustrated in Fig. 06-024. However this one has a ribbed bas-relief-like surface as the 30th Inf Div SSI illustrated in Fig. 06-023 which can clearly be seen. Also detail scans of this patch can be seen below.

Some findings:

- In the detailed scan of the fronts of the three patches (see Fig. 06-026 below), a certain similarity can be seen when one looks at the dense red embroidery in the three "X"s of the 30th Inf Div SSI [see (a)] and the red background of the 76th Inf Div insignia illustrated in Fig. 06-024 [see (b)]. It has almost the same kind of dense, single thread loop embroidery style;
- Another similar feature on these two patches [see (a) and (b) of the detail scan of their backs illustrated in Fig. 06-027] is the back thread color. Both have the same black-grey-colored catch thread at the back;
- The 30th Inf Div and the second 76th Inf Div insignia (illustrated in Fig. 06-025) have a bas relief-like surface and were embroidered with such rows. These apparent vertical pattern rows to the embroidery can clearly be seen in Fig. 06-027;
- The pattern of all three SSI is also very regular and structured, which is characteristic of German embroidery;
- Both 76th Inf Div patches have the same kind (thickness) and the same colors of design thread; also the border of those two SSI has the same kind of thread.

REMARK: For an easy comparison of the details, the 30th Inf Div patch needs to be turned to see a similar direction of the thread loops.

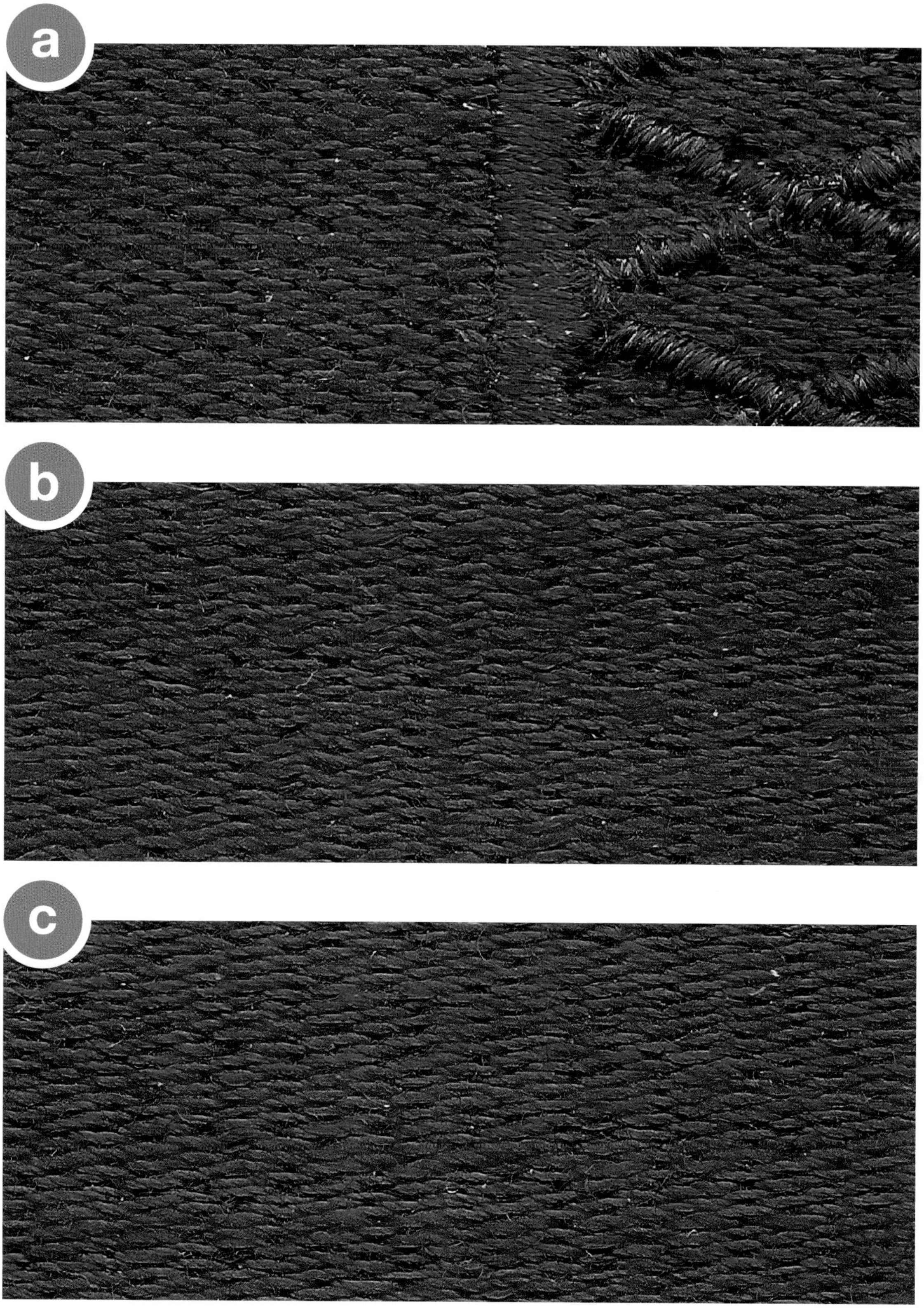

Fig. 06-026: The embroidery in the "X"s of the 30th Inf Div patch at (a) is almost similar and as dense as the embroidery of the 76th Inf Div patch at (b).

a Detail scan of a part of the 30th Inf Div SSI illustrated in Fig. 06-023 (turned 90°)

b Detail scan of a part of the red background of the 76th Inf Div SSI illustrated in Fig. 06-024

c Detail scan of a part of the red background of the 76th Inf Div SSI illustrated in Fig. 06-025

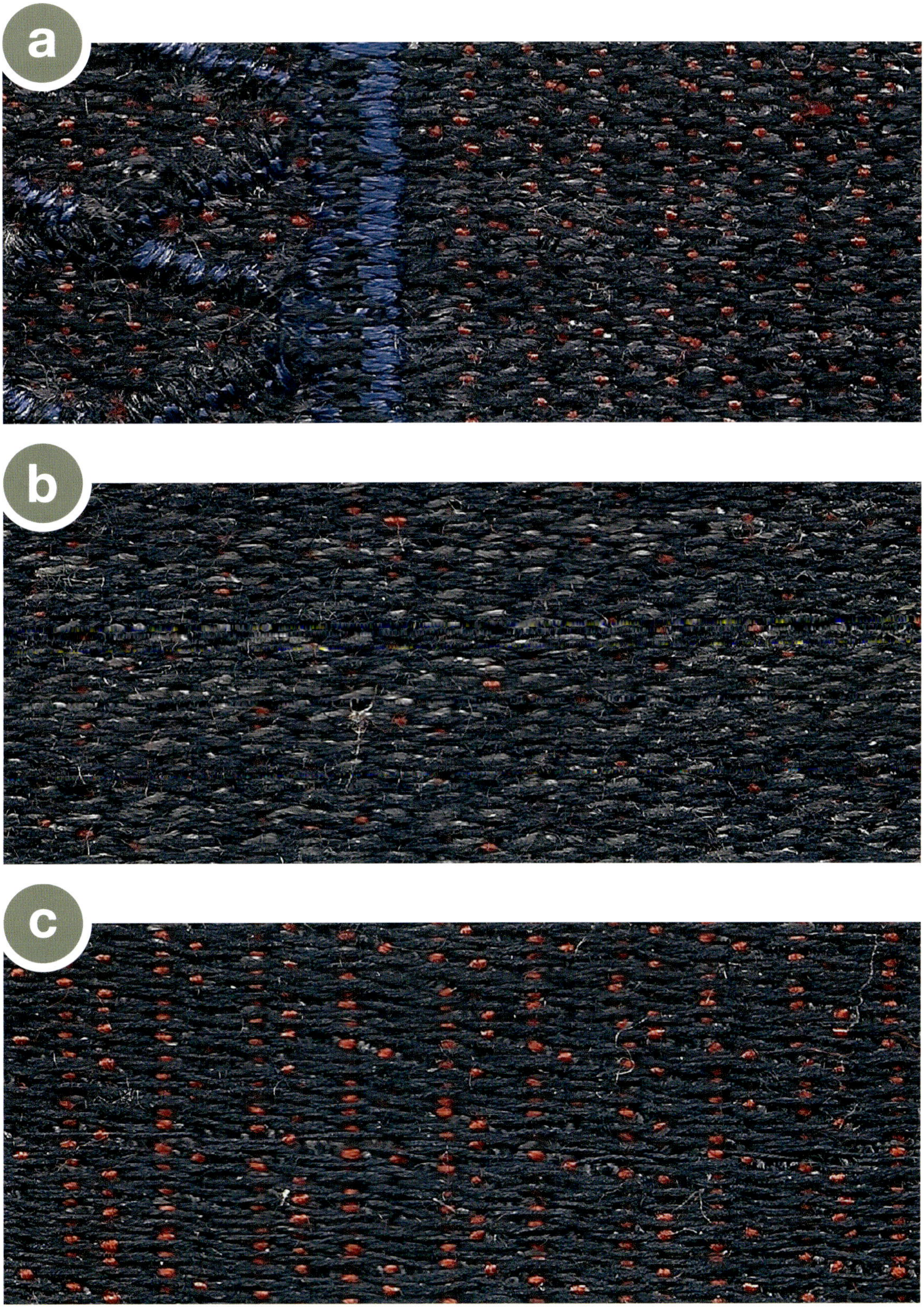

Fig. 06-027:
a Detail scan of a part of the back of the 30th Inf Div SSI illustrated in Fig. 06-023 (turned 90°). The embroidery rows which create the bas relief-like surface can clearly be seen
b Detail scan of a part of the back of the 76th Inf Div SSI illustrated in Fig. 06-024
c Detail scan of a part of the back of the 76th Inf Div SSI illustrated in Fig. 06-025. Also here the vertical embroidery rows which create the bas relief-like surface can clearly be seen

Fig. 06-028: The route of both the 30th and 76th Inf Div in the European Theater. During their occupation duties in Germany (May to August 1945) these Divisions were practically neighbors.

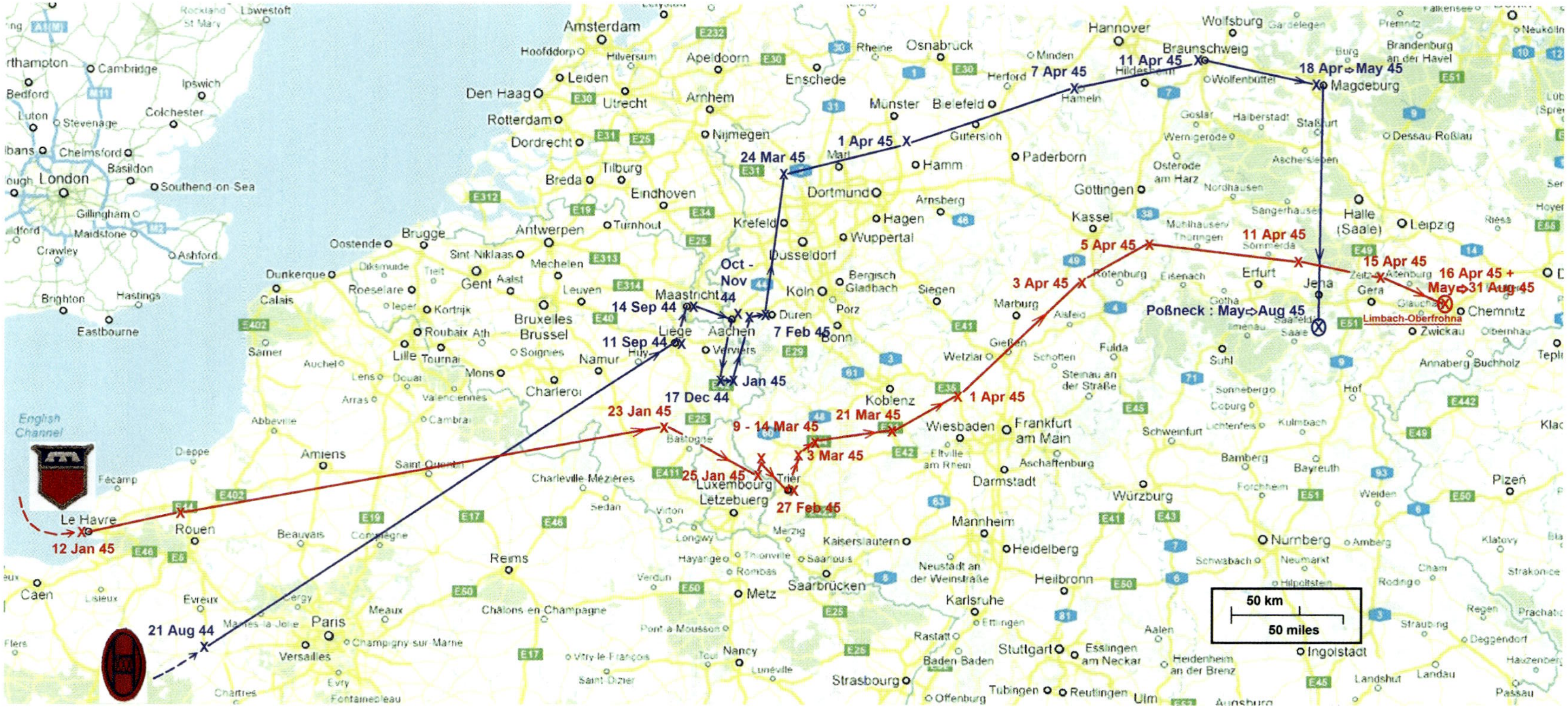

During this period of reinforcing the 30th Inf Div, the Division likely needed more 30th Inf Div SSI for the new troops coming from the 76th, as well as 76th Inf Div SSI for the same troops to wear on the right shoulder. During their stay, both patches were probably ordered with some local manufacturers, with almost similar embroidery techniques in their occupation area. They were nevertheless made on three different embroidery machines, if one sees the slight differences in pattern. This kind of embroidery technique and resulting pattern is possibly specific to that area. It is not certain whether the 30th and 76th Inf Div SSI were made by the same manufacturer or not. However, because of their (similar) appearance, it is clear that both 76th Inf Div patches were made by one and the same manufacturer, and on two different embroidery machines.

Between the few months after VE-Day, the transfers/reinforcements and their departure (30th), or the inactivation (76th), this could be a period for those patches to manufacture for the reason mentioned above. There was enough time to complete those orders in Germany.

Because of these particular similar features – the black back, the very thin and supple appearance, and the particular history of both Divisions, which were neighbors in occupation duty in Germany at the end of the war – these patches were very likely German made. Also, this kind of embroidery is seen only on the SSI of those two Divisions.

When returning, the 30th Inf Div's trip through France and their stay there was too short to order a large number of SSI. When units are being transported, the staff officers' time is being fully used up with details of moving a large body of men over a distance, and it takes time to negotiate a contract for a large number of SSI, get approvals, and have the firm then manufacture the items. It is doubtful that troops on the move ever had anything manufactured, so it is unlikely these patches are of French manufacture.

Also, these patches can not be British made either, because of the very short embroidery loops each insignia has. WWII British embroidered insignia have much longer thread loops than these two, even longer than the U.S. made fully machine-embroidered, cut-edge SSI. If someone should think of Belgian manufacture, these could not be Belgian made either, if one should consider the following: only these two Divisions had such patches, while dozens of U.S. divisions passed through Belgium in 1945 (and our country is not that big). Why shouldn't other Divisions have ordered their patches to be made with this (or these) specific manufacturer(s) here in Belgium? Also, was there enough time in the period of the "Battle of the Bulge" to make the orders? Looking at the map in Fig. 06-028, the 30th Inf Div was not even near the 76th, nor in a same region or town at the same dates when they were in the offensive. And an offensive also meant "no time for something else."

The most likely conclusion is they are German made, regarding the few months time frame the 30th Inf Div was in Germany before being shipped to the U.S., the very structured embroidery pattern both patches have (German style was always very regular), and the black back. They don't look German made like the usual "salt and pepper" look made patches, but the theory mentioned above creates the least doubt of this opinion.

CHAPTER 7
Comparison with the WWII British Made, Fully Machine-embroidered, Cut-edge SSI for U.S. Units

During WWII, SSI for the U.S. Armed Forces were also made in Great Britain. These were manufactured in both felting implementation (machine-embroidered on felt, with the color of the felt as main color of the SSI, and afterwards cut in the necessary form and size), as fully machine-embroidered on a piece of cotton base fabric, and then cut. With the latter, the cut-edge principles were also applied from their U.S. counterparts.

One of the clear differences with these SSI made in the U.S. is the color of the main thread and the border. In most cases, the color of the British made SSI is much less pronounced (less bright) than their U.S. made counterparts. Possibly the reason could be found in the lack of certain raw materials and products because of the war. In Great Britain lesser products were available, while the U.S., as a WWII economic superpower, had an enormous stock and a variety of products (such as threads with a range of shades and colors to choose). The British manufacturers took the thread with that shade of color, probably the only they had in stock, which was the closest to the specified one of the U.S. made design. However, SSI of British manufacture do exist in the same colors of design as their U.S. counterparts. To distinguish those similarly colored SSI, the two following characteristics (length of the embroidery loops and the color of the back thread) are important.

The thread loops (of the embroidery technique) of the British made SSI are a little longer than the U.S. made ones. Because of this, the embroidery style of the threads appears to be a bit looser and less regular with the British made patches, although their manufacturing style is just as dense and contiguous as the ones made in the U.S.

Following are examples of the WWII cut-edge 1st U.S. Army: the first of British manufacture, the second of U.S. manufacture.

Fig. 07-001: A WWII British made, cut-edge 1st U.S. Army SSI. Note the GI's later added red detail of the Army's Artillery component.

Fig. 07-002: A WWII U.S. made, cut-edge 1st U.S. Army Ordnance SSI.

The detail pictures of both patches can be seen below. With this particular example, the embroidery style of the (OD) background of the British made SSI is very irregular. No pattern can be seen. With the U.S. made example, what appear to be parallel diagonal pattern rows to the embroidery can be seen.

The British manufacture style certainly does not compare with the German made SSI, where a clear recurring drawing in the pattern can be seen (see earlier in chapter 6).

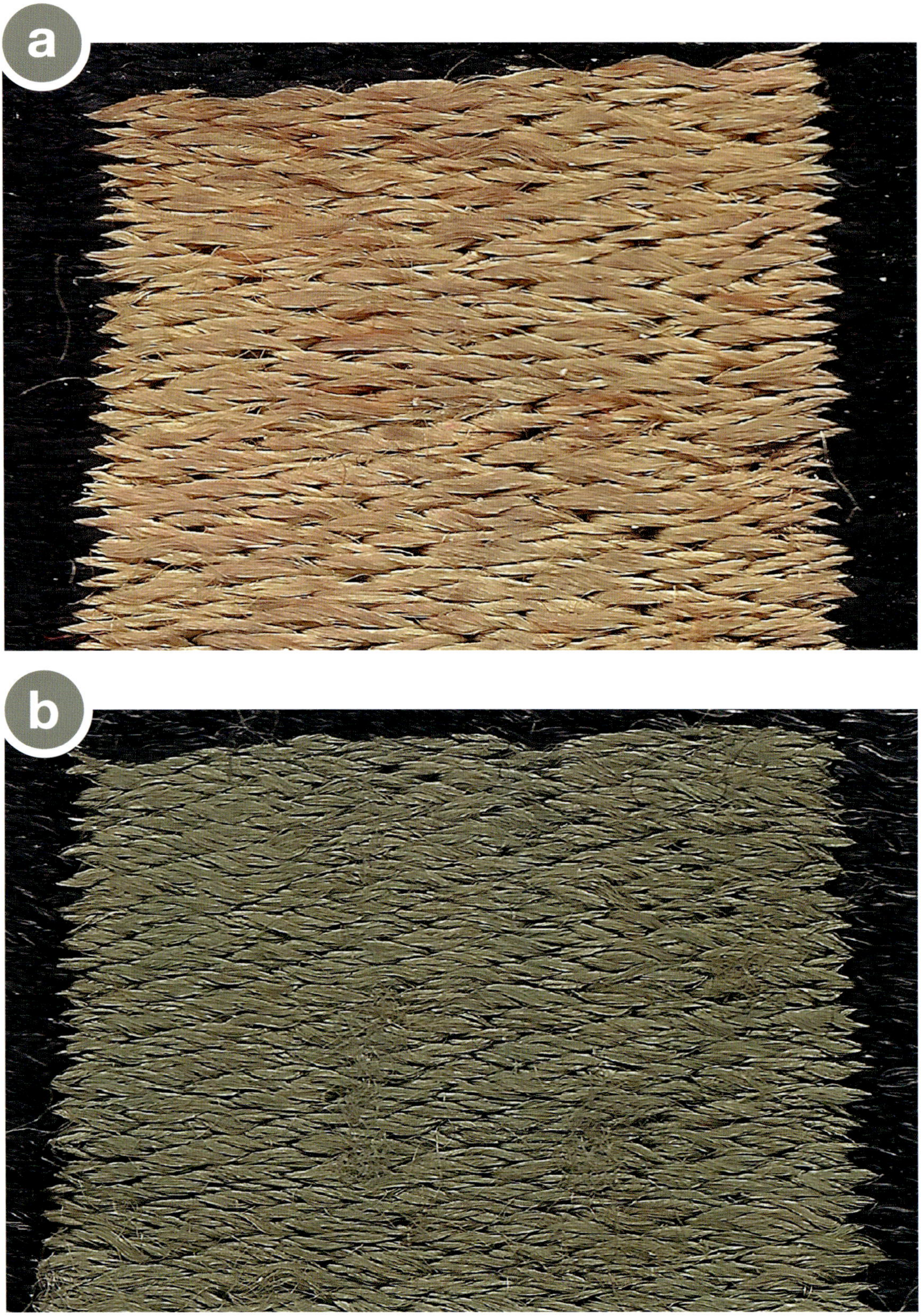

Fig. 07-003: The differences in both embroideries and design colors can clearly be seen.
a Detail of the WWII British made, cut-edge 1st U.S. Army SSI of Fig. 07-001
b Detail of its WWII U.S made, cut-edge counterpart illustrated in Fig. 07-002

The back thread of the British made SSI also vary from the U.S. made ones. Like the patches of U.S. manufacture, the British manufactured patches can also have different colors. But in addition to the white colored back or catch thread, black, orange, yellow, and purple are common colors in patches of British manufacture. With the U.S. made SSI, some of these back thread colors can never or barely be found. I have yet to see a British made SSI with OD-colored back.

In some cases, the shape and the design of the British made SSI are also slightly different from the U.S. made ones.

On the following pages, examples of the same WWII era made patch are illustrated, but one is of British manufacture, while the other is American made.

Fig. 07-004: Front and back of a WWII British made, cut edge 34th Inf Div black back SSI.

Fig. 07-005: Front and back of a WWII U.S. made, cut-edge 34th Inf Div SSI with OD back thread.

Fig. 07-006: Front and back of two WWII British made, cut-edge 29th Inf Div SSI, both with black back thread. The difference in color of the used blue design thread and OD-colored border thread can clearly be seen.

Fig. 07-007: Front and back of a WWII U.S. made, cut-edge 29th Inf Div white back SSI.

Fig. 07-008: Front and back of a WWII British made, cut-edge 17th AB Div black back SSI. Also the "Airbornc" tab is of British manufacture: partially machine-embroidered on black felt with black mesh reinforcement (also called stabilizer) and cut into the arc-shape.

Fig. 07-009: Front and back of a WWII U.S. made, cut-edge 17th AB Div SSI with white back thread. This is an unused patch where the tab is still fixed on the shield.

Fig. 07-010: Front and back of a WWII British made, cut-edge 82nd AB Div black back SSI. The 'Airborne'-tab is also of British manufacture: a fully machine-embroidered cut-edge tab. The tab is not attached and is most likely manufactured separately from the shield comparing the width of both.

Fig. 07-011: Front and back of a WWII U.S. made, cut-edge 82nd AB Div SSI with white back thread and ribbed embroidery style. The patch has an attached tab to the shield by the manufacturer. The khaki colored cotton twill between the two parts has already been cut by the paratrooper.

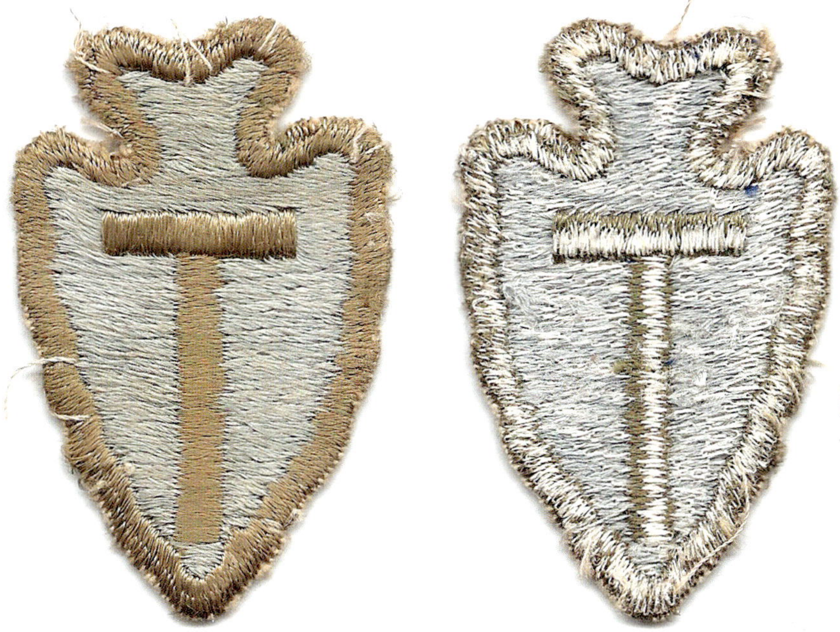

Fig. 07-012: Front and back of a WWII British made, cut-edge 36th Inf Div SSI with white back thread.

Fig. 07-013: Front and back of a WWII U.S. made, cut-edge 36th Inf Div SSI with white back thread.

Fig. 07-014: Front and back of a WWII British made, cut-edge 8th USAAF SSI with white back thread.

Fig. 07-015: Front and back of a WWII U.S. made, cut-edge 8th USAAF SSI with white back thread.

Fig. 07-016: Front and back of a WWII British made, cut-edge 80th Inf Div SSI with black back thread.

Fig. 07-017: Front and back of a WWII U.S. made, cut-edge 80th Inf Div SSI with white back thread.

Fig. 07-018: The front of three WWII, cut-edge SSI of Advanced Section, Communications Zone – European Theater of Operations, U.S. Army. The one on the left with the OD border is of U.S. manufacture; the two others are of British manufacture. One can also clearly see the differences in design. Here, the color of the threads used by the two British manufactured patches does not differ from their U.S. made counterpart.

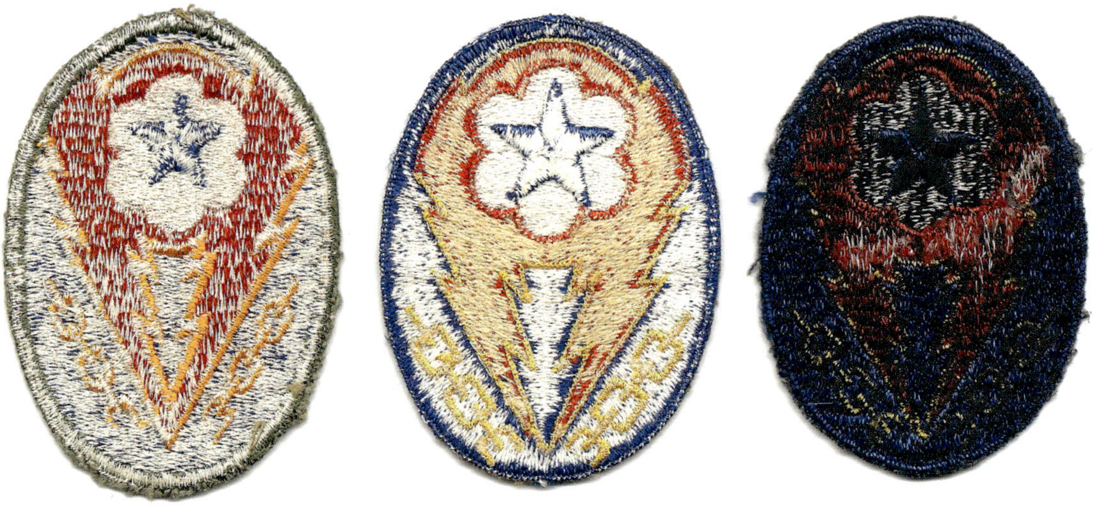

Fig. 07-019: The backs of the same SSI illustrated in Fig. 07-018. The U.S. made patch on the left has white back thread; the one of British manufacture in the middle has partially yellow and white back thread; the British made one on the right has an almost completely black back.

CHAPTER 8
Variations of WWII U.S. Made, Fully Machine-Embroidered Cut-Edge SSI (EXAMPLES)

1 | IN GENERAL – "THE INSTITUTE OF HERALDRY"

Various features of a WWII military patch, including the design, form, and the colors and images portrayed, all had a significance of some sort. Every subject (specific colors, persons/figures, fauna or flora) or item was used to contribute to the building of the morale of the unit as being one that was strong and invincible, and often included symbols of a region of the U.S. where the units were formed and/or trained (often during the First World War, when the SSI designs were originally approved). When units were organized abroad, often the symbols of the country in which the unit was formed can be seen in that unit's SSI (e.g., the second design of the U.S. 5th Army SSI. The outlined design of this patch is a mosque, representative of Morocco, North Africa, where the army was activated). Often the unit's numerical designation is depicted, either by the shape of the shield of the SSI (e.g., the number of angles, such as the six-pointed star of the 6th Inf Div SSI or the octagonal shaped patch of the U.S. XIII Corps), by the SSI's design itself (e.g., the 69th Inf Div SSI), or by the addition of a Roman or Arabic numeral.

How a SSI of a given unit should look and how it should be worn is determined, certified, and protected by The Institute of Heraldry (Office of the Administrative Assistant to the Secretary of the Army), and codified by certain drawings. These drawings were directives relating to the form, colors, designs, and sizes of the SSI. When SSI were ordered, the U.S. Army provided "The Institute of Heraldry" drawings to the civilian manufacturers.

But, due to the different companies during WWII, sometimes several variations of the same SSI were created and circulated. This led to a wide variety of SSI that will certainly not diminish the interest of the collector (differences in hue, detail differences in design, etc.). Some of these variants are illustrated on the following pages. It is impossible to do this for all SSI, because it cannot be determined which variations pertain and how many there should be. The collector will have to decide for himself how many different variations he wishes to include in his collection.

See below some examples of "The Institute of Heraldry" drawings used during WWII. They were assembled on a Master Sheet with a color legend at the bottom corner. The illustrated Master Sheet is dated May 16, 1925. Look at the dates on the separate drawings. These original drawings can go back to the WWI era.

The Institute of Heraldry, Office of the Administrative Assistant to the Secretary of the Army, describes itself thusly:

> The Institute of Heraldry has a long and distinguished record of support to the United States Army. Its roots were firmly planted in 1919 when President Woodrow Wilson directed the creation of the Heraldic Program Office under the War Department General Staff. Its purpose was to take responsibility for the coordination and approval of coats of arms and other insignia for Army organizations. By the end of WWII, its role expanded to include the other military services. In 1957 Public Law 85-263 directed the Secretary of the Army to furnish heraldic services to all branches of the federal government. The Institute's wide range of heraldic services include decorations, flags, streamers, agency seals, coats of arms, badges, and other forms of official emblems and insignia. (http://www.tioh.hqda.pentagon.mil)

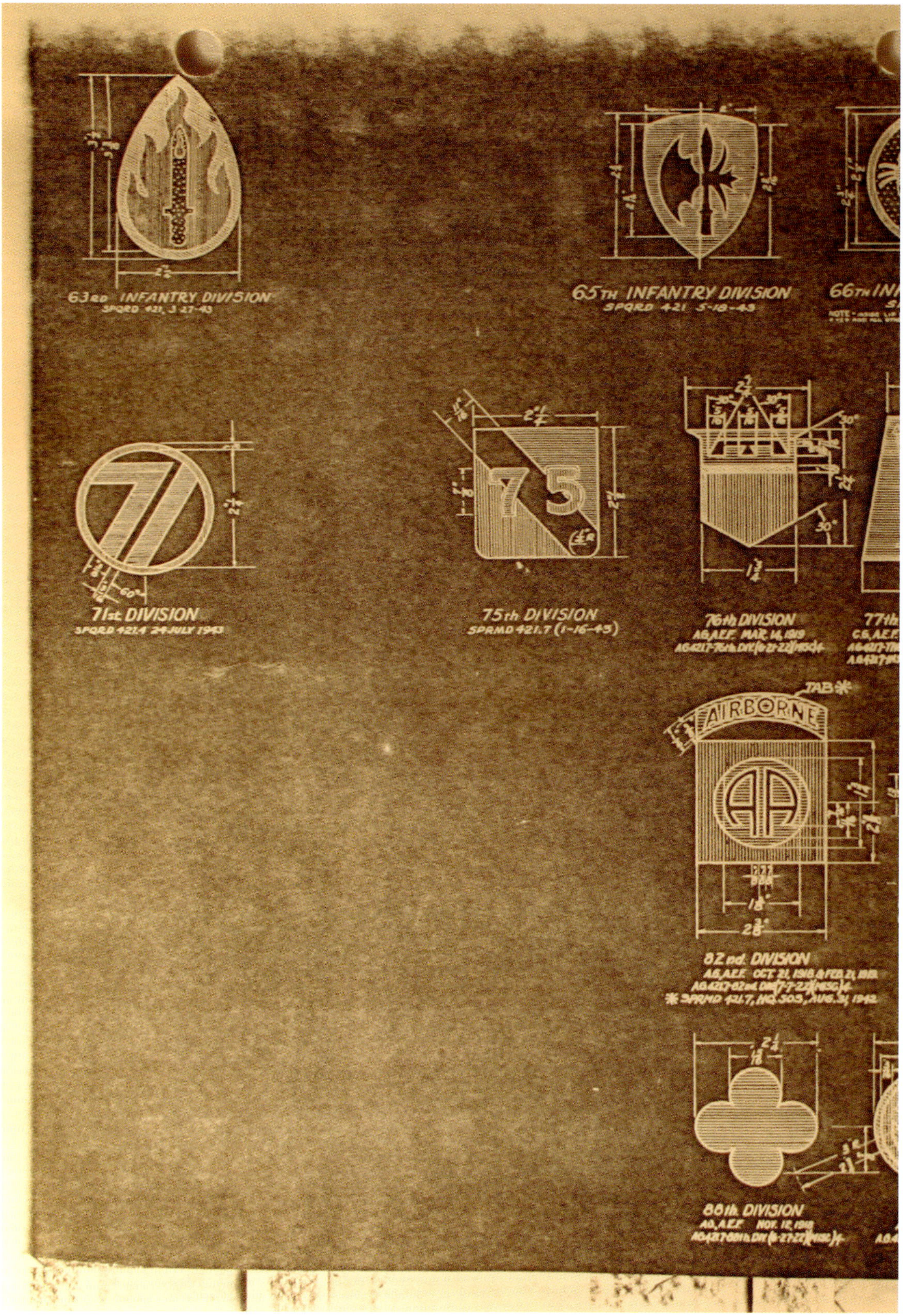

Fig. 08-101: An example of a Master Sheet assembled with some of the TIOH-Drawings of SSI used during WWII. *(Courtesy of Craig Pickrall)*

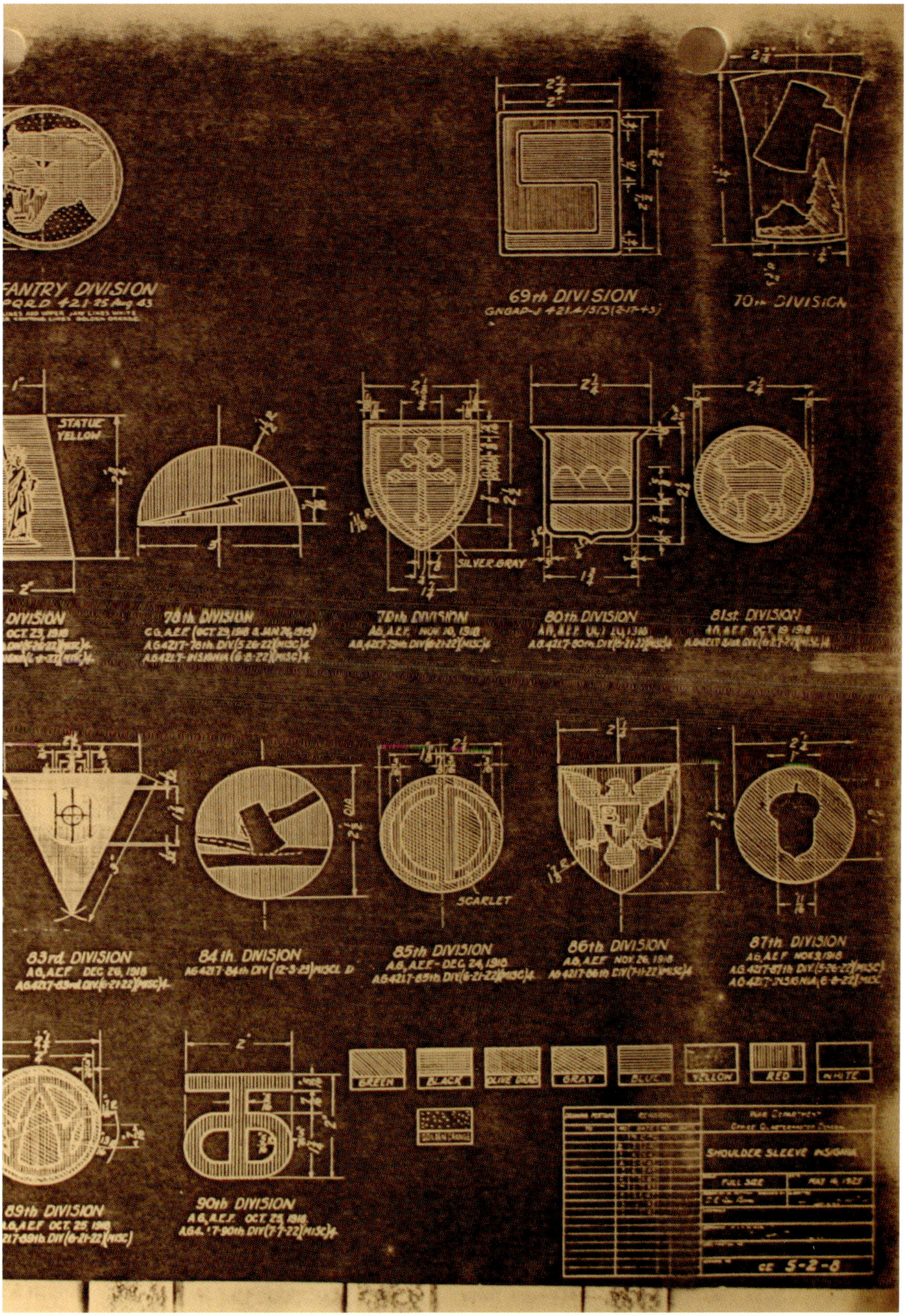
FANTRY DIVISION
69th DIVISION
70th DIVISION
STATUE
YELLOW
DIVISION
78th DIVISION
79th DIVISION
SILVER GRAY
80th DIVISION
81st. DIVISION
83rd. DIVISION
84 th. DIVISION
SCARLET
85th DIVISION
86th DIVISION
87th. DIVISION
89th DIVISION
90th DIVISION
GREEN
BLACK
OLIVE DRAB
GRAY
BLUE
YELLOW
RED
WHITE
SHOULDER SLEEVE INSIGNIA
FULL SIZE
CE 5-2-8

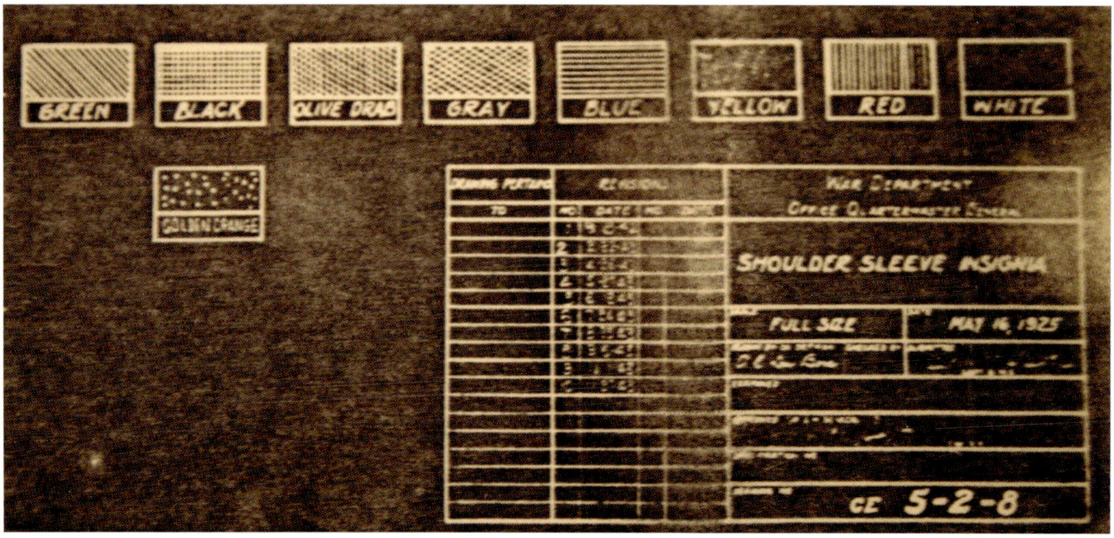

Fig. 08-102: The color legend at the bottom right corner of the illustrated Master Sheet. *(Courtesy of Craig Pickrall)*

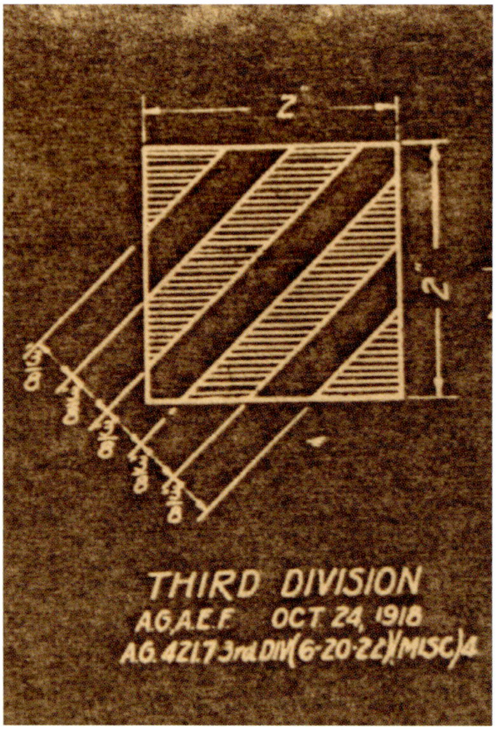

Fig. 08-103: The Institute of Heraldry-Drawing of the 3rd Inf Div SSI used during WWII. *(Courtesy of Craig Pickrall)*

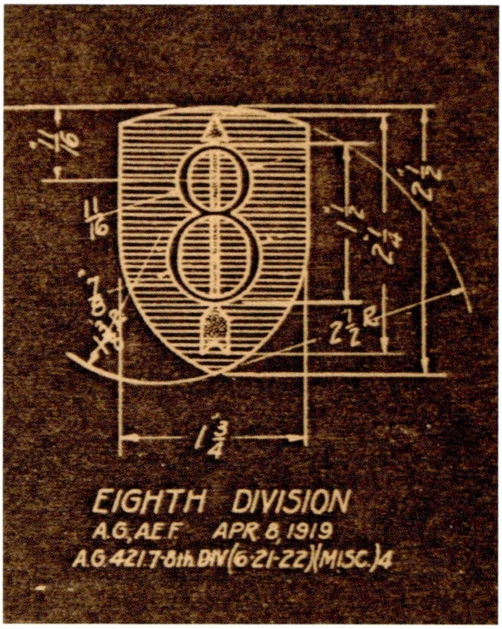

Fig. 08-104: The Institute of Heraldry-Drawing of the 8th Inf Div SSI used during WWII. *(Courtesy of Craig Pickrall)*

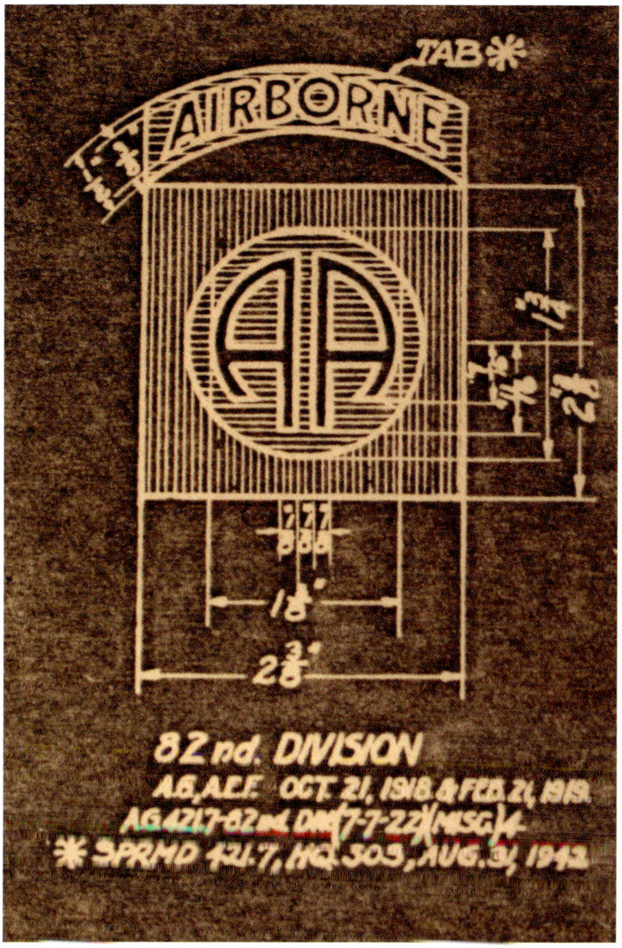

Fig. 08-105: The 1942 Institute of Heraldry-Drawing of the 82nd Airborne Div SSI used during WWII. *(Courtesy of Craig Pickrall)*

In the post-WWII era all of the patch drawings were redrawn. Each patch was put on a separate drawing instead of using the master sheet. By doing this, the legend for the colors was eliminated. The actual color was specified on the drawing itself. Even the number of stitches was included on the new drawing for each patch. Below examples of the post-WWII drawings of the 1st Inf Div and 82nd AB Div insignia are illustrated.

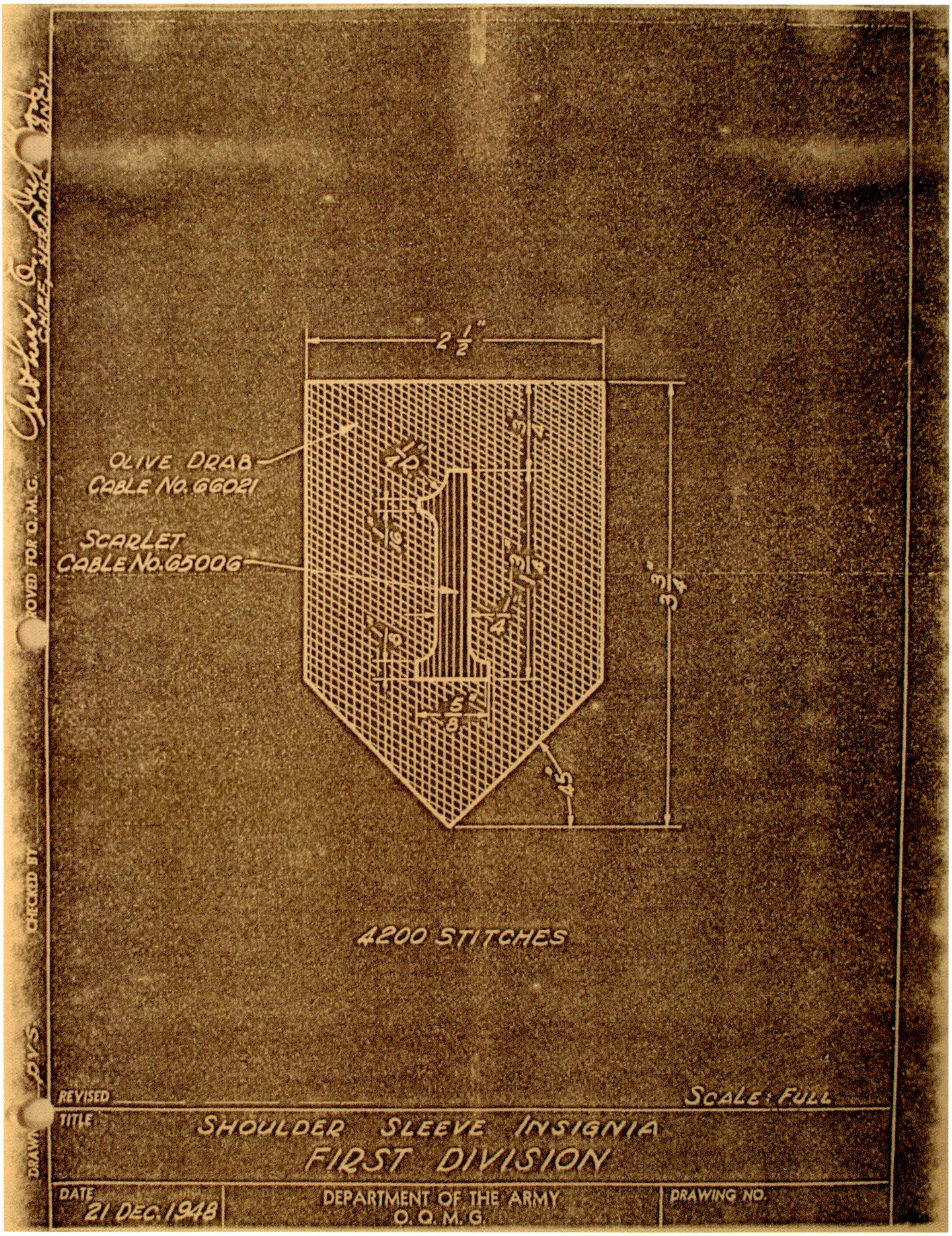

Fig. 08-106: Post-WWII TIOH-Drawing of the 1st Inf Div SSI. *(Courtesy of Craig Pickrall)*

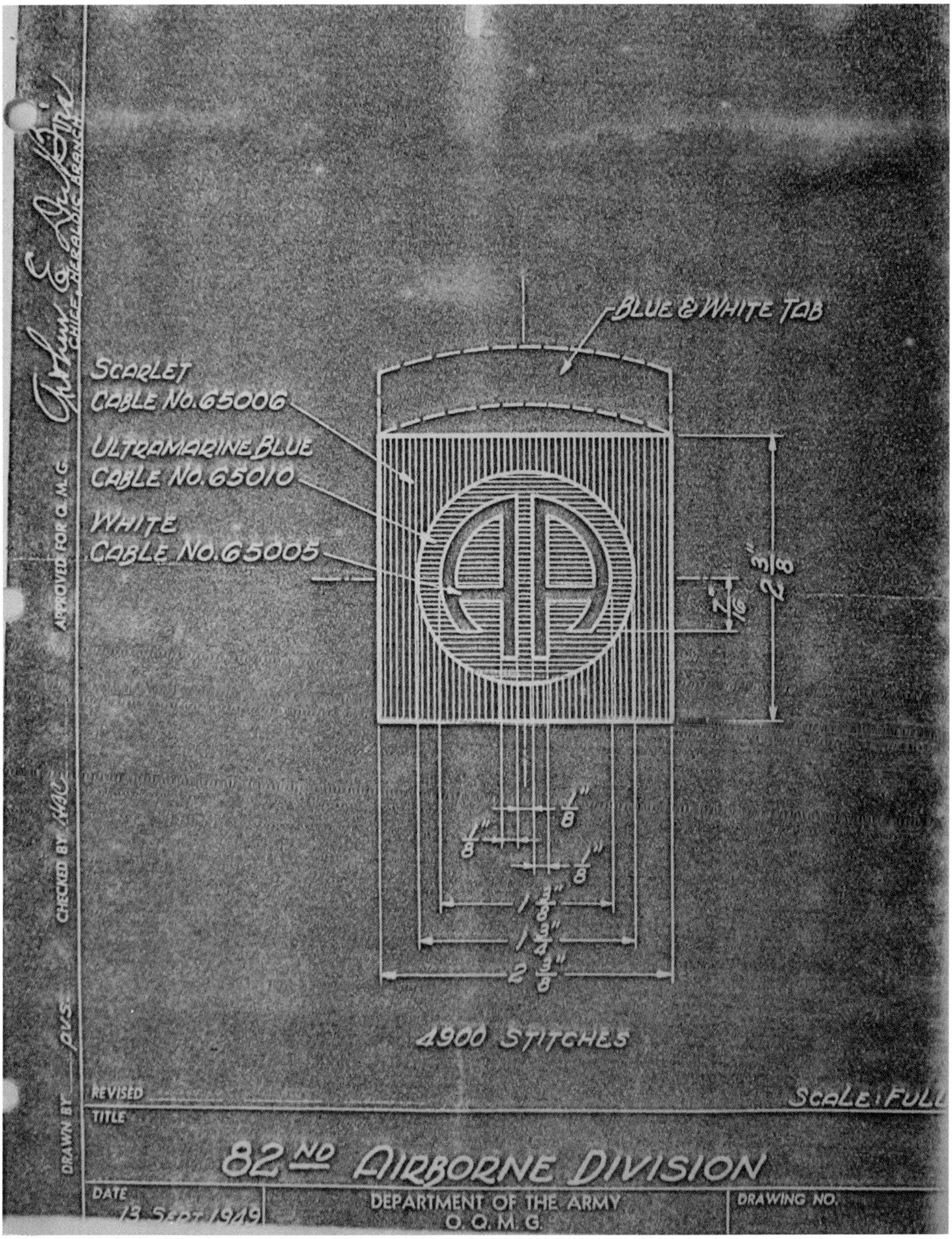

Fig. 08-107: Post-WWII TIOH-Drawing of the 82nd AB Div SSI. *(Courtesy of Craig Pickrall)*

2 | ERRORS

A patch that contains a mistake is considered a manufacturer's error. These errors could be:

- Typically in spelling, size, and/or thread colors;
- A little part of the cotton twill-base fabric that is not covered with threads and is still visible (see the example of the 94th Inf Div SSI illustrated in Fig. 05-031);
- Or a part of the design or lettering is not embroidered on the right place according to "The Institute of Heraldry" drawings (e.g., a small shift of a part of the design/lettering).

Error patches are often rejected by the ordering unit/organization, but in some cases the unit/organization used the error patches. Some examples:

Example below: 100th Inf Div SSI – Reversed white / yellow color of the "100":

Fig. 08-201: Correct SSI.

Fig. 08-202: Error SSI.

Example below: 119th Inf "Phantom" Div SSI – Reversed OD / blue colors:

Fig. 08-203: Correct SSI.

Fig. 08-204: Error SSI – Opposite colors.

Example below: 38th Inf Div SSI – Reversed blue / red colors:

Fig. 08-205: Correct SSI.

Fig. 08-206: Error SSI – Opposite colors.

Example below: 99th Inf Div SSI – Reversed white / blue colors:

Compare the colors of the chessboard: these are reversed (blue and white squares).

Fig. 08-207: Correct SSI.

Fig. 08-208: Error SSI.

Example below: 83rd Inf Div SSI – Lettering on the SSI – Errors in color:

Fig. 08-209: Usual SSI with yellow lettering…

Fig. 08-210: …and with the rare OD border.

Fig. 08-211: Error SSI – White lettering.

Example below: 101st AB Div SSI – Errors in color:

The white "AIRBORNE" lettering on the tab and the white tongue are manufacturer's errors.

Fig. 08-212: SSI with the usual yellow lettering and usual red tongue.

Fig. 08-213: Error SSI – White "Airborne"-lettering.

Fig. 08-214: Error SSI – A white tongue instead of the usual red tongue. 101st AB Div "White tongue"-patches were used during WWII and can be seen on many pictures.

Example below: 69th Inf Div and 1st Marine Amphibious Corps SSI – A shift in the embroidery:

Fig. 08-215:
Correct manufactured SSI.

Fig. 08-216:
Error by a slight shift in the embroidery.

Fig. 08-217:
Correct manufactured SSI.

Fig. 08-218:
Error by a slight shift in the embroidery.

Example below: 95th Inf Div SSI – Errors in design:

With the first example, the two legs of the "V" were embroidered on the upper part of the border, which is a manufacturer's error. It is not a shift of that particular part of the design, because the lower part of the "V" is embroidered on the correct place, just above the border as it should be. This also means that the "V" was embroidered after the blue background and border were completed. In any usual case, the design always stays within the border (see Fig. 08-220).

Fig. 08-219: Front and back of an error 95th Inf Div SSI (slight shift in the embroidery – "V").

With the second example of the 95th Inf Div SSI below, both legs of the "V" were embroidered on top of the "9." The correctly made 95th Inf Div SSI should have the upper part of the left leg under the "9," while the upper part of the right leg is above.

Fig. 08-220: Front and back of an error 95th Inf Div SSI (both legs of the "V" in front of the "9").

Example below: 5th U.S. Marine Div SSI – Errors in design:

The correct SSI on the right has the same size as the red background of the error patch, which means the yellow border made the left one larger. Also, both design details (the "V" and spearhead) are larger on the left SSI. This could be a good example of a misinterpretation of an order of a SSI: the description of the yellow border was likely not well explained enough and/or misunderstood.

Fig. 08-221: Front and back of two 5th U.S. Marine Div SSI, with the one on the left being oversized.

Example below: SSI of the U.S. Strategic Air Forces in Europe – Errors in text:

The SSI on the right has inverted letters (should be "USSTAF").

Fig. 08-222: Front and back of two SSI of the U.S. Strategic Air Forces in Europe. The one the right has inverted embroidered letters, a manufacturer's error.

3 | VARIATIONS

There are variations in embroidery pattern, color, tints of a color, form, design, back thread, and border, which is proof that many different manufacturing companies were used.

It is impossible to show all the different types of SSI and their respective variations because of the enormous amounts of SSI that were made during WWII. Each Division SSI could easily be depicted in a range of all these variations, depending on the period of manufacture and the firms which made them. Here are some examples. Each collector will have to decide for himself how many different variations he wishes to include in his collection.

Example below: 46th Inf "Phantom" Div SSI:

Fig. 08-301: Thin flames variation.

Fig. 08-302: Thick flames variation.

Yet, to this 46th Inf "Phantom" Div patch, the one is an inverted version of the design with inverted colors. When one turns the thin flames variation 180°, one can see the thick flames variation, but with the thick flames in the black main design thread.

Fig. 08-303: The thin flames variation (turned 180°) versus the thick flames variation. The same design can be seen but with reversed colors (black / red).

Example below: 5307th Composite unit (Merrill's Marauders) SSI – Variations in design:

These two different SSI are from one and the same unit.

Fig. 08-304

Fig. 08-305

Example below: 17th Airborne Div SSI – Differences in design:

Next to the details in feathers, compare the direction of the claws.

Fig. 08-306: Normal variation.

Fig. 08-307: Opposed claw variation: the second claw from the right is reversed.

Example below: 11th Airborne Div SSI – Differences in design:

Compare the "11" and the height of the "Airborne" tab.

Fig. 08-308: Variation with short type "Airborne"-tab.

Fig. 08-309: Variation with tall type "Airborne"-tab.

Example below: 104th Inf Div SSI – Differences in embroidery pattern and color:

Compare the color of the main thread and the method of embroidery (technique). Also, the designs of the wolf have slight differences.

Fig. 08-310: Common variation.

Fig. 08-311: Darker green variation with Gemsco embroidery style.

Example below: 98th Inf Div SSI
– Differences in shades of colors, thickness of the border, details, etc.:

Compare the different colors of the Indian head, and also the width of the SSI and the thickness of the border. Even more variations than illustrated below do exist.

Fig. 08-312: Darker orange – Wide variation.

Fig. 08-313: Lighter orange – Wide variation, with ribbed embroidery style.

Fig. 08-314: Orange color – Smaller variation.

Fig. 08-315: Bright orange – Wide variation, with wider border.

Example below: 94th Inf Div SSI – Differences in style and design:

Of the first design, (a) and (b) have an OD-colored border and are genuine, while (c) has a grey border and is likely a post-WWII reproduction, given the lack of detail on the Pilgrim's head and hat design and the less qualitative finishing (embroidery) on the edges of the galley.

Fig. 08-316: (a), (b) and (c) are first design 94th Inf Div SSI; (d) and (e) are second design used from September 1942. (c) is likely a post-WWII reproduction.

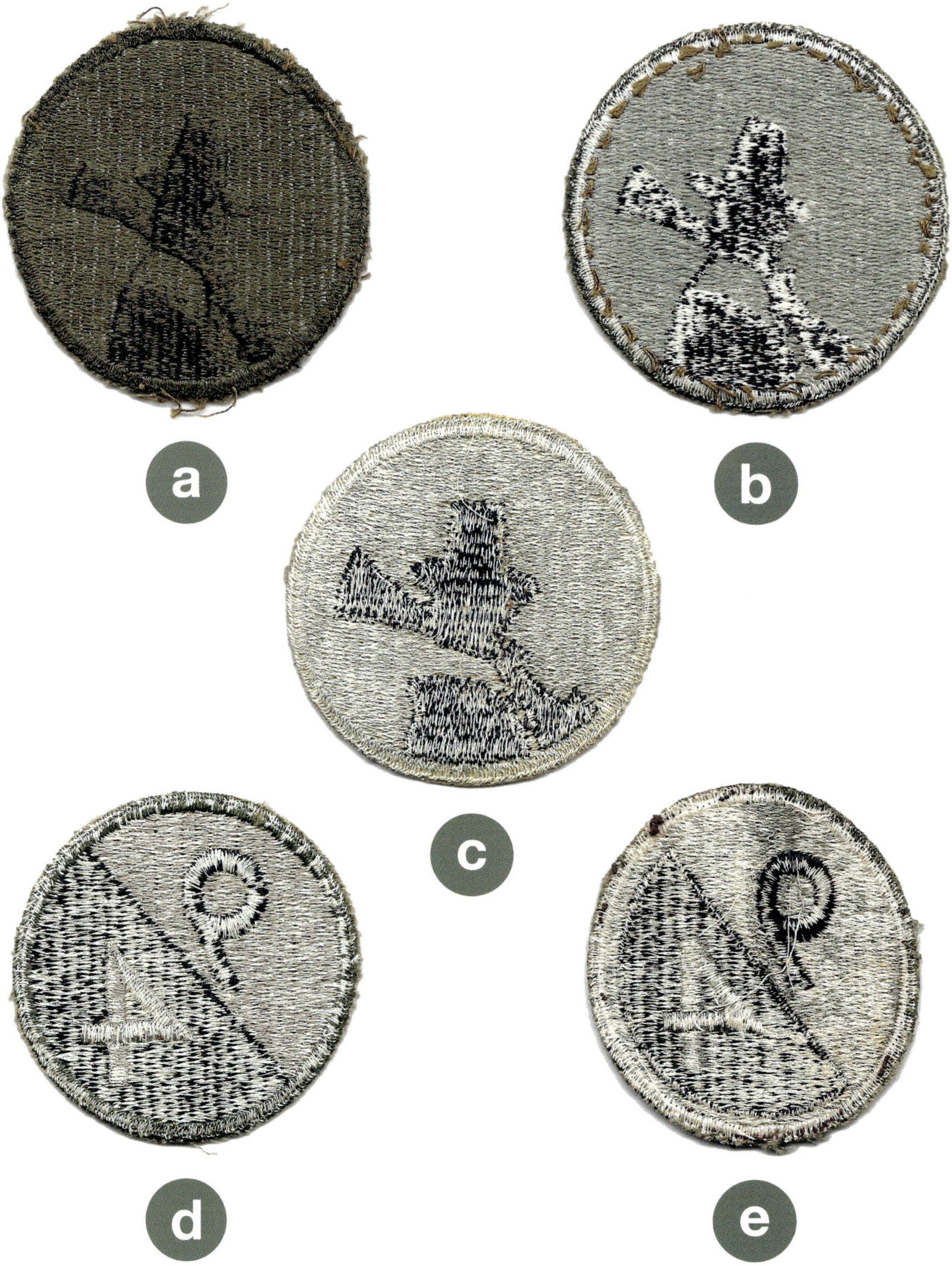

Fig. 08-317: The backs of the same 94th Inf Div SSI illustrated in Fig. 08-316.

Example below: 90th Inf Div SSI – Different variations in forms and colors:

Fig. 08-318: Square shape.

Fig. 08-319: Early-WWII round shape with darker red- and OD-colored thread.

Example below: 80th Inf Div SSI – Different variations in colors:

Fig. 08-320:
A light blue mountain variation.

Fig. 08-321:
A dark blue mountain variation.

Example below: IV Armored Corps SSI – Different variations in colors:

Fig. 08-322: A WWII U.S. made, cut-edge IV Armored Corps SSI with the usual golden-yellow apex.

Fig. 08-323: A WWII U.S. made, cut-edge IV Armored Corps SSI with the lemon-yellow apex. Also the "IV" is different with the previous.

Example below: 95th Inf Div SSI – Different variations:

Fig. 08-324: Error patch: Two legs of the "V" before the "9"; and the bottom curve of the "9" has vertical embroidery loops.

Fig. 08-325: Detail of the bottom curve of the "9" with vertical embroidery loops seen with the SSI illustrated in Fig. 03-324 above.

Fig. 08-326: Error patch because of the slight shift of the "V" (partially machine-embroidered on the border) – One leg of the "V" before the "9" as the usual SSI should have, and the bottom curve of the "9" has horizontal embroidery loops.

Fig. 08-327: Detail of the bottom curve of the "9" with horizontal embroidery loops seen with the SSI illustrated in Fig. 03-326 here above.

Fig. 08-328: Thin "V" and "9" – No outlined "9". The SSI is foreign theater made: likely British made given the typical longer thread loops.

Fig. 08-329: Outlined "9" by the manufacturer.

Fig. 08-330: "9" with machine-added outline by either the soldier or someone else different than the manufacturer.

Fig. 08-331: With OD border and outlined "9", plus usual embroidery.

Fig. 08-332: With OD border and outlined "9", plus Gemsco embroidery style.

Fig. 08-333: WWII fully machine-embroidered, cut-edge 1st design of the 95th Inf Div (used until 1942).

Example below: Alaska Defense Command SSI – Differences in detail:

Fig. 08-334

Fig. 08-335

Fig. 08-336

Example below: 78th Inf Div SSI – Differences in embroidery pattern and design:

Fig. 08-337: With a wider lightning bolt and OD back thread.

Fig. 08-338: With a smaller lightning bolt and white back thread.

Fig. 08-339: Ribbed embroidery variation and white back.

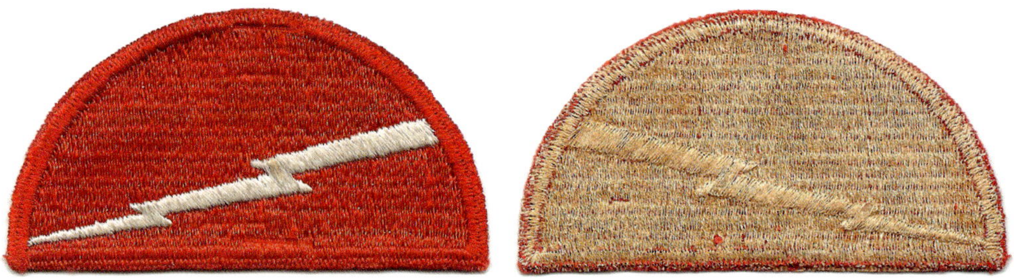

Fig. 08-340: Gemsco embroidery variation with complete white back and unusual red border.

Example below: 77th Inf Div SSI
– Differences in colors (shades of blue and yellow) and details:

These SSI have either an OD back or white back.

Fig. 08-341

Fig. 08-342

Fig. 08-343

Fig. 08-344

Fig. 08-345: With the rare OD border.

Fig. 08-346: With the less common, light blue background.

Example below: 2nd U.S. Marine Div SSI – Differences in design and color:

Fig. 08-347: The unauthorized WWII cut-edge, first design of the 2nd U.S. Marine Div SSI.

The unauthorized WWII cut-edge, first design of the 2nd U.S. Marine Div SSI. From 1943, the patch was manufactured in similarity with the 1st U.S. Marine Div SSI, but was changed very quickly into the second design (see pictures below) during WWII due to that resemblance. Each unit had to propose their own design. Afterwards, as in all cases of official SSI designs, some higher authority had to approve them.

Fig. 08-348: 2nd design of the 2nd U.S. Marine Div SSI with large '2'.

Fig. 08-349: 2nd design of the 2nd U.S. Marine Div SSI with small '2'.

NOTE

The hands and torches were also differently manufactured.

Fig. 08-350: 2nd design of the 2nd U.S. Marine Div SSI with white hand.

Fig. 08-351: 2nd design of the 2nd U.S. Marine Div SSI with golden-yellow colored hand.

NOTE

Although the same type of patch, the embroidered "2" in Fig. 08-349 is even thinnor than it is in Fig. 08-350.

Fig. 08-352: Another design of the 2nd U.S. Marine Div SSI, but applied with pattern #8 (see chapter 3, heading 5). This patch is wider than the previous 2nd design SSI.

Fig. 08-347a: An unauthorized variation ("heart"- or "kidney"-shaped) of the 2nd U.S. Marine Division SSI which can be cataloged as an error (chapter 8, heading 2 earlier in this book). The patch is the result of an incorrect color drawing that appeared in a WWII publication, and was copied by a manufacturer that way. According to literature, the drawing in this publication was made after verbal instructions over the telephone which were misinterpreted by the editor.

Example below: 13th Airborne Div SSI – Differences in design (drawing) and color:

eye, mouth of the unicorn, wings, shades of orange, with or without OD border, embroidered on khaki- or olive drab-colored cotton twill-base fabric, etc.:

Fig. 08-353: With partial OD border between "Airborne"-tab and shield, and brighter shade of orange.

Fig. 08-354: No OD border, darker shade of orange, more detailed wings and large eye.

Fig. 08-355: No OD border, brighter orange and small eye.

Fig. 08-355a: With a total OD border and darker shade of orange, embroidered on olive drab-colored cotton twill base fabric.

Fig. 08-355b: The same as in Fig. 08-355a above but embroidered on khaki-colored cotton twill backing.

Example below: 4th Inf Div SSI
– Differences in embroidery pattern, in OD color and in shape of the SSI:

Fig. 08-356: The usual diamond-shaped 4th Inf Div SSI – With the normal OD-colored background.

Fig. 08-357: The usual diamond-shaped 4th Inf Div SSI – With a darker OD-colored background (a darker shade of OD color).

Fig. 08-358: The larger diamond-shaped version of the 4th Inf Div SSI – Ribbed embroidery variation – Lighter shade of OD color.

Fig. 08-359: The larger diamond-shaped version of the 4th Inf Div SSI – Ribbed embroidery variation – Lighter shade of OD color. Note the oblique embroidery pattern of the ribbed embroidery (45° turned position during the manufacturing process).

Fig. 08-360: The larger diamond-shaped version of the 4th Inf Div SSI – Standard embroidery variation – Darker shade of OD color.

Example below: 10th Mountain Div SSI – Differences in detail (the hilt of the sword and crossed swords):

Fig. 08-361: SSI detail: The upper sword goes to the upper right and has a detailed design of the hilt of the sword.

Fig. 08-362: SSI detail: The upper sword goes to the upper right and has no detailed design of the hilt of the sword.

Fig. 08-363: SSI detail: The upper sword goes to the upper left and has no detailed design of the hilt of the sword. This patch also has an Italian theater made, woven 'Mountain'-tab.

4 | WWII VARIETIES OF SSI WITH OD BACKGROUND

In the early-WWII period, and in some cases, an OD-colored background was not always specified for certain SSI. This was still the result of the descriptions and drawings of these SSI in the telegrams sent to GHQ, AEF by the Commanding Generals during the WWI period (1918-early 1920s) for the approval of the SSI. In those telegrams no background color was mentioned, but only the descriptions of the details of these insignia (see *Shoulder Sleeve Insignia of the American Expeditionary Forces 1918-1919* by Ross H. Ford). This fact is also illustrated by certain SSI appearing in the 1942 printed booklet "A Guide to U.S. Insignia and Decorations" (see figure below) where, for example, only a black letter "A" without background is illustrated as the 1st U.S. Army SSI (page 27 of the guide).

Fig. 08-401: The cut black felt letter "A" as the WWI period 1st U.S. Army SSI which was put directly on the WWI uniform coat.

Because only a black letter "A" was approved during the WWI period, the SSI's background color was not predetermined. Ergo a cut black felt letter "A" as the WWI-period 1st U.S. Army SSI was put directly on the WWI uniform coat. At that early period the background of the "A" was the fabric of the OD-colored uniform on which the cut black felt letter was sewn.

To a lesser extent during WWI, but certainly during the Interwar period, the black letter "A" was either sewn (a cut black felt "A") or machine-embroidered on OD wool. This way of manufacturing was to reinforce the SSI a bit more, and also to sew the SSI much easier and much nicer, because of the OD wool border, to the OD-colored uniform.

When the higher quality fully machine-embroidered on cotton twill 1st U.S. Army cut-edge SSI was introduced (in 1941), the background was fully embroidered with OD-colored threads to imitate the OD wool base fabric.

From 1950, the SSI's background color became red and white, the usual colors of a field army.

Fig. 08-402: The 1942 Revised edition with hardcover.

In the booklet, the same can be found of the 2nd U.S. Army, 4th Inf Div, and 90th Inf Div, patches which normally also have OD-colored backgrounds when manufactured.

It is wrong if one thinks that the OD color was not printed in the booklet, because the 1st, 9th, and 26th Inf Div SSI are in fact illustrated with OD background. The fact that an OD background for these insignia was foreseen at the time can also be seen in their pre-WWII dated "The Institute of Heraldry" drawing below. One can see these dates at the bottom of the drawing. The information in the booklet thus comes from those drawings.

In the cases of the 4th and 90th Inf Div SSI, the lack of OD background with certain early-WWII illustrations is the reason why there are different sizes or different shapes. Because of this, SSI like the larger sized square-shaped 4th Inf Div SSI and 90th Inf Div patch with round shaped bottom (instead of the square form) are more likely early-WWII manufactured (1941-1942). Varieties of both SSI are illustrated above in heading 3 of this chapter (see Fig. 08-319 and 08-356).

The fact that these fully machine-embroidered cut-edge varieties on cotton twill-base fabric are probably early-WWII can be demonstrated with "The Institute of Heraldry" drawings. The one of the 4th Inf Div SSI is dated October 30, 1918 (see figure below). Here, only the regulations on the ivy leaves are specified. In the early-WWII period, certain companies which received the "TIOH" drawing manufactured, among others, the larger sized square-shaped SSI. Different theories could be stated here:

- The pre-WWII contracted company continued making them in the same shape as they manufactured the OD wool variant during the 1930s. This patch is the same size as the fully machine-embroidered cut-edge counterpart (see figure 08-403 below). This is the most likely;

Fig. 08-403: Front and back of a 1930s partially machine-embroidered, square-shaped, OD wool 4th Inf Div SSI, reinforced with black mesh (as stabilizer).

- Or prior to the machine embroidering, the early-WWII newly contracted manufacturer received an example of such large square 1930s OD wool patch from someone to use it for drawing the template of the patch at the Schiffli embroidery machine;
- Or the early-WWII newly contracted manufacturer had only the "TIOH" drawing to begin with and did not know the patch should be diamond-shaped and manufactured them as illustrated above in chapter 8, heading 3.

The reason for making them square-shaped can only be found in the nonexistence of background in the "TIOH" drawing. Afterwards, when issued, the corners of the square 4th Inf Div SSI were simply folded into the normal diamond shape by the GI before sewing the patch on the uniform. These SSI are not often seen, because they were probably not made in large amounts before being corrected.

The same can be said about the 90th Inf Div SSI. The square shape of the patch is not specified in the "TIOH" drawing, which led to the SSI with the round bottom neatly embroidered around the specified flat "O."

Fig 08-404: 90th Inf Div SSI from different periods:
a a WWI period patch
b a WWI / 1920s period patch
c a late 1920s – early 1930s partially machine-embroidered SSI on OD wool
d an early-WWII fully machine-embroidered cut-edge patch with round bottom

As mentioned earlier, below are the pre-WWII dated "The Institute of Heraldry" drawings of the SSI, which are pictured in the booklet with or without OD background. The link can easily be made with the existence of a number of varieties of the 4th and 90th Inf Div SSI described above. The "TIOH" drawings of these two SSI show no drawn shape of the SSI, but only the specifications of the ivy leaves of the 4th Inf Div and the "Tough Ombres" design of the 90th Inf Div. Likely early-WWII newly contracted manufacturers which received this drawing made that insignia in a different shape and size. They needed a correction afterwards. On the other hand, most pre-WWII contracted companies probably already had the knowledge of the diamond shape and correct size to manufacture them as correct fully machine-embroidered cut-edge SSI.

The other drawings (1st, 9th, and 26th Inf Div SSI) all had OD-colored background, which also determined the correct shape and size of these insignia.

Fig. 08-405: TIOH-drawing of the 1st Inf Div SSI. *(Courtesy of Craig Pickrall)*

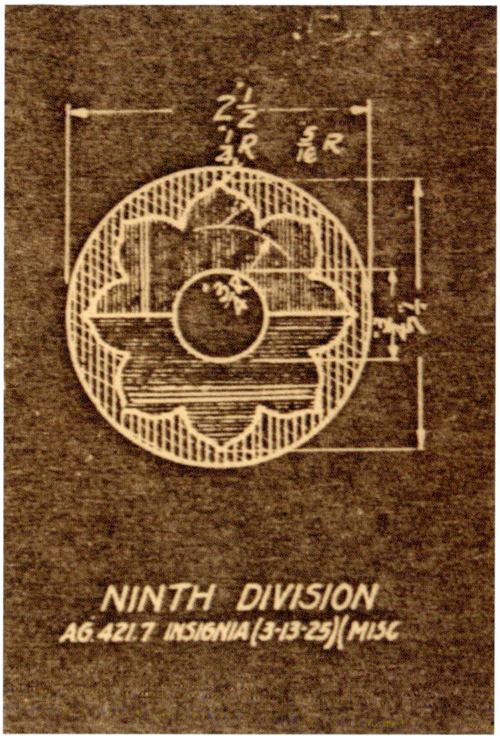

Fig. 08-406: TIOH-drawing of the 9th Inf Div SSI. *(Courtesy of Craig Pickrall)*

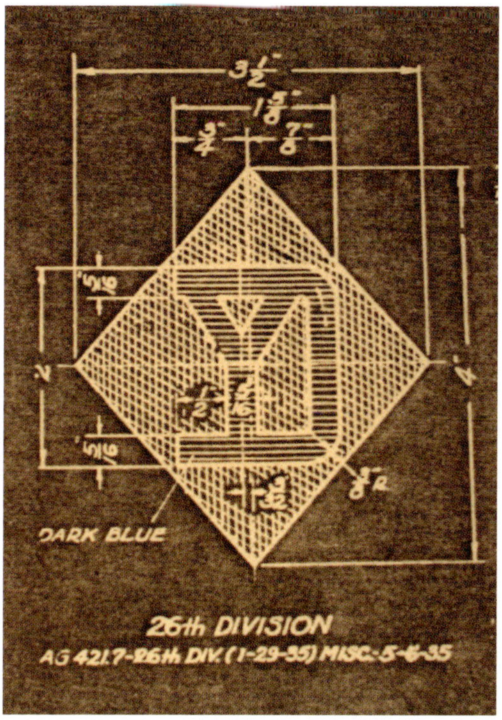

Fig. 08-407: TIOH-drawing of the 26th Inf Div SSI. *(Courtesy of Craig Pickrall)*

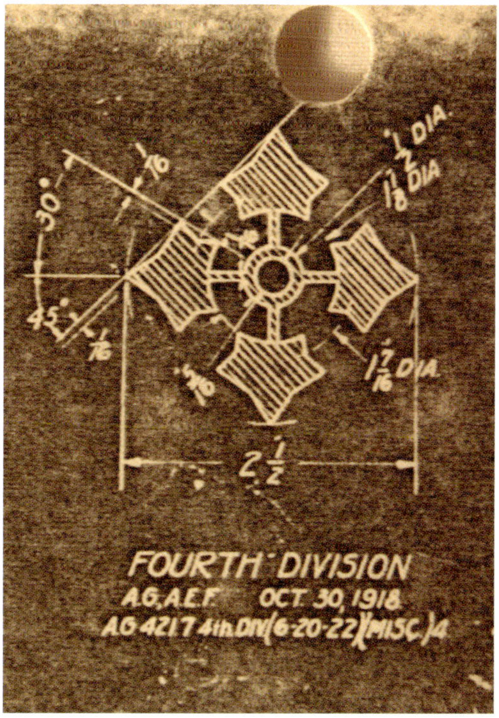

Fig. 08-408: TIOH-drawing of the 4th Inf Div SSI. *(Courtesy of Craig Pickrall)*

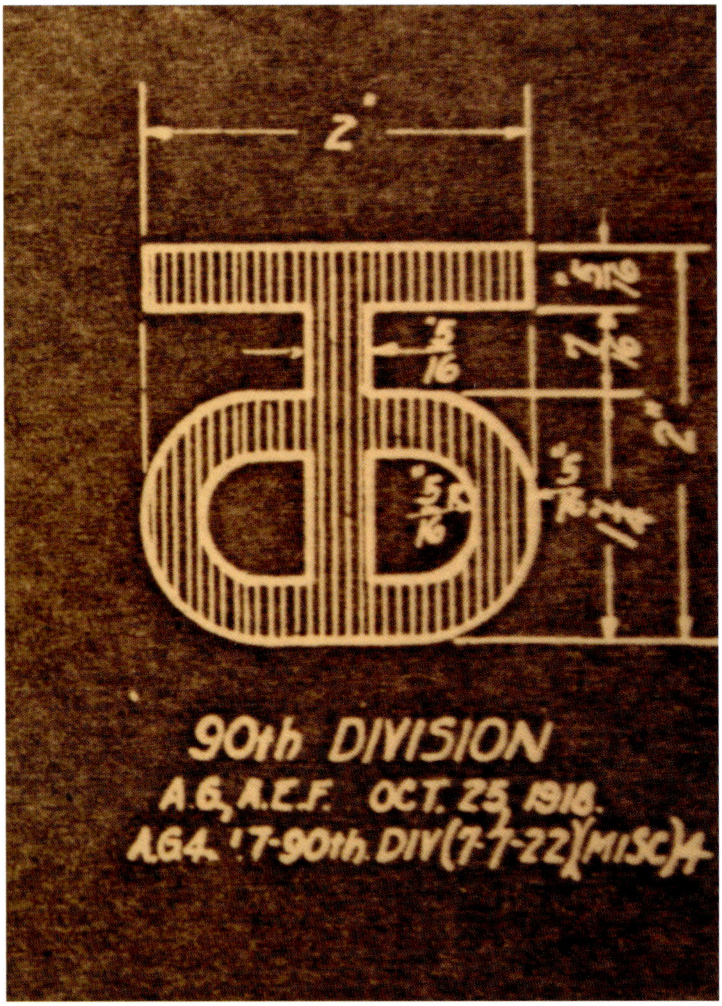

Fig. 08-409: TIOH-drawing of the "Tough Ombres"-design of the 90th Inf Div SSI. (Courtesy of Craig Pickrall)

CHAPTER 9
Ways of Collecting

Each collector has his own personal ideas and interests about collecting WWII items. This is no different in the case of WWII insignia. It is up to the collector how much he wants to spend on the collection, or which SSI of which period(s) he wants to collect.

When the word period is used, I am referring to WWI, Interwar, WWII in general, WWII Normandy Campaign, WWII Battle of the Bulge, post-WWII, Korean War, and so many other campaigns in which the collector could find his interests. Within the WWII period, also different kinds of styles (techniques) of embroidery could be a topic of the collection: different embroidery styles mean different manufacturers, SSI with and/or without OD border, OD backs, varieties of design, etc. Another way of collecting could be the SSI of all Divisions, Army Groups, and Armies. It could be one SSI or a certain number of SSI of each U.S. military unit.

This list is endless. The previous chapter provides some examples. But what will be in the collection is dependant on the collector and is their choice only!

Of course one can only speak for one's self, but my interests at the beginning were not the same as now. They changed over the years with the collection of different SSI and pocket and cap patches. Starting with the WWII Normandy Campaign SSI, my own interests evolved to the collecting of patches from WWI to WWII, and examples of the various kinds of manufacture that developed during the period. However, one must realize that it is possible to acquire only a fraction of the varieties of SSI that really exist. This fact makes collecting SSI something very interesting to continue doing over a long time. Every new added piece is a personal upgrade to something that is endless, which is, after all, the purpose of collecting and building a hobby that lasts for a lifetime.

Not only the collection will enlarge, but also the knowledge of the collector. Even after years of collecting and with the benefit of knowledge gained from more knowledgeable collectors, it remains fun to look for and find that exceptional and unusual SSI to add to your collection.

As mentioned earlier in this book, creating a time line in your collection could be one of the collector's ways of collecting. Considering the guidelines in this book, and if one should have more than one SSI of the same unit, one could try to store them in a certain order of periods (time frames).

Here, the manufacturing method plays a major role. This means not only the different periods in which the SSI of a certain unit was made, but also the evolution of manufacturing within a certain period (like WWII).

Below is an example of the 45th Inf Div SSI starting from the Interwar period to WWII. Some illustrated patches are not WWII, fully machine-embroidered, or even U.S. made. But these additions show and complete the created time line, as well as the SSI's evolution. The most important thing to show will be the SSI's evolution within WWII. Dating WWII SSI is not an exact science. Because it is more than 65 years ago, certain motives and ways of manufacture can only be presumed. But the added WWII periods would be very possible, considering the guidelines and theories mentioned in this book.

The 45th Inf Div SSI:

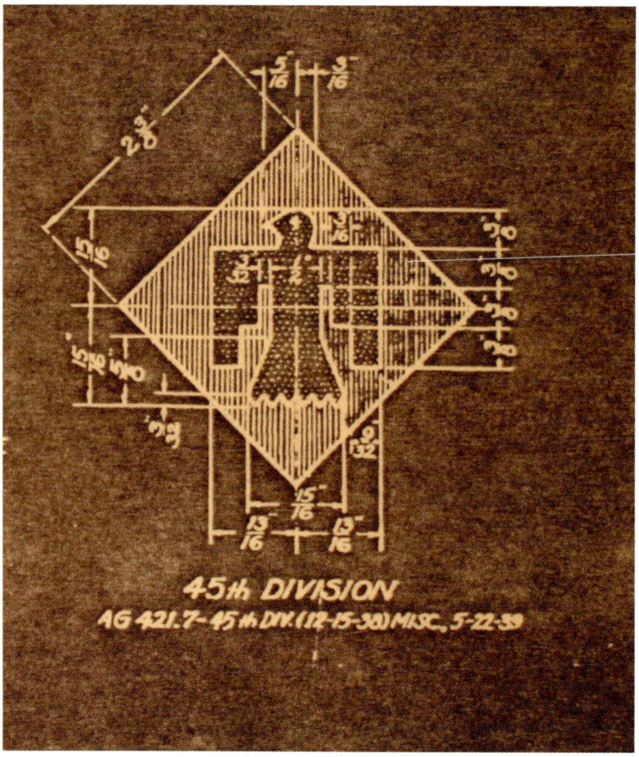

Fig. 09-001: "The Institute of Heraldry"-Drawing with the "Thunderbird"-design – Dated May 22, 1939. *(Courtesy of Craig Pickrall)*

1 An early 1930s U.S. made felt on felt example of the 45th Inf Div SSI worn prior to 1939. The swastika changed into the Thunderbird design because of the resemblance to the national symbol of Nazi Germany.

Fig. 09.002: Front and back of #1.

2

A 1939/early 1941 period U.S. made SSI, fully machine-embroidered on OD wool and reinforced with black mesh. After 1939, the Thunderbird design appears based on the TIOH drawings (see Fig. 09-001 above).

Fig. 09.003: Front and back of #2.

3

A 1939/early 1941 period U.S. made SSI, fully machine-embroidered on OD wool. The SSI has the same thickness as the previous one and has the same thin machine-embroidered border. The thicker embroidered border became a specific feature of the later (wartime period) cotton twill cut-edge SSI. Here, the OD wool border has been cut off.

Fig. 09.004: Front and back of #3.

4

A 1941/early 1943 period U.S. made SSI, fully machine-embroidered on cotton twill with cut-edge. The embroidered OD border (which replaces the OD wool border) and OD back are typical for that period. Probably this manufacturer already made OD wool SSI prior to WWII, before continuing to make them on cotton twill during the war.

Fig. 09.005: Front and back of #4.

5

A 1941/early 1943 period U.S. made SSI, fully machine-embroidered on cotton twill with cut-edge. This is an early-WWII example because of the embroidered OD border (which replaces the OD wool border). Also it has a pre-/early-WWII manufacturing style (see earlier in this book). Probably this manufacturer already made OD wool SSI prior to WWII, before making them on cotton twill during the war. This company probably never had the intention (stock) to use the OD threads as back thread as with the previous example.

Fig. 09.006: Front and back of #5.

6

A 1944-1945 period Italian theater made SSI. The reversed colors on the back of the SSI demonstrate it is woven and not embroidered. The division was in Italy from 1943 (assaulted Sicily in July 1943, assaulted Salerno in September 1943, and assaulted Anzio in January 1944), and left for the assault on Southern France in August 1944. Prior to these dates this SSI could never be made.

Fig. 09.007: Front and back of #6.

7 Such a SSI is more difficult to catalogue. Two theories can be set here:

- A U.S. made SSI without OD border manufactured from 1943 by a pre-WWII contracted manufacturer who omitted the OD border and embroidered a red one, making the SSI according to the "TIOH" drawings. Maybe this company also utilized OD colored back thread in early war time and changed it into white during the course of the war (see earlier). But this is just an assumption;
- A second theory: a U.S. made SSI manufactured certainly after 1941, because it is fully machine-embroidered on cotton twill with cut-edge. It does not have an old style manufacture and has no OD border and back. For these reasons it could also be made by a WWII newly contracted manufacturer making the SSI according to the TIOH drawings.

In both ways, and the most likely, the mint condition of the SSI and the presence of lots of white back thread could tell us this is a (likely late-) WWII patch (1944-1945), or made just after.

Fig. 09.008: Front and back of #7.

BIBLIOGRAPHY

Brown, Christopher P. *U.S. Military Patches of WWII.* (Paducah, KY: Turner Publishing Company, 2003)

Conejos, Sean. *Synthetically Speaking, WWII won't have Synthetic Threads.* [The Trading Post: the official quarterly publication of the American Society of Military Insignia Collectors (ASMIC), Edition Oct-Dec 2011]

Dalessandro, Robert J. and Michael G. Knapp. *Organization and Insignia of the American Expeditionary Force – 1918-1923.* (Atglen, PA: Schiffer Publishing Ltd, 2008)

History – *The Schiffli Lace and Embroidery Manufacturers.* Available at http://www.schiffli.org/history.htm

Ford, Ross H. *Shoulder Sleeve Insignia of the American Expeditionary Forces 1918-1919 (Authorized by Approval of General Headquarters, American Expeditionary Forces – By Order of General John J. Pershing, Commander-in-Chief).* (Atglen, PA: Schiffer Publishing Ltd, 2012)

Kaufman, David A. *Patch Styles and Manufacture.* [The Trading Post: the official quarterly publication of the American Society of Military Insignia Collectors (ASMIC), Edition Apr-Jun 2002]

Keller, Kurt H. *Emblems of Honor – Patches and Insignia of the US Army from the Great War to the Early Cold War – Armor, Cavalry, Tank Destroyer, Constabulary.* (Twin Pond, 2005)

Keller, William and Kurt Keller. *United States Army Shoulder Patches and Related Insignia from World War I to Korea – 41st Division to 106th Division.* (Atglen, PA: Schiffer Publishing Ltd, 2002)

Keller, William and Kurt Keller. *United States Army Shoulder Patches and Related Insignia from World War I to Korea – Army Groups, Armies and Corps.* (Atglen, PA: Schiffer Publishing Ltd, 2004)

Keller, William. *United States Army Shoulder Patches and Related Insignia from World War I to Korea – 1st Division to 40th Division.* (Atglen, PA: Schiffer Publishing Ltd, 2007)

Morgan Jr, James L. and Ted A. Thurman. *American Military Patch Guide.* (Fountain Inn, SC: Medals of America Press – illustrated edition, 1997)

Packaging Today – packagingtoday.com. *An Introduction to the History of Plastics – Cellulose Based Plastics: Celluloid and Rayon*: available at http://www.packagingtoday.com/introcelluloid.htm

Petersen, Gordon A. J. *A Guide to U.S. Insignia and Decorations* (Revised edition prepared with the assistance of Lieut. Robert H. Rankin, St. John's Military Academy). (Racine, Wisconsin: Whitman Publishing Company; Copyright 1941 – Printed in 1942)

Sindle, Kevin. *Liberty Loan Shoulder Patches of the A.E.F.* [The Trading Post: the official quarterly publication of the American Society of Military Insignia Collectors (ASMIC), Edition Jul-Sep 1992]

Smith, Richard W. *Shoulder Sleeve Insignia of the U.S. Armed Forces 1941-1945 (2nd Edition).* (ISBN 0-9618883-3-4, Richard W. Smith, 1981)

Stein, Barry Jason. *U.S. Army Patches, Flashes and Ovals: An Illustrated Encyclopedia of Cloth Unit Insignia.* (Greenwich, CT: Insignia Ventures Inc.; 1st edition, 2007)

Stanton, Shelby L., Capt. *WWII Order of Battle: An Encyclopedic Reference to U.S. Army Ground Forces from Battalion through Division, 1939-1946 (Revised edition).* (Mechanicsburg, PA: Stackpole Books; 2 Rev Upd edition, 2006)

The Institute of Heraldry, Office of the Administrative Assistant to the Secretary of the Army. Available at http://www.tioh.hqda.pentagon.mil/

U.S. Militaria Forum (U.S. Militaria Discussions – Shoulder Sleeve Insignia & Patches). *Green back Patch List, Chart of Known Green backs.* Available at http://www.usmilitariaforum.com/forums/index.php?showtopic=105377&mode=linear or http://www.usmilitariaforum.com/forums/index.php?showtopic=105377&st=0&start=0

U.S. Militaria Forum [Reference – Shoulder Sleeve Insignia (Ref)]. Available at http://www.usmilitariaforum.com/forums/index.php?showforum=17

U.S. Militaria Forum (U.S. Militaria Discussions – Shoulder Sleeve Insignia & Patches). *Using the Burn Test to Identify Fibers in Patches, A Guide.* Available at http://www.usmilitariaforum.com/forums/index.php?showtopic=43652

U.S. Militaria Forum (US Militaria Discussions – Research sources). *Manufacturers of US Militaria Emblems WWI onward, List of Manufactures by Name.* Available at http://www.usmilitariaforum.com/forums/index.php?showtopic=36888

Wikipedia – The Free Encyclopedia. *1-thread formation overlock.* Available at http://en.wikipedia.org/wiki/Overlock and http://en.wikipedia.org/wiki/File:Merrow_300204.jpg

Wikipedia – The Free Encyclopedia. *Rayon.* Available at http://en.wikipedia.org/wiki/Rayon

Wikipedia – The Free Encyclopedia. *Embroidered patch.* Available at http://en.wikipedia.org/wiki/Embroidered_patch.

AIRBORNE